Colloquial

Korean

THE COLLOQUIAL SERIES
Series Adviser: Gary King

The following languages are available in the Colloquial series:

Afrikaans
Albanian
Amharic
Arabic (Levantine)
Arabic of Egypt
Arabic of the Gulf and Saudi Arabia
Basque
Bengali
Breton
Bulgarian
Cambodian
Cantonese
Catalan
Chinese
Croatian
Czech
Danish
Dutch
English
Estonian
Finnish
French
German
Greek
Gujarati
Hausa (forthcoming)
Hebrew
Hindi
Hungarian
Icelandic
Indonesian
Irish
Italian
Japanese
Korean
Latvian
Lithuanian
Malay
Mongolian
Norwegian
Panjabi
Persian
Polish
Portuguese
Portuguese of Brazil
Romanian
Russian
Scottish Gaelic
Serbian
Slovak
Slovene
Somali
Spanish
Spanish of Latin America
Swahili
Swedish
Tamil
Thai
Turkish
Ukrainian
Urdu
Vietnamese
Welsh
Yoruba
Zulu (forthcoming)

COLLOQUIAL 2s series: *The Next Step in Language Learning*

Chinese
Dutch
French
German (forthcoming)
Italian
Portuguese of Brazil
Russian
Spanish
Spanish of Latin America

All these Colloquials are available in book & CD packs, or separately. You can order them through your bookseller or via our website www.routledge.com.

Colloquial
Korean

The Complete Course for Beginners

Danielle Ooyoung Pyun and
In-Seok Kim

NEW YORK AND LONDON

First edition by In-Seok Kim
Published 1996 by Routledge
Reprinted 1997, 2000, 2001, 2004, 2005, 2007 (twice)
Revised edition 1999

This edition first published 2010
by Routledge
270 Madison Ave, New York, NY 10016

Simultaneously published in the UK
by Routledge
2 Park Square, Milton Park, Abingdon, Oxon OX14 4RN

Routledge is an imprint of the Taylor & Francis Group, an informa business

Typeset in Avant Garde and Helvetica by Graphicraft Limited, Hong Kong
Printed and bound in Great Britain by
TJ International Ltd, Padstow, Cornwall

Library of Congress Cataloging in Publication Data
Pyun, Danielle Ooyoung.
Colloquial Korean : the complete course for beginners / Danielle Ooyoung Pyun and In-Seok Kim. — 2nd ed.
p. cm. — (Colloquial series)
Includes index.
1. Korean language—Conversation and phrase books English.
2. Korean language—Textbooks for foreign speakers—English.
I. Kim, In-Seok, 1950– II. Title.
PL913.P98 2008
495.7′83421—dc22
2008048435

British Library Cataloguing in Publication Data
A catalogue record for this book is available from the British Library

ISBN13: 978–0–415–44478–1 (pbk)
ISBN13: 978–0–415–44479–8 (audio CDs)
ISBN13: 978–0–415–77446–8 (pack)
ISBN13: 978–0–415–49691–9 (MP3)

Contents

Preface

Korean is a language spoken by about 72 million Koreans living on the Korean peninsula—a population of about 48.5 million in South Korea and about 23.3 million in North Korea (as of 2007)—as well as approximately 11 million ethnic Koreans living in other countries including China, Japan, the US, and Russia. By learning Korean, you are one step closer to an understanding of the dynamic and vibrant culture of Korea, a nation that has preserved a unique traditional heritage over a five-thousand-year history, yet also has one of the most advanced and fastest-growing science and technology sectors. Learning Korean will also benefit you with increased business opportunities, as the Korean economy and Korean companies—such as Samsung, Hyundai, LG, Kia, and SK—become increasingly globalized. Language acquisition is the best way to understand the heart of a local culture and to connect with its people.

Colloquial Korean: The Complete Course for Beginners is designed to help you develop communicative ability in Korean through a variety of useful functions and tasks that are likely to be encountered in real life. Along with a range of communicative situations in context, *Colloquial Korean* provides detailed explanations on the structure of Korean and the cultural practices embedded in language forms, both of which it is necessary to acquire to communicate successfully in Korean.

This book's target audience is the beginning-level learner who has little or no prior knowledge of Korean and aims to build communicative skills as well as basic literacy in Korean. This book is useful to learners who need to visit or travel through Korea, communicate in a business setting, and live or work with Korean speakers. While it can be used as a course text, it is also a comprehensive manual for independent, self-directed study without any assistance from a course instructor.

A key feature of *Colloquial Korean* is its introduction of authentic and contextualized colloquial language that is frequently used in contemporary Korea. This colloquial language component is derived from real Korean language data collected from various sources. In designing dialogues, drills, and activities, the author focused particularly on essential functions and cultural knowledge needed to negotiate and overcome communicative challenges.

This book begins with an introduction to *Hangŭl*, the Korean alphabet, followed by seventeen instructional units. Each unit is structured around learning points, one or two model dialogues, words and expressions, grammar points, and exercises. Cultural points relevant to unit themes and functions are also discussed throughout the book. The audio materials accompanying *Colloquial Korean* contain recordings of the Introduction, dialogues, vocabulary, and listening exercises. References at the end of the text include the answer key to exercises, Korean—English and English—Korean glossaries, and a grammar index.

Introduction This section presents Korean vowels and consonants, and their combination into syllables. Some useful pronunciation rules are also presented in this section, but you don't need to be overly conscious of these rules or try to memorize them. You will become familiar with the conventions of Korean pronunciation as you listen repeatedly to the dialogues and compare the sounds with their matching written forms. Pronunciation rules are guidelines that you can refer to later as needed.

Learning points At the beginning of each unit is a section entitled "In this unit you will learn about:", which is structured according to the essential functions, grammar patterns, and communicative goals that the learner is expected to achieve by the end of the unit.

Dialogue Each unit contains model dialogue(s) which demonstrate authentic communicative exchanges among the characters featured in *Colloquial Korean*. Each dialogue is contextualized with a setting description and utilizes key functions and grammar points presented in the unit. Listen to the dialogue carefully and repeat after the speaker until you become comfortable with both the pronunciation and speed of conversation. Each dialogue is accompanied by Romanization and English translation. This text uses the McCune—Reischauer Romanization system, since it is the easiest to pronounce for speakers of

English. At the outset of the course, you might need to depend on Romanized forms to some degree, but it is best to pay attention to the audio program and try to read the *Hangŭl* script first before looking at the Romanized script. As you progress, you will become less dependent on the Romanized forms, and you will be able to read and pronounce *Hangŭl* without referring to the corresponding Romanization. A supplemental English translation is given for each dialogue, to ensure that self-study learners accurately comprehend expressions and contextual meanings. When you reach the end of each unit, it is recommended that you go back to the dialogues and rehearse or role-play them again to internalize the key functions and structures of each unit.

Vocabulary This section presents words and expressions that are introduced in each dialogue. In addition to dialogue vocabulary, some units have extra words and expressions related to the unit topic. Some words that were introduced in the previous units may be re-listed in the later units for review purposes.

Grammar points These are provided in a systematic and manageable way to help you to understand the structure of Korean and to build on what you learned in previous units. The author also made efforts to explain basic grammar patterns using concrete and authentic examples. In the construction of grammar points, two main objectives were considered: (1) providing grammar patterns that are useful or necessary to perform key functions introduced in each unit, and (2) sequencing grammar points as much as possible according to frequency of use and level of difficulty. A comprehensive grammar reference is listed at the end of the book and includes sentence ending charts and the appropriate verb or adjective variations according to grammar patterns.

Exercises Designed to check your comprehension of the vocabulary, grammar points, and functions introduced in each unit, exercise questions are both a review of unit content and an application of acquired knowledge: these activities extend what you practiced from the model dialogue. Exercise items include both structural drills and communicative tasks. Structural drills mostly provide guided questions that reinforce the functions and grammar points studied in the unit.

Communicative tasks encourage the learner to produce more creative answers.

When an exercise question includes any previously un-introduced words or expressions, separate notes or English definitions are provided. From Unit 8, the Exercise sections include a listening task in which you will listen to a short dialogue or passage and answer comprehension check questions. This listening passage utilizes the unit's grammar points. Answer keys for exercise questions, as well as the listening exercise scripts and their translations, are all given at the end of the book.

Cultural point These sections present up-to-date cultural information relevant to the unit content and useful tips for visitors navigating daily life in the Republic of Korea.

Acknowledgments

In completing this book, I am indebted to many people. I would like to thank the Routledge staff for their help and guidance in writing and publishing this book as well as the reviewers commissioned by Routledge who provided valuable suggestions and feedback. I am particularly grateful to Perry Miller for her thorough review of the draft manuscript as well as to Carrie Middleditch for her illustrations included in this book. I am also indebted to the Ohio State University's College of Humanities for funding the field-test and proof-reading of the early manuscript of this book. Friends and co-workers including Eunjo Lee and Kwang Hee Hong helped me with taking the photos that are used in this book. I also thank my family for their support and encouragement throughout this project.

The Ohio State University
Columbus, Ohio
Danielle Ooyoung Pyun

Map of Korea

RUSSIA
CHINA
Pyongyang
East Sea
Gaeseong
KOREA
Incheon
Seoul
Yellow Sea
Daejeon
Daegu
Ulsan
Gwangju
Busan
Jeju
JEJU-DO
JAPAN
Capital
City
Demarcation line
100 km

Introduction

The Korean alphabet, *Hangŭl*

While the origin of the Korean language is not definitively established, the most commonly accepted hypothesis is that Korean belongs to the Altaic language family. Other languages in this family include Mongolian, Turkish, Manchu-Tungus, Korean, and Japanese.

The Korean alphabet *Hangŭl* (meaning *Koreans' writing*) was created in 1446 by King Sejong. Before the fifteenth century, Koreans did not have their own writing system and borrowed Chinese characters to record their speech. However, as the Korean language is structurally very different from Chinese (while Japanese is genetically very similar to Korean), it was difficult and inconvenient for Koreans to represent speech using Chinese characters. For this reason, the Korean King Sejong (1397–1450) and his scholars created an alphabetic script consisting of consonants and vowels that would best suit the Korean speech.

Hangŭl is a phonetic alphabet that can be easily acquired within a few days or even a few hours. Today, linguists around the world cite the Korean alphabet as an excellent script that is original, logical, and easy to learn. Due to the easiness and efficiency of Hangŭl, illiteracy hardly exists in Korea. In 1997, the United Nations Educational, Scientific, and Cultural Organization (UNESCO) designated Hangŭl as an international archive property.

This Introduction provides a step-by-step presentation of Hangŭl in order to prepare the learner to read, pronounce, and understand conversations presented in each unit of this book. Throughout this section, the learner is encouraged to repeatedly listen to each sound recording, in order to become familiarized with Korean sounds and to pronounce them correctly.

Hangŭl vowels and consonants

One of the characteristics of Hangŭl is that letters (consonants and vowels) are combined into syllabic blocks. In English, letters are written linearly to form words, but in Korean, letters are first clustered into syllabic units to form words. A syllabic block is composed of at least one consonant and at least one vowel. One or more syllabic blocks are then used to form words. The following section will introduce the sounds of Hangŭl consonants and vowels, and later the way that syllabic blocks are formed.

A. Vowels

■ 1. Simple vowels **(CD1; 2)**

These are the eight simple vowel symbols and their Romanization.

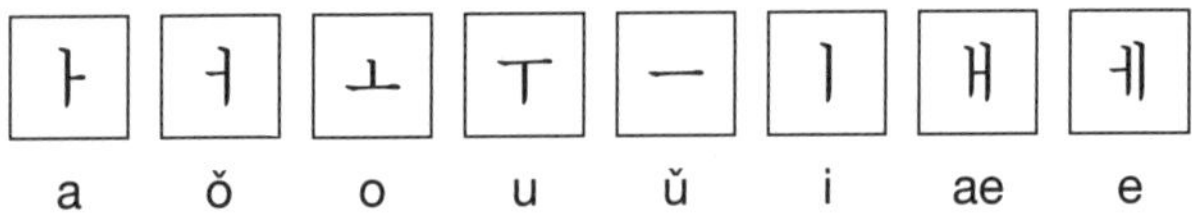

In modern Korean speech, the difference between ㅐ *ae* and ㅔ *e* is often not observed and their sounds are perceived as the same, particularly with younger generation speakers.

Symbol	Romanization	Pronunciation
ㅏ	a	as in *father*
ㅓ	ŏ	as in *saw*
ㅗ	o	as in *orange*
ㅜ	u	as in *June*
ㅡ	ŭ	as in *spoken*
ㅣ	i	as in *eat*
ㅐ	ae	as in *mat*
ㅔ	e	as in *met*

Note:

The purpose of Romanization is to help learners with pronunciation of Korean characters in the beginning stage of their learning process. Do not depend on Romanziation, but try to remember and match characters and their sounds as soon as possible so that you can move on to read Korean by Hangŭl characters.

■ 2. Compound vowels

(1) Y-ADDED VOWELS **(CD1; 3)**

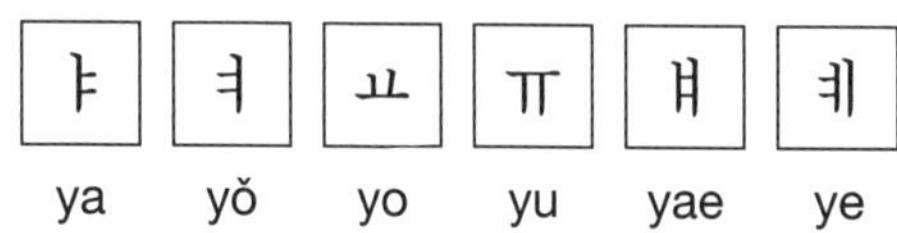

Adding one more stroke to ㅏ, ㅓ, ㅗ, ㅜ, ㅐ, ㅔ creates the y-added vowels (ㅑ, ㅕ, ㅛ, ㅠ, ㅒ, ㅖ respectively). In modern Korean speech, the difference between ㅒ *yae* and ㅖ *ye* is often not observed and their sounds are perceived as the same, particularly with younger-generation speakers.

Symbol	Romanization	Pronunciation
ㅑ	ya	as in *yard*
ㅕ	yŏ	as in *yawn*
ㅛ	yo	as in *yo-yo*
ㅠ	yu	as in *you*
ㅒ	yae	as in *yap*
ㅖ	ye	as in *yes*

(2) OTHER COMPOUND VOWELS **(CD1; 4)**

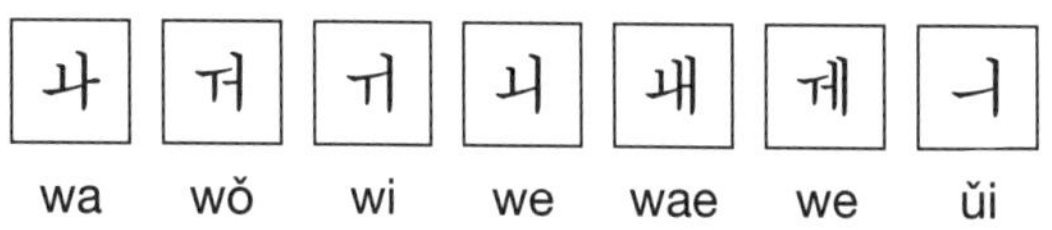

The vowels ㅘ, ㅝ, ㅟ, ㅚ, ㅙ, ㅞ, ㅢ are combinations of two simple vowels.

ㅗ + ㅏ → ㅘ   ㅜ + ㅓ → ㅝ
ㅜ + ㅣ → ㅟ   ㅗ + ㅣ → ㅚ
ㅗ + ㅐ → ㅙ   ㅜ + ㅔ → ㅞ
ㅡ + ㅣ → ㅢ

Symbol	Romanization	Pronunciation
ㅘ	wa	as in *wash*
ㅝ	wŏ	as in *wonderful*
ㅟ	wi	as in *we*
ㅚ	we	as in *wet*
ㅙ	wae	as in *wax*
ㅞ	we	as in *wedding*
ㅢ	ŭi	combination of *e* as in *spoken* and *e* as in *we*

Note:
Many Korean speakers pronounce ㅚ and ㅞ virtually the same. Also, the difference between ㅚ, ㅙ and ㅞ is not noticeable and thus they sound the same [*we*] in casual speech.

Exercise 1 **(CD1; 5)**

Now you'll hear the vowels in a different order. Listen to the speakers and repeat what you hear. Each vowel will be pronounced twice.

1 ㅏ	2 ㅜ	3 ㅓ	4 ㅔ
5 ㅛ	6 ㅕ	7 ㅡ	8 ㅟ
9 ㅝ	10 ㅞ	11 ㅐ	12 ㅣ

Exercise 2 **(CD1; 6)**

Circle the vowel you hear. Each vowel will be pronounced twice.

1 ㅗ ㅏ ㅔ ㅚ ㅠ
2 ㅜ ㅖ ㅡ ㅓ ㅝ
3 ㅘ ㅑ ㅛ ㅕ ㅢ
4 ㅐ ㅙ ㅗ ㅠ ㅔ
5 ㅜ ㅣ ㅡ ㅗ ㅞ
6 ㅓ ㅠ ㅏ ㅝ ㅚ

■ 3. Writing of Korean vowels

The general rule of stroke order is to write left to right for horizontal lines and to write top to bottom for vertical lines.

Practice writing the following vowels, observing the correct stroke order. As you write, try to recall the sound value of each vowel.

vowel	stroke order	writing practice			
ㅏ a	ㅏ ①②	ㅏ	ㅏ	ㅏ	ㅏ
ㅑ ya	ㅑ ①②③	ㅑ	ㅑ	ㅑ	ㅑ
ㅓ ŏ	ㅓ ①②	ㅓ	ㅓ	ㅓ	ㅓ
ㅕ yŏ	ㅕ ①②③	ㅕ	ㅕ	ㅕ	ㅕ
ㅗ o	ㅗ ①②	ㅗ	ㅗ	ㅗ	ㅗ
ㅛ yo	ㅛ ①②③	ㅛ	ㅛ	ㅛ	ㅛ
ㅜ u	ㅜ ①②	ㅜ	ㅜ	ㅜ	ㅜ
ㅠ yu	ㅠ ①②③	ㅠ	ㅠ	ㅠ	ㅠ

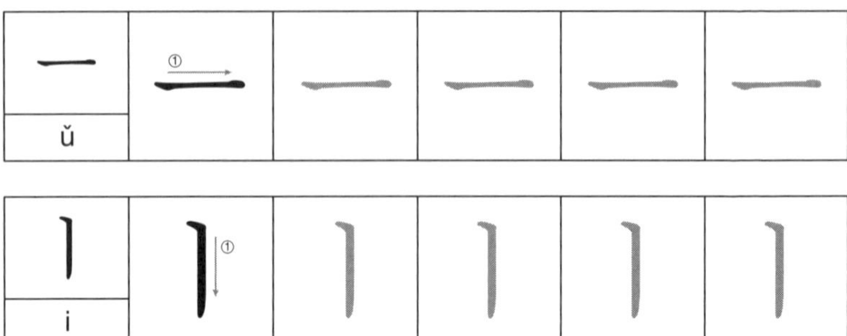

Exercise 3

1 Practice writing the following simple vowels. Refer to the stroke order provided above.

ㅏ, ㅓ, ㅗ, ㅜ, ㅡ, ㅣ, ㅐ, ㅔ

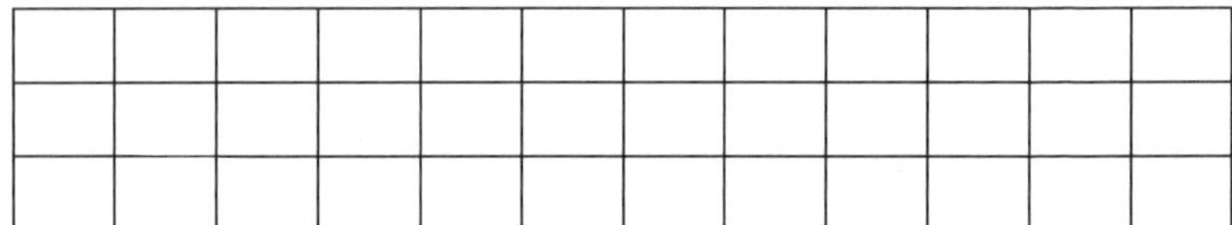

2 Practice writing the following compound vowels. Also, pay attention to the stroke order of each vowel.

ㅑ, ㅕ, ㅛ, ㅠ, ㅒ, ㅖ, ㅘ, ㅝ, ㅟ, ㅢ, ㅙ, ㅞ, ㅚ

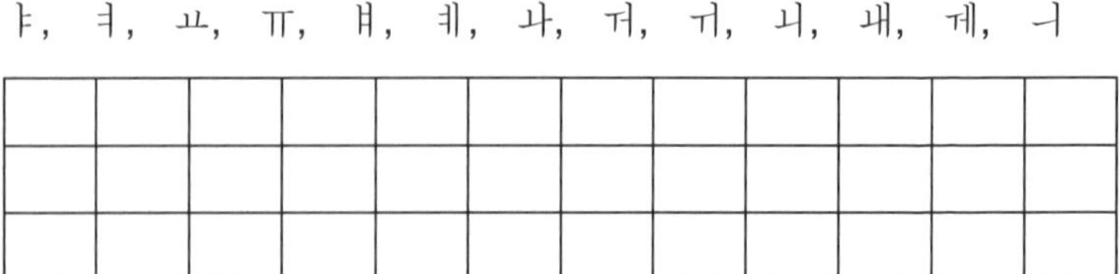

B. Consonants

■ 1. Simple and double consonants

Familiarize yourself with the following Korean consonants.

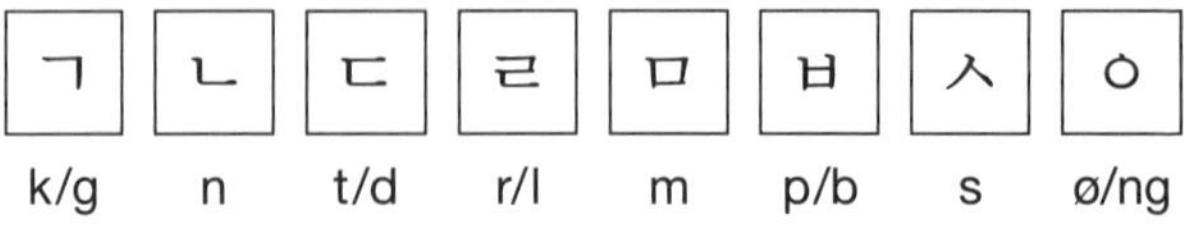

ㄱ	ㄴ	ㄷ	ㄹ	ㅁ	ㅂ	ㅅ	ㅇ
k/g	n	t/d	r/l	m	p/b	s	ø/ng

Symbol	**Romanization**	**Pronunciation**
ㄱ	k/g	k as in *kind*, but weaker and more relaxed; or g as in *goose*
ㄴ	n	n as in *nose*
ㄷ	t/d	t as in *tall*, but weaker and more relaxed; or d as in *doll*
ㄹ	r/l	r as in *river* or l as in *liver*
ㅁ	m	m as in *my*
ㅂ	p/b	p as in *pine*, but weaker and more relaxed; or b as in *bite*
ㅅ	s	s as in *sky*, but weaker and more relaxed
ㅇ	ø/ng	zero (no) sound at the beginning of a syllable; ng as in *finger* at the end of a syllable
ㅈ	ch/j	ch as in *China*, but weaker and more relaxed; or j as in *jar*
ㅊ	ch'	ch as in *church*, with a strong aspiration
ㅋ	k'	k as in *kite*, with a strong aspiration
ㅌ	t'	t as in *tie*, with a strong aspiration
ㅍ	p'	p as in *pie*, with a strong aspiration
ㅎ	h	h as in *height*
ㄲ	kk	k as in *ski*, but more tensed
ㄸ	tt	t as in *stuck*, but more tensed
ㅃ	pp	p as in *spy*, but more tensed
ㅆ	ss	s as in *sippy*, but more tensed
ㅉ	tch	ts as in *shirts*, but more tensed

PRONUNCIATION OF ㅋ, ㅌ, ㅍ, ㅊ

ㅋ, ㅌ, ㅍ, ㅊ are aspirated (or h-added) sounds of ㄱ, ㄷ, ㅂ, ㅈ, respectively. You can pronounce ㅋ, ㅌ, ㅍ, ㅊ by adding a strong aspirated sound [h] to ㄱ, ㄷ, ㅂ, ㅈ. Try to puff the air out of your mouth, when pronouncing ㅋ, ㅌ, ㅍ and ㅊ.

PRONUNCIATION OF ㄲ, ㄸ, ㅃ, ㅆ, ㅉ

ㄲ, ㄸ, ㅃ, ㅆ, ㅉ are doubled forms of ㄱ, ㄷ, ㅂ, ㅅ, ㅈ, respectively. You can pronounce ㄲ, ㄸ, ㅃ, ㅆ, ㅉ by reinforcing and tightening the sounds of ㄱ, ㄷ, ㅂ, ㅅ, ㅈ.

PRONUNCIATION OF ㅅ

ㅅ is pronounced like English *s* as in *sky* but weaker and more relaxed. When ㅅ is followed by a vowel ㅣ [i] or ㅟ [wi], it is pronounced more like *sh* as in *dish*.

PRONUNCIATION OF ㅇ

At the beginning of a syllable, ㅇ is a zero consonant. It has no sound value, but instead serves only as a place marker. At the end of a syllable, it is pronounced [ng].

Syllabus initial position	[Ø]	아 [a]
Syllable ending position	[ng]	앙 [a**ng**]

All Korean syllables start with a consonant. Thus, to write a vowel alone as a syllable, it should always be written with ㅇ in zero-consonant position. That is, the vowel symbol ㅏ becomes a syllable 아 when ㅇ is added.

Example	vowel symbol	→	syllable
	ㅏ	→	아
	ㅝ	→	워
	ㅐ	→	애

■ 2. Writing of Korean consonants

The general rule for stroke orders is that you write left to right for horizontal lines and top to bottom for vertical lines. Practice writing the following consonants, paying attention to the stroke order.

cons./name	stroke order	writing practice			
ㄱ kiyŏk	ㄱ ①	ㄱ	ㄱ	ㄱ	ㄱ
ㄴ niŭn	ㄴ ①	ㄴ	ㄴ	ㄴ	ㄴ
ㄷ tigŭt	ㄷ ① ②	ㄷ	ㄷ	ㄷ	ㄷ
ㄹ riŭl	ㄹ ① ② ③	ㄹ	ㄹ	ㄹ	ㄹ
ㅁ miŭm	ㅁ ① ② ③	ㅁ	ㅁ	ㅁ	ㅁ
ㅂ piŭp	ㅂ ① ② ③ ④	ㅂ	ㅂ	ㅂ	ㅂ
ㅅ siot	ㅅ ① ②	ㅅ	ㅅ	ㅅ	ㅅ
ㅇ iŭng	ㅇ ①	ㅇ	ㅇ	ㅇ	ㅇ

Letter	Stroke order				
ㅈ chiŭt	ㅈ ①②	ㅈ	ㅈ	ㅈ	ㅈ
ㅊ ch'iŭt	ㅊ ①②③	ㅊ	ㅊ	ㅊ	ㅊ
ㅋ k'iŭk	ㅋ ①②	ㅋ	ㅋ	ㅋ	ㅋ
ㅌ t'iŭt	ㅌ ①②③	ㅌ	ㅌ	ㅌ	ㅌ
ㅍ p'iŭp	ㅍ ①②③④	ㅍ	ㅍ	ㅍ	ㅍ
ㅎ hiŭt	ㅎ ①②③	ㅎ	ㅎ	ㅎ	ㅎ

C. Combining vowels and consonants
(CD1; 7, 8, 9)

Recall that in Hangŭl, each syllable starts with a consonant. So, to write a syllable that has only a vowel sound, you must add the zero consonant ㅇ before the vowel as in the following example.

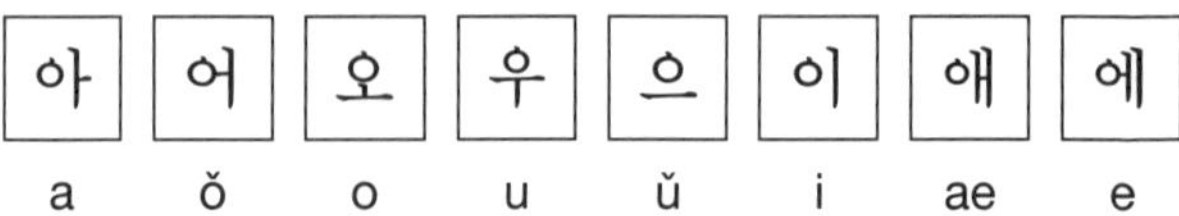

To write *ka, kŏ, ko, ku, kŭ, ki, kae, ke*, replace ㅇ with ㄱ.

가	거	고	구	그	기	개	게
ka	kŏ	ko	ku	kŭ	ki	kae	ke

Here are more examples of vowel-consonant combinations.

1 ㄴ (n) + ㅏ (a) → 나 (na)

2 ㅁ (m) + ㅓ (ŏ) → 머 (mŏ)

3 ㅋ (k’) + ㅜ (u) → 쿠 (k’u)

4 ㅎ (h) + ㅣ (i) → 히 (hi)

Now let’s examine the patterns of vowel-consonant combination in more detail in the following section.

■ 1. Syllable blocking I (consonant + vowel) **(CD1; 10, 11, 12)**

Vowels with a vertical main stroke such as ㅏ, ㅑ, ㅓ, ㅕ, ㅣ are attached to the right side of a consonant. Vowels with a horizontal main stroke such as ㅗ, ㅛ, ㅜ, ㅠ, ㅡ are written under a consonant.

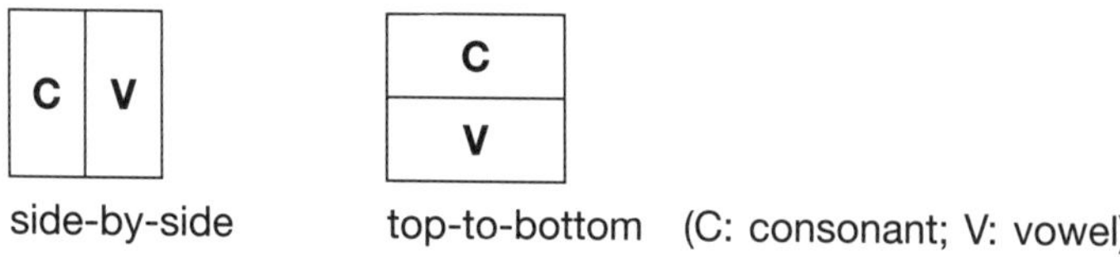

side-by-side top-to-bottom (C: consonant; V: vowel)

Side-by-side arrangement:

아	야	어	여	이	애	얘	에	예
a	ya	ŏ	yŏ	i	ae	yae	e	ye

Top-to-bottom arrangement:

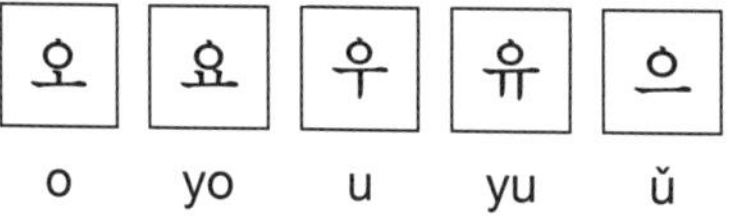

Now let's look at more examples of consonant-vowel combination.

1	ㄴ + ㅏ	→	나		5	ㅍ + ㅛ	→	표
	n a		na			p' yo		p'yo
2	ㅈ + ㅓ	→	저		6	ㅎ + ㅠ	→	휴
	ch ŏ		chŏ			h yu		hyu
3	ㄹ + ㅡ	→	르		7	ㅅ + ㅗ	→	소
	r ŭ		rŭ			s o		so
4	ㅁ + ㅐ	→	매		8	ㅋ + ㅣ	→	키
	m ae		mae			k' i		k'i

Exercise 4

(CD1; 13)

1 Look at the following table of consonant and vowel combinations, and follow along with the audio recording.

	ㅏ a	ㅓ ŏ	ㅗ o	ㅜ u	ㅡ ŭ	ㅣ i	ㅐ ae	ㅔ e
ㄱ k, g	가	거	고	구	그	기	개	게
ㄴ n	나	너	노	누	느	니	내	네
ㄷ t, d	다	더	도	두	드	디	대	데
ㄹ r, l	라	러	로	루	르	리	래	레
ㅁ m	마	머	모	무	므	미	매	메
ㅂ p, b	바	버	보	부	브	비	배	베
ㅅ s	사	서	소	수	스	시	새	세
ㅇ ø	아	어	오	우	으	이	애	에

(CD1; 14)

2 Look at the following table of consonant and vowel combinations. Fill in the boxes with the appropriate syllables. Pay attention to the stroke order and the positioning of consonants with vowels. After you've written all of them, follow along with the audio recording.

	ㅏ a	ㅑ ya	ㅓ ŏ	ㅕ yŏ	ㅗ o	ㅛ yo	ㅜ u	ㅠ yu	ㅡ ŭ	ㅣ i
ㄱ k, g	가	갸	거	겨	고	교	구	규	그	기
ㄴ n	나		너		노		누		느	
ㄷ t, d			더			됴		듀		
ㄹ r, l	라			려			루			
ㅁ m		먀			모					미
ㅂ p, b	바						부			
ㅅ s		샤			소				스	
ㅇ ø							우			
ㅈ ch, j		쟈				죠				
ㅊ ch'						쵸				
ㅋ k'			커							키
ㅌ t'	타							튜		
ㅍ p'				펴						
ㅎ h					호				흐	

Exercise 5 (CD1; 15)

Read the following Korean words aloud. Check your reading with the model pronunciation.

1	나라	country	6	캐나다	Canada
2	아기	baby	7	커피	coffee
3	오이	cucumber	8	다리미	iron
4	가요	go	9	소리	sound
5	주세요	give	10	초	candle

Exercise 6 (CD1; 16)

Listen to the model voice and circle the word you hear. Each word will be pronounced twice.

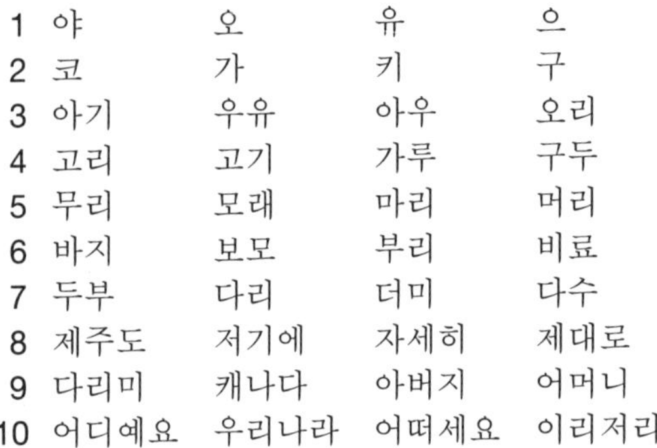

1	야	오	유	으
2	코	가	키	구
3	아기	우유	아우	오리
4	고리	고기	가루	구두
5	무리	모래	마리	머리
6	바지	보모	부리	비료
7	두부	다리	더미	다수
8	제주도	저기에	자세히	제대로
9	다리미	캐나다	아버지	어머니
10	어디예요	우리나라	어떠세요	이리저리

Exercise 7 (CD1; 17)

Listen to the model voice and complete the following words. Each word will be pronounced twice.

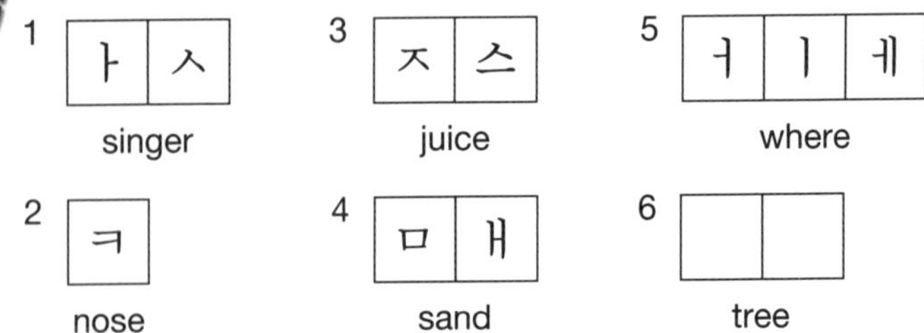

Exercise 8 (CD1; 18)

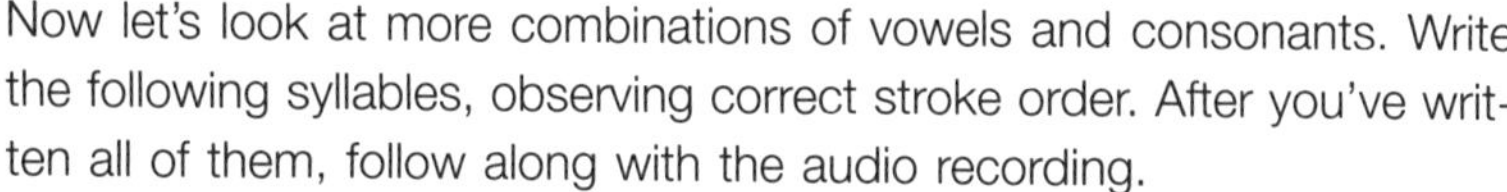

Now let's look at more combinations of vowels and consonants. Write the following syllables, observing correct stroke order. After you've written all of them, follow along with the audio recording.

(1)	에	예	애	얘	와	워	위	외	왜	웨	의
	에	예	애	얘	와	워	위	외	왜	웨	의
(2)	게	계	개	걔	과	궈	귀	괴	괘	궤	긔
(3)	네	녜	내	냬	놔	눠	뉘	뇌	놰	눼	늬

Exercise 9 (CD1; 19)

Continue to practice writing Hangŭl with the following syllables; follow along with the recorded pronunciations.

(1)	도	과	나	쥐	웨	뷔	페	뻬	빼	헤	휴
(2)	태	떼	째	꿰	꾀	꽈	씌	솨	래	뮈	춰

Exercise 10 (CD1; 20)

Read the following Korean words aloud. Check your reading with the model pronunciation.

1	예	yes	4	개	dog	7	의도	intention
2	왜	why	5	귀	ear	8	꾀꼬리	oriole
3	위	up	6	뷔페	buffet	9	의사	doctor

■ 2. Syllable blocking II **(CD1; 21)** (consonant + vowel + consonant)

In syllable blocking I, syllables that end in a vowel were introduced. However, not all syllables end in a vowel in Korean. There are many words that end in a consonant, and some syllables have multiple consonants. When final consonants are added, syllable blocks are formed in the following patterns. (C: consonant; V: vowel)

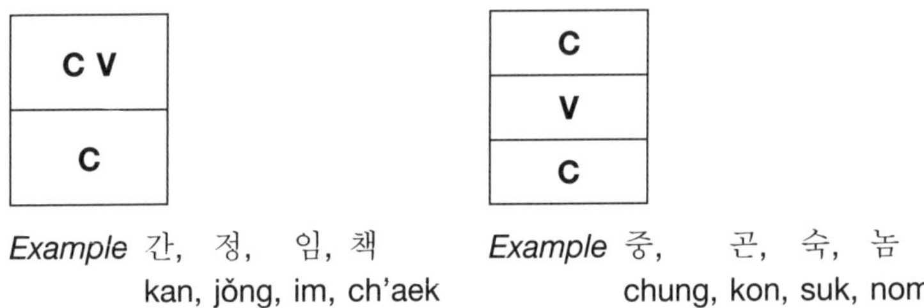

Take a look at the following syllables containing final consonants; follow along with the recorded pronunciations.

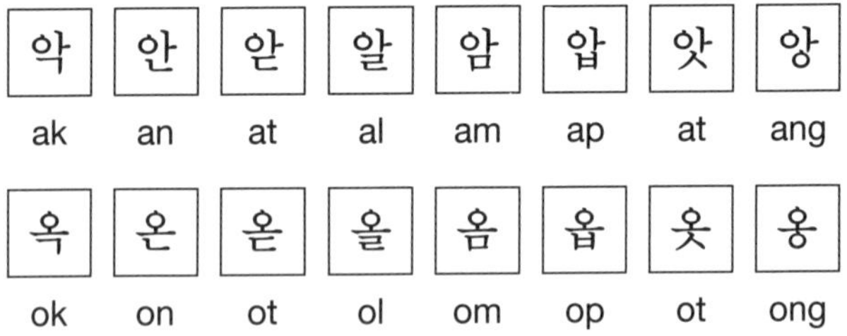

■ Pronunciation of the final consonants

Some consonants change pronunciation slightly when they occur at the end of a syllable. As final consonants, ㄱ, ㅋ, ㄲ are pronounced [k], ㅂ, ㅍ are pronounced [p], and ㄷ, ㅌ, ㅅ, ㅆ, ㅈ, ㅊ, ㅎ are pronounced [t]. This pronunciation change is summarized below:

syllable-final position		**pronunciation**	**example**	
ㄱ, ㅋ, ㄲ	→	k	낙	nak
ㅂ, ㅍ	→	p	돕	dop
ㄷ, ㅌ, ㅅ, ㅆ, ㅈ, ㅊ, ㅎ	→	t	있	it

These consonants in syllable-final position (ㄱ, ㅋ, ㄲ, ㅂ, ㅍ, ㄷ, ㅌ, ㅅ, ㅆ, ㅈ, ㅊ or ㅎ) are unreleased stops. Pronounce them without releasing air; stop the sound in the middle of the pronunciation. You can do this by shortening or tightening its sound.

Exercise 11 **(CD1; 22)**

Listen to the following words and repeat aloud after the speaker. Each word will be pronounced twice. Focus on the final consonants. After you've become familiar with their pronunciation, practice writing the following words, recalling their pronunciations.

1	한국	Korea	11	발	foot
2	서울	Seoul	12	팔	arm
3	사람	person	13	악수	hand-shaking
4	영어	English	14	못	nail
5	선생님	teacher	15	밥	rice; meal
6	옷	clothes	16	국	soup
7	목	neck	17	영국	the UK
8	눈	eye	18	뉴욕	New York
9	입	mouth	19	부엌	kitchen
10	손	hand	20	앞	front

Exercise 12 **(CD1; 23)**

Listen to the following word pairs and repeat aloud after the speaker. Each pair has two syllables that sound identical. Focus on the pronunciation of the final consonants.

1	같–갓	6	솟–솥
2	깍–깎	7	넣–넛
3	숟–숫	8	끝–끗
4	팟–팥	9	햇–했
5	덥–덮	10	억–엌

Exercise 13 **(CD1; 24)**

The following words are English loanwords used in Korean. Read them aloud and try to guess the original English words. Then compare your reading with the model pronunciation. The original English words are provided in the Answer Key to Exercises.

1 커피	6 컴퓨터	11 케이크
2 라디오	7 팩스	12 치즈
3 바나나	8 프린터	13 카메라
4 아이스크림	9 컵	14 초콜릿
5 아메리카	10 커피숍	15 샌드위치

Exercise 14

Combine the following vowels and consonants into syllabic units. Pay attention to the position of each vowel and consonant.

Example ㄱ + ㅏ + ㅇ → 강

1 ㅈ + ㅣ + ㅂ	6 ㅇ + ㅝ + ㄴ
2 ㅆ + ㅏ + ㄹ	7 ㅅ + ㅟ + ㅂ
3 ㅋ + ㅓ + ㅁ	8 ㄱ + ㅜ + ㄱ
4 ㅁ + ㅜ + ㄹ	9 ㄴ + ㅠ + ㄱ
5 ㅇ + ㅗ + ㄱ	10 ㅇ + ㅕ + ㅍ

■ 3. Syllable blocking III (C + V + C + C)

There are syllables with two final consonants, as shown in the two figures below.

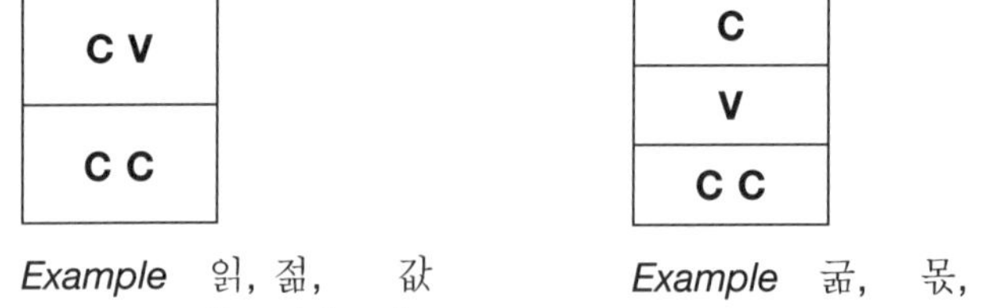

Example 읽, 젊, 값
il, chŏm, kap

Example 굶, 몫, 옮
kum, mok, om

You'll learn more about the pronunciations of two final consonants in the next section, "Pronunciation Guidelines."

Note:
When stacking vowels and consonants into syllabic blocks, try to balance the size and shape of vowels and consonants so that each consonant and vowel fits proportionately into a syllabic box. Each syllabic block should appear to be the same size. Thus, as the number of vowels and consonants increase, you'll need to write them smaller.

ka kap

D. Pronunciation guidelines

The following are major pronunciation rules that will assist you with speaking and reading Korean. Other pronunciation tips and details are also provided in lessons throughout this book.

(CD1; 25)

■ 1. Pronunciation of ㄱ, ㄷ, ㅂ, ㅈ (k/g, t/d, p/b, ch/j)

ㄱ, ㄷ, ㅂ, ㅈ (k, t, p, ch) are sounded g, d, b, j when they occur between two vowels. That is, in that position these consonants are voiced. Compare the sounds of the following pairs by carefully listening to the model voice and repeating after the speaker.

a. 가수 **k**asu singer
휴가 hyu**g**a vacation

b. 다리 **t**ari leg; bridge
바다 pa**d**a sea

c. 비 **p**i rain
준비 chun**b**i preparation

d. 자주 **ch**aju often
모자 mo**j**a hat

(CD1; 26)

■ 2. Pronunciation of ㄹ (r/l)

ㄹ is pronounce d [r] at the syllable-initial position or in between two vowels.

a. 라면 **r**amyŏn ramen, instant noodles
b. 머리 mŏ**r**i head; hair; brain

ㄹ is pronounced [l] at the syllable-final position or when it is preceded by another ㄹ.

c. 말 ma**l** language
d. 빨래 ppal-**l**ae laundry

(CD1; 27)

■ 3. Pronunciation of syllables

Joining syllables can sometimes alter their pronunciation. When a consonant-ending syllable is followed by a vowel, the final consonant is pronounced as the second syllable's initial consonant.

a. 할아버지 ha-**ra**-bŏ-ji grandfather
(pronounced [하라버지])

b. 있어요 i-**ssŏ**-yo to exist
(pronounced [이써요])

c. 도서관에 do-sŏ-gwa-**ne** to the library
(pronounced [도서과네])

d. 작아요 cha-**ga**-yo be small
(pronounced [자가요])

(CD1; 28)

■ 4. Pronunciation of ㅎ (h)

1 Between two voiced sounds (vowels or ㄹ consonant), the sound of ㅎ is usually weakened, almost silent.

a. 좋아요 cho-a-yo be good
(pronounced [조아요])

b. 미안해요 mi-an-**hae**-yo or mi-a-n**ae**-yo I am sorry.
(pronounced [미안해요] or [미아네요])

2 When ㅎ occurs before or after ㄱ, ㄷ, ㅂ, ㅈ, the combined sound is ㅋ, ㅌ, ㅍ, ㅊ, respectively.

ㅎ + ㄱ, ㄷ, ㅂ, ㅈ → ㅋ, ㅌ, ㅍ, ㅊ
h + k, t, p, ch → k', t', p', ch'

c. 어떻게 ŏ-ttŏ-**k'**e how
(pronounced [어떠케])

d. 좋다 cho**t'**a good
(pronounced [조타])

e. 입학 **ip'**ak entering a school
(pronounced [이팍])

f. 그렇지만 kŭrŏ**ch'i**man but, however
(pronounced [그러치만])

(CD1; 29)

■ 5. Nasal pronunciation

A consonant followed by nasal consonants ㄴ or ㅁ (n or m) is also nasalized for ease of pronunciation.

ㄱ, ㅋ, ㄲ → ㅇ [ng]
ㄷ, ㅌ, ㅅ, ㅆ, ㅈ, ㅊ, ㅎ → ㄴ [n]
ㅂ, ㅍ → ㅁ [m]

a. 죽는 chu**ng**-nŭn (pronounced [중는])
b. 끝나요 kkŭ**n**-na-yo (pronounced [끈나요])
c. 옷만 o**n**-man (pronounced [온만])
d. 밥맛 pa**m**-mat (pronounced [밤맛])

(CD1; 30)

■ 6. Pronunciation of two final consonants

1 When there are two final consonants in a syllable, one of the two final consonants is silenced. Which one of the two consonants becomes silent? It depends on the word; thus you'll just need to learn the pronunciation of such words as you encounter them. Syllables with two final consonants are not too common, so there are not too many to memorize.

a. 값 kap [갑] price
b. 닭 tak [닥] chicken
c. 앉 an [안] to sit

2 However, when a syllable containing two final consonants is followed by a vowel, both of the final consonants are pronounced. The second final consonant sound carries over to the following syllable (pronouncing the second consonant as the initial consonant sound of the following syllable).

d. 읽어요 il-gŏ-yo [일거요] I read
e. 앉아요 an-ja-yo [안자요] I sit

(CD1; 31)

■ 7. Tensed pronunciation

When ㄱ, ㄷ, ㅂ, ㅅ, ㅈ (k, t, p, s, ch) are preceded by ㄱ, ㄷ, ㅂ (k, t, p), they are intensified and pronounced as ㄲ, ㄸ, ㅃ, ㅆ, ㅉ (kk, tt, pp, ss, tch) respectively.

a. 학교	**hak-kkyo**	[학꾜]	school
b. 식당	**shik-ttang**	[식땅]	restaurant
c. 입다	**ip-tta**	[입따]	wear
d. 집주인	**chip-tchu-in**	[집쭈인]	home owner
e. 한국분	**han-kuk-ppun**	[한국뿐]	Korean person
f. 한국산	**han-kuk-ssan**	[한국싼]	Korean-made

■ 8. Stress in Korean

In general, Korean words do not have the kind of stress found in English words (for example, the English word *language* has a stress on *a* in the syllable *lang*). So, Korean words may sound flatter. However, to sound more like a native speaker, pay attention to the intonation of sentences by listening carefully to the native speaker's voice provided in the accompanying audio tape/cd.

Exercise 15 (CD1; 32)

Read the following words aloud. Compare your pronunciation with the model pronunciation, and then practice writing the following words.

1 태권도 Taekwondo
2 의자 chair
3 전화 telephone
4 회사 company
5 식사 (eating) meal
6 있어요 exist; have
7 빨리 fast
8 영어 the English language
9 화장실 restroom
10 없어요 not exist; not have
11 읽어요 read
12 입니다 is; am; are
13 어떻게 how
14 좋아요 be good

Exercise 16 (CD1; 33)

Circle the word that you hear. The word will be pronounced twice.

1 괜찮아요—귀찮아요
2 누구예요—구두예요
3 계세요—겠어요
4 겠어요—계세요
5 여행—유행
6 파리—빨리
7 외국—왜곡
8 번호—보모
9 책상—책방
10 좋고—작고

Exercise 17 **(CD1; 34)**

Read the following words aloud and write them at least twice. Also compare your reading with the model pronunciation.

1 British person

영	국	사	람	영	국	사	람				

2 waiter

웨	이	터									

3 subway

지	하	철									

4 doctor

의	사										

5 movie theater

극	장										

6 coffee shop

커	피	숍									

7 bank employee

은	행	원									

8 price

값											

9 telephone number

전	화	번	호								

10 department store

백	화	점									

11 Korean language

한	국	말									

12 university

대	학	교									

13 fast, quickly

빨	리										

14 parking lot

주	차	장									

E. Summary of Romanization

The table below summarizes the Roman letters used in this book for Korean consonants and vowels. While you get more used to Hangŭl consonants and vowels, Romanization may help you with pronunciation. However, keep in mind that the best way to practice pronunciation is by listening to and repeating the native speaker's pronunciation.

Hangŭl consonants	Romanization	Hangŭl vowels	Romanization
ㄱ	k, g	ㅏ	a
ㄴ	n	ㅑ	ya
ㄷ	t, d	ㅓ	ŏ
ㄹ	r, l	ㅕ	yŏ
ㅁ	m	ㅗ	o
ㅂ	p, b	ㅛ	yo
ㅅ	s, sh	ㅜ	u

Hangŭl consonants	Romanization	Hangŭl vowels	Romanization
ㅇ	ø, ng	ㅠ	yu
ㅈ	ch, j	ㅡ	ŭ
ㅊ	ch'	ㅣ	i
ㅋ	k'	ㅐ	ae
ㅌ	t'	ㅒ	yae
ㅍ	p'	ㅔ	e
ㅎ	h	ㅖ	ye
ㄲ	kk	ㅘ	wa
ㄸ	tt	ㅝ	wŏ
ㅃ	pp	ㅟ	wi
ㅆ	ss	ㅚ	we
ㅉ	tch	ㅙ	wae
		ㅞ	we
		ㅢ	ŭi

F. Basic sentence structure of Korean

There are four basic sentence structures in Korean.

Sentence types	
1. subject + noun + be (is/am/are) verb	
메리 + 가	학생 + 이에요.
Noun + subject marker	Noun + be-verb
Mary	**student + is**
Mary is a student	
2. subject + adjective	
날씨 + 가	더워요.
Noun + subject marker	Adjective
Weather	**hot**
The weather is hot. (It's hot.)	

Sentence types		
3. subject + verb		
비 + 가	와요.	
Noun + subject marker	Verb	
Rain	**comes**	
It is raining.		
4. subject + object + verb		
메리 + 가	책 + 을	읽어요.
Noun + subject marker	Noun + object marker	Verb
Mary	**book**	**reads**
Mary reads a book.		

■ 1. Subject

The subject of a Korean sentence is usually placed at the beginning of a sentence, as in English. However, unlike English, subjects in Korean (particularly *I* and *you*) are frequently deleted when they are contextually apparent. Therefore, when a subject is deleted, the verb *go* in Korean could mean "I go" or "you go" or "she/he goes" or "they go"; use context to decide the correct meaning.

■ 2. Word order

While English is an SVO (subject + verb + object) language, Korean is an SOV (subject + object + verb) language: the verb is usually at the end of a sentence.

■ 3. Subject marker and object marker

In colloquial speech, subject or object markers are frequently omitted. When sentence subjects or objects are marked using a subject or object marker, the positioning of a subject or an object becomes more flexible than it is in English. This is because subject and object marking clarifies which is which, regardless of sentence position.

4. Verbs and adjectives

Verbs represent actions or processes, while adjectives describe states, conditions, or shapes. Here are some examples of Korean verbs and adjectives.

verbs			adjectives		
가다	kada	*to go*	바쁘다	pappŭda	*be busy*
하다	hada	*to do*	예쁘다	yeppŭda	*be pretty*
먹다	mŏk-tta	*to eat*	크다	k'ŭda	*be big*
주다	chuda	*to give*	작다	chak-tta	*be small*
만나다	man-nada	*to meet*	맛있다	mashit-tta	*be delicious*

In the dictionary, verbs and adjectives all end in 다. So the…다 form of a verb or an adjective is called its dictionary form. The part before 다 is the base of a verb or adjective.

"to go"	가다	: dictionary form
	가	: base
"be busy"	바쁘다	: dictionary form
	바쁘	: base

5. Auxiliary verbs

Auxiliary verbs follow verbs, adjectives, or nouns and give further information or meaning. Compare the position of auxiliary verbs in Korean and in English:

English	Korean
can go	go-can (가 to go + ㄹ 수 있어요 can)
will do	do-will (하 to do + ㄹ 거예요 will)

G. Useful expressions in Korean (CD1; 35)

The following is a list of useful expressions that are most frequently used in daily life. These expressions are also introduced throughout the book.

	Korean	Romanization	English definition
1	안녕하세요?	**Annyŏng-haseyo?**	How are you?/Hello.
2	감사합니다.	**Kamsa(h)amnida.**	Thank you.
3	고마워요.	**Komawŏyo.**	Thank you. (casual)
4	고맙습니다.	**Komapsŭmnida.**	Thank you.
5	뭘요.	**Mwŏlyo.**	Not at all. (You are welcome.)
6	별말씀을요.	**Pyŏlmalssŭmŭlyo.**	Don't mention it. (You are welcome.)
7	미안해요.	**Mian(h)aeyo.**	I'm sorry. (casual)
8	미안합니다.	**Mian(h)amnida.**	I'm sorry. (formal)
9	죄송해요.	**Chwesong(h)aeyo.**	I'm truly sorry. (casual)
10	죄송합니다.	**Chwesonghamnida.**	I'm truly sorry. (formal)
11	괜찮아요.	**Kwaenchanayo.**	That's okay. (casual)
12	괜찮습니다.	**Kwaenchansŭmnida.**	That's okay. (formal)
13	네.	**Ne.**	Yes.
14	예.	**Ye.**	Yes.
15	아니오.	**Anio.**	No.
16	안녕히 가세요.	**Annyŏng(h)i kaseyo.**	Good-bye. (to the one leaving) [lit. Go in peace.]
17	안녕히 계세요.	**Annyŏng(h)i kyeseyo.**	Good-bye. (to the one staying) [lit. Stay in peace.]
18	...한국말로 뭐라고 해요?	**...hangungmallo mwŏrago-haeyo?**	How do you say... in Korean?

Unit One
인사
Greetings

In this unit you will learn about:

- How to greet people
- How to introduce yourself
- Identify something or someone using ...이에요/입니다
- Idiomatic expressions for first meetings
- Asking for someone's name
- How to write Korean names
- How to address Korean adults
- How to use the verb 이다 "to be"
- How to say "to not be" in Korean
- The use of ...는요/은요? to shift topics

Dialogue 1

(CD1; 36, 37)

James Smith, a new employee at the Global Printing Company, is meeting his co-worker Ms Mira Kim for the first time. They are being introduced to each other.

제임스	안녕하세요? 제임스 스미스입니다.
김미라	안녕하세요? 처음 뵙겠습니다.
제임스	성함이 어떻게 되세요?
김미라	김미라입니다.
제임스	반갑습니다.
김미라	예, 반갑습니다.
제임스	이거 제 명함입니다.
김미라	감사합니다.

JAMES	Annyŏng-haseyo? Cheimsŭ Sŭmisŭ-imnida.
KIM MIRA	Annyŏng-haseyo? Ch'ŏ-ŭm pwekket-ssŭm-ni-da.
JAMES	Sŏng-(h)a-mi ŏ-ttŏ-k'e dwe-se-yo?
KIM MIRA	Kim Mira im-ni-da.
JAMES	Pan-gap-sŭm-ni-da.
KIM MIRA	Ye, Pan-gap-sŭm-ni-da.
JAMES	I-gŏ je myŏng-(h)am-im-ni-da
KIM MIRA	Kamsa-ham-ni-da.

JAMES	*How are you?* *I am James Smith.*
KIM MIRA	*Hello.* *How do you do? [lit. It's the first time to see you.]*
JAMES	*What is your name?*
KIM MIRA	*I am Kim Mira.*
JAMES	*It's nice to see you.*
KIM MIRA	*Yes, it's nice to see you.*
JAMES	*This is my business card.*
KIM MIRA	*Thank you.*

Vocabulary

안녕하세요?	How are you?, Hello, Hi
제임스 스미스	James Smith
입니다	is, am, are
처음 뵙겠습니다.	How do you do? [lit. I will see you for the first time]
처음	first time; for the first time
뵙겠습니다	I see you 뵙다 (see) + 겠(will) + 습니다 (sentence ending)
성함이 어떻게 되세요?	What is your name? [lit. How does your name become?)
성함	name
...이	subject marker
어떻게 되세요	how to become
김미라	Kim Mira (last name: Kim, first name: Mira)
반갑습니다.	It's nice to meet you./Glad to see you. [lit. Be glad (to see).]
예	Yes (= 네)
이거	this
제	my
명함	business card
감사합니다.	Thank you.

Note:

- 입니다 is pronounced [imnida], as [p] in 입 becomes [m] before the nasal sound ㄴ [n] in 니.
- 습니다 is pronounced [sŭmnida] not [sŭp-nida].
- 명함 is pronounced either [myŏng-ham] or [myŏng-am] with the "h" sound weakened.
- 감사합니다 is pronounced either [kamsa-hamnida] or [kamsa-amnida] with the "h" sound weakened.

(Refer also to "Pronunciation guidelines" in the Introduction.)

Grammar points

1.1 Greetings in Korean

Annyŏnghaseyo? (안녕하세요?) is the most commonly used greeting expression which can be used at any time of day. When someone greets you with 안녕하세요?, you can return the greeting with 안녕하세요?

A: 안녕하세요? How are you?, Hello.
B: 안녕하세요? How are you?, Hello.

1.2 Introducing oneself

You can introduce a person, including yourself by just adding 입니다 [imnida] after the person's name.

존입니다	**Jon-imnida**	I am John.
메리입니다	**Meri-imnida**	I am Mary.

Depending on context, 입니다 can mean: *I am; you are; he is; she is; they are.* So, 존입니다 can mean *I am John; He is John; It is John.*

1.3 Korean names

In Korean, the surname is written before the given name. Here are some common Korean last names and their typical transcription in English:

김	Kim	이	Lee; Yi	박	Park; Pak
조	Cho	최	Choi; Choe	정	Chong; Jeong
장	Chang; Jang	홍	Hong	서	Suh; Seo
남	Nam; Nahm	노	No; Noh; Roh	강	Kang; Gang
신	Shin	한	Han	윤	Yoon; Yun

1.4 Asking someone's name

Sŏng-a-mi ŏ-ttŏ-k'e twe-se-yo? (성함이 어떻게 되세요?) is an idiomatic expression asking someone's name. Another expression that has the same meaning is **I-rŭ-mi Mwŏ-e-yo?** (이름이 뭐예요?). **Sŏngami ŏttŏk'e dweseyo?** (성함이 어떻게 되세요?), which is frequently used between adults, is a more formal and polite expression than **Irŭmi Mwŏeyo?** (이름이 뭐예요?).

Exercise 1 **(CD1; 38)**

How would you greet your co-worker when you meet her at the following times:

1 9:00 a.m. 2 1:00 p.m. 3 6:30 p.m.

Exercise 2

Introduce yourself in Korean.

Exercise 3

You meet a person at a conference. Ask her what her name is.

Exercise 4

Complete the dialogue by filling in the blanks with the appropriate idiomatic expression.

James Smith:	______________	How do you do?
	제임스 스미스입니다.	I am James Smith.
Mira Kim:	______________	Glad to see you.
	김미라입니다.	I am Mira Kim.

Cultural point

Greeting with a bow

When greeting, Koreans will often bow to each other. The degree of a bow may vary depending on who you are greeting. To a person who is much older or whose social status is higher than your own, you can bend at the waist, but to a close friend, you may simply nod your head. To a much younger person such as a young child, *annyong?* (안녕?) instead of *annyonghaseyo?* (안녕하세요?) can be used without bowing or head-nodding.

Exchanging business cards

It is a very common practice in Korea to exchange business cards at the first meeting. When handing your business card, you are expected to use both hands. Generally, to show courtesy to a person, two hands should always be used when giving an object to someone.

Dialogue 2

(CD1; 39)
James has an appointment with Mr Han Sangho from Hangook Electronics, whom he first met several months ago. James arrives at Mr Han's office and knocks on the door.

한상호 네, 들어오세요.
제임스 안녕하세요?
한상호 아, 제임스씨. 오래간만이에요.
제임스 요즘, 어떻게 지내세요?
한상호 잘 지내요. 제임스씨는요?
제임스 조금 바빠요.
한상호 아, 그래요?
제임스 한과장님은 고향이 서울이에요?
한상호 아니오. 서울이 아니에요. 대구예요.

MR HAN Ne, Tŭrŏ-o-se-yo.
JAMES An-nyŏng-ha-se-yo?
MR HAN Ah, Che-im-sŭ ssi. O-re-gan-mani-eyo.
JAMES Yojŭm, ŏttŏk'e ji-nae-se-yo?
MR HAN Chal ji-nae-yo. Che-im-sŭ-ssi-nŭn-yo?
JAMES Cho-gŭm ba-ppa-yo.
MR HAN Ah, kŭ-rae-yo?
JAMES Han kwa-jang-ni-mŭn ko-(h)yang-i Sŏu-ri-eyo?
MR HAN Aniyo. Sŏuri ani-eyo. Taegu-(y)eyo.

MR HAN *Yes, come in.*
JAMES *Hello.*
MR HAN *Ah, (Mr) James. It's been a long time.*
JAMES *How are you doing these days?*
MR HAN *I am doing well. How about you, (Mr) James?*
JAMES *I am a little busy.*
MR HAN *Oh, really? [lit. Ah, is that so?]*
JAMES *Mr Han, are you from Seoul?*
[lit. As for Manager Han, is your hometown Seoul?]
MR HAN *No. It is not Seoul. It is Daegu.*

Vocabulary

네	yes
들어오세요.	Come in.
오래간만이에요.	It's been a while, It's been ages. (an idiomatic expression used when seeing somebody after a long while) 오래간만 (long time no see) + 이에요 (is/am/are)
요즘	these days
어떻게 지내세요?	How are you doing? [lit. How are you spending days?]
어떻게 [ŏttŏk'e]	how
지내세요	to spend days (honorific form of 지내요)
잘 지내요.	I am doing fine. [lit. I am spending days well.]
잘	well
지내요	to spend days
[name] + 씨	Mr/Ms...
제임스씨는요?	What about you, James?
...는요?	What about...?, How about...?
조금	a little (조금can be contracted to 좀)
바빠요	be busy
그래요?	Is that so?, Is that right?
과장님	section chief; manager of a department 한과장님 Manager Han
...은	topic marker

고향이	고향 "hometown" + 이 subject marker
서울	Seoul, the capital city of South Korea
...이에요	am/are/is (= ... 입니다)
아니오	no
...이 아니에요	to not be...
대구	Daegu (name of a Korean city)
예요	am/are/is (variation of 이에요, attached to vowel-ending nouns) ... 예요 is pronounced either [yeyo] or [eyo].

Grammar points

1.5 Name + 씨 "Mr/Mrs/Ms/Miss..."

...씨 *ssi* is a title word used after somebody's name. It is equivalent to Mr/Mrs/Ms/Miss in English.

김영수씨	Mr Kim Youngsoo
박지영씨	Ms Park Jiyoung
브라운씨	Mr Brown

...씨 is used to address or refer to somebody other than the speaker him/herself. It is never used to refer to oneself.

제임스 스미스씨예요?	Are you James Smith?
네. 제임스 스미스예요. (correct)	Yes, I'm James Smith.
네. 제임스 스미스씨예요. (incorrect)	Yes, I'm James Smith.

Pronouns are much less frequently used in Korean than in English. In particular, Koreans tend to avoid using the pronoun *you* when addressing a person. Instead of the pronoun *you*, Koreans typically use the listener's name or the name plus a title. For example, to ask Mr Kim Youngsoo if he is a student, use "Is Mr Kim Youngsoo a student?"

1.6 Link verb 이다 "to be (am, are, is)"

The dictionary form of 입니다 is 이다. "입니다, 이에요, 예요" are three different forms of 이다.

Attached to a noun, …이다 is used to link the noun with the subject of the sentence. The two major functions of 이다 (입니다, 이에요/예요) are:

1 Identify someone or something

Example 제임스입니다 I'm James.

2 Equate someone/thing with some other person/thing.

Example 고향이 서울이에요. (My) hometown is Seoul.

The meaning of 이에요/예요 is the same as that of 입니다. However, 입니다 sounds more formal or deferential than 이에요/예요. The choice between 이에요 and 예요 depends on the preceding noun. If the preceding noun ends in a consonant, 이에요 is used and if the preceding noun ends in a vowel, 예요 is used.

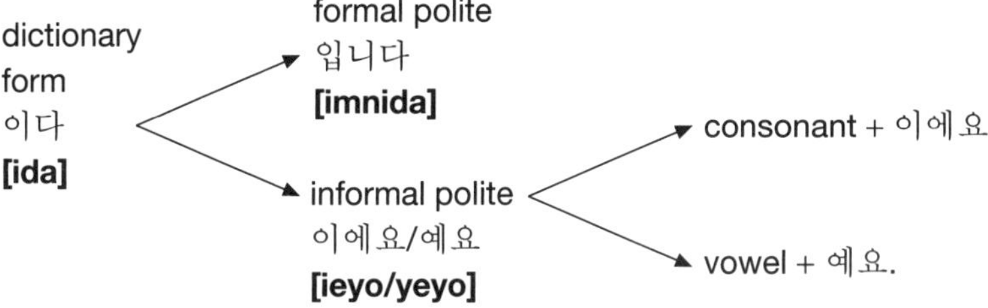

김미라입니다 or 김미라예요.	I am Mira Kim.
제임스입니다 or 제임스예요.	I am James.
제니예요.	I am Jenny.
마이클이에요.	I am Michael.

제임스입니다 "I am James" literally means "*James am*" because the subject "I" is often deleted in Korean when it is contextually apparent.

1.7 Creating questions using 이에요?/예요? "Are you…?"

Note that by raising the tone just like in English, the 이에요/예요? ending can also make the sentence a question.

김지연이에요.	(statement)	I am Kim Jiyŏn.
김지연이에요?	(question)	Are you Kim Jiyŏn?
커피예요.	(statement)	It is coffee.
커피예요?	(question)	Is it coffee?

1.8 Shifting topics using ...는요/은요? "What about...?; How about...?"

...는요/은요? is used when shifting a topic to something else. When preceded by a word ending in a consonant, 은요? is used and when preceded by a word ending in a vowel, 는요? is used.

김미라씨는요?	What about you (Kim Mira)?
이거는요?	What about this?
성함은요?	What about your name?

1.9 The negative form of "Noun 이에요/예요"

Noun 이/가 아니에요	It is not Noun

[noun] + 입니다 or [noun] + 이에요/예요 means "It is/I am/He is/She is/They are [noun]." The negative form of "[noun] 입니다" or "[noun] 이에요/예요" is "[noun] 이/가 아니에요."

영국 사람이에요.	I am a British [person].
미국 사람이 아니에요.	I am not an American [person].

(영국: the UK, 미국: the US, 사람: person)

When the preceding noun ends in a consonant, ...이 아니에요 is used, and when the preceding noun ends in a vowel, ...가 아니에요 is used. Note the use of 이 or 가 and the preceding noun in the following examples.

서울이 아니에요.	It is not Seoul.
대구가 아니에요.	It is not Daegu.
제임스가 아니에요.	I am not James. He is not James.
김미라가 아니에요.	I am not Kim Mira. She is not Kim Mira.
학생이 아니에요.	I am not a student. (학생: student)

Exercise 5

Choose the correct form, paying attention to the usage of 입니다/이에요/예요.

Example 박수미이에요/(박수미예요.) I'm Park Sumi.

1 피터 브라운이에요/피터 브라운예요. I'm Peter Brown.
2 한국이에요/한국예요. It is Korea.
3 존입니다/존예요. He is John.
4 한국어이에요/한국어예요. It is Korean language.
5 조문기입니다/조문기이에요. I am Cho Munki.

Exercise 6

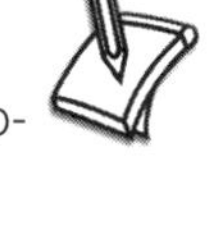

You are showing your friend the following photo of you with your co-workers. Identify each person for your friend using 이에요 or 예요.

1 사라 Sarah 3 마이클 밀러 Michael Miller
2 존 John 4 이미영 Lee Miyoung

Exercise 7 **(CD1; 40)**

You are asked the following questions. Answer the question using the negative form of the sentence given.

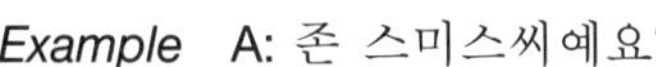

Example A: 존 스미스씨예요? Is he John Smith?
B: 존 스미스씨가 아니에요. No. He is not.

1 영국사람이에요? Are you British? (영국사람: a British person)
2 서울이에요? Is it Seoul?
3 한국어예요? Is it Korean?
4 스티브예요? Are you Steve?

Exercise 8

Imagine that you are James Smith who is from the UK. You work in Korea for the Global Printing Company.

1 Introduce/identify yourself.

2 Answer the following questions.
   a. 미국 사람이에요? (미국 사람: an American)
   b. 학생이에요? (학생: a student)
   c. 존 밀러씨예요? (존 밀러: John Miller)

Exercise 9 (CD1; 41)

How would you respond in the following situations?

1 Greeting a person that you met for the first time.

2 Greeting Manager Park, whom you haven't seen for a long time.

3 Asking Manager Park how he is doing these days.

Unit Two
어디 가세요?
Where are you going?

In this unit you will learn about:

- The polite sentence ending ...아요/어요
- The honorific polite sentence endings ...(으)세요 and ...(이)세요
- Constructing negative sentences using 안... "not..."
- Asking someone where he/she is going
- Providing a destination
- Names of public places
- Expressing existence or possession using 있어요
- Expressing the location of something using ...에 있어요
- How to use 별로 "not really"

Dialogue 1

(CD1; 42, 43)
James is on his way to a café inside the company building when he runs into Mira in the hallway.

김미라	어디 가세요?
제임스	카페에 가요.
김미라	회의에 안 가세요?
제임스	오늘 회의 있어요?
김미라	네. 지금 시작해요.
제임스	회의실 어디에 있어요?
김미라	이층에 있어요.
	같이 가요.

KIM MIRA	Ŏdi-ga-se-yo?
JAMES	K'ap'e-e gayo.
KIM MIRA	Hwe-i-e an kaseyo?
JAMES	Onŭl hwe-i-i-ssŏ-yo?
KIM MIRA	Ne, Chigŭm shijak-haeyo.
JAMES	Hwei-sil ŏdi-e-i-ssŏ-yo?
KIM MIRA	I-ch'ŭng-e i-ssŏ-yo.
	Kach'i gayo.

KIM MIRA	*Where are you going?*
JAMES	*I am going to the café.*
KIM MIRA	*Aren't you going to the meeting?*
JAMES	*Do we have a meeting today?*
KIM MIRA	*Yes, it's starting now.*
JAMES	*Where is the conference room?*
KIM MIRA	*It's on the second floor.*
	Let's go together.

Vocabulary

어디	Where
가세요	to go (< dic. form: 가다) 가다 "to go" dictionary form 가요. "to go" polite sentence ending 가세요. "to go" honorific polite sentence ending

카페	café, coffee shop = 커피숍
...에	to (attached to locations, 에 marks the destination) 카페에 to café 서울에 to Seoul 뉴욕에 to New York
회의	conference, meeting
안	not (negative marker, followed by a verb/adjective) 안 가요. I don't go [lit. Not go] 안 가요? Don't you go? [lit. Not go?]
지금	now
시작해요	to start (< dic. form: 시작하다) 시작하다 (to start) + 어요/아요 (polite sentence ending)
회의실	conference room, meeting room
어디예요?	Where is it? 어디 (where) + 예요 (is)?
이층	second floor 이 (two) + 층 (floor)
...에 있어요.	It is [located] in/on/at... 서울에 있어요. It is in Seoul. 대구에 있어요. It is in Daegu.
있어요	1 to exist 2 to have, to possess
같이	together
같이 가요.	Let's go together.

Note:
같이 is pronounced like [kachi] not [kati].
회의 is pronounced either [hwe-ŭi] or [hwe-i].

Grammar points

2.1 The polite sentence ending ...아요/어요 ayo/ŏyo (CD1; 44)

아요/어요 is a polite sentence ending form that is attached to verb and adjective bases. The base part of a verb or adjective is the part that appears before –다 in the dictionary.

Dictionary form	Base
가다 to go	가
오다 to come	오

1 When the last vowel of the verb or adjective base ends in 아 [a] or 오 [o], 아요 [ayo] is used.

앉다	to sit	앉 + 아요 → 앉아요	[**anjayo**]
좋다	be good	좋 + 아요 → 좋아요	[**choayo**]

When the base ends in [a] or [o], vowel contraction occurs.

가다	to go	가 + 아요 → 가요	[**kayo**]
자다	to sleep	자 + 아요 → 자요	[**chayo**]
오다	to come	오 + 아요 → 와요	[**wayo**]
보다	to see	보 + 아요 → 봐요	[**pwayo**]

2 When the last vowel of the verb or adjective base ends in a vowel other than 아 [a] or 오 [o], 어요 [ŏyo] is used.

먹다	to eat	먹 + 어요 → 먹어요	[**mŏgŏyo**]
읽다	to read	읽 + 어요 → 읽어요	[**ilgŏyo**]
있다	to exist, to have	있 + 어요 → 있어요	[**issŏyo**]

When the preceding vowel is 애, 어 is dropped to contract the vowel.

지내다	to spend days	지내 + 어요 → 지내요	[**chinaeyo**]
보내다	to send	보내 + 어요 → 보내요	[**ponaeyo**]

3 When the verb or adjective ends with 하다, 해요 is used.

공부하다	to study	→	공부해요	[**kongbu-haeyo**]
일하다	to work	→	일해요	[**il-haeyo**]
하다	to do	→	해요	[**haeyo**]
시작하다	to start	→	시작해요	[**shijak-haeyo**]
운동하다	to exercise	→	운동해요	[**undong-haeyo**]

4 Irregular verbs/adjectives
Some verbs/adjectives do not follow the regular **ayo/ŏyo** rule. These irregular verbs/adjectives require special attention.

Example 바쁘다 be busy → 바빠요 [**pappayo**]

2.2 The honorific polite sentence ending ...(으)세요 (CD1; 45)

...(으)세요 is an honorific form of 아요/어요 that is used to show respect or courtesy to a person. (으)세요 is used to elevate someone, thus is never used to refer to the speaker him/herself. When the base of a verb or an adjective ends in a consonant, 으세요 is used and when the verb/adjective base ends in a vowel, 세요 is used.

dic. form		polite ending	honorific polite ending
가다	to go	가요	가세요.
앉다	to sit	앉아요	앉으세요.
오다	to come	와요	오세요.
있다	to have	있어요	있으세요.
만나다	to meet	만나요	만나세요.
하다	to do	해요	하세요.
시작하다	to start	시작해요	시작하세요.

2.3 ...에 가요 "go to..."

...에 is a location marker. Used with a location, ...에 가요 means "go to the destination." ...에 가세요 is an honorific form of ...에 가요.

[Destination] 에 가요.

은행에 가요.	I am going to the bank.
도서관에 가요.	I am going to the library.
백화점에 가세요?	Are you going to the department store?

To ask where he/she is going, the question word 어디 "where" is used. After 어디, the location marker 에 is frequently omitted.

어디에 가세요?	Where are you going? [lit. where-to go?]
= 어디 가세요?	Where are you going? [lit. where go?]

2.4 Constructing negatives using 안 "not..."

In Unit 1, you learned the negative of [noun] 이에요/예요, which is [noun] 이/가 아니에요. To express the negative of a verb or an adjective, the negation word 안 is placed before the verb/adjective.

안 가요. I don't go. [lit. Not go.]
안 바빠요. I am not busy. [lit. Not busy.]
안 좋아요. It is not good. [lit. Not good.]

While 안 is most frequently used in colloquial speech to negate a verb/adjective, there is another negative form used to negate a verb/adjective, which is ...지 않아요. "...지 않아요" is attached to the base of a verb or adjective and denotes the same meaning as 안.

안 가요 = 가지 않아요. I don't go.
An kayo Kaji anayo.
안 바빠요 = 바쁘지 않아요. I am not busy.
An pappayo Pappŭji anayo.

Dictionary form	Short negative	Long negative
좋다 be good	안 좋아요	좋지 않아요
만나다 to meet	안 만나요	만나지 않아요
보다 to see	안 봐요	보지 않아요
마시다 to drink	안 마셔요	마시지 않아요
힘들다 be difficult	안 힘들어요	힘들지 않아요

2.5 The verb 있다 "to have; to exist"

있어요 (I-ssŏ-yo) can express either "existence" or "possession." Its two meanings are (1) "to exist," "there is," and (2) "to have/possess."

커피 있어요. There is coffee *or* I have coffee
커피 있어요? Is there coffee? *or* Do you have coffee?
민수 있어요? Is Minsu (there)?

2.6 ...에 있어요 "to be/exist in/on/at..."

[location]+에 있어요 expresses the location of an object/person.

백화점에 있어요. I am in the department store.
이층에 있어요. I am/It is on the second floor.
카페에 있어요. I am/he is in the café.

The question word 어디 "where" can be used to ask the location of an object or a person.

어디에 있어요?	Where is it/he/she?, Where are you?
=어디 있어요?	Where is it/he/she?, Where are you?
카페 어디에 있어요?	Where is the café?
마이클 어디에 있어요?	Where is Michael?

Exercise 1

Select the correct *ayo/ŏyo* form of the following words.

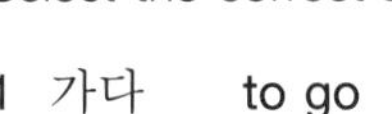

1	가다	to go	a. 가아요.	b. 가요.
2	오다	to come	a. 오아요.	b. 와요.
3	먹다	to eat	a. 먹어요.	b. 먹아요.
4	만나다	to meet	a. 만너요.	b. 만나요
5	하다	to do	a. 해요.	b. 하아요.
6	있다	to exist, to have	a. 있아요.	b. 있어요.

Exercise 2

Make a polite question using ...(으)세요?

Example 바쁘다 be busy → 바쁘세요? Are you busy?

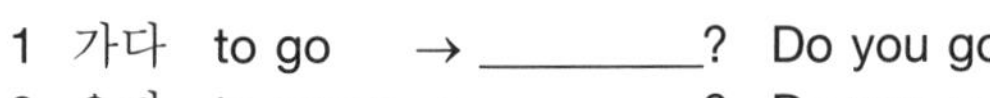

1 가다 to go → ________? Do you go?
2 오다 to come → ________? Do you come?
3 하다 to do → ________? Do you do?
4 있다 to have → ________? Do you have?

Exercise 3

Make a polite request using ...(으)세요.

Example 가다 to go → 가세요. Please go.

1 하다 to do → ________. Please do.
2 오다 to come → ________. Please come.

Exercise 4

Your friend is on the phone asking where you are now. Following the example, tell her you are at each one of the following locations.

Example A: 어디 있어요? Where are you?
B: 백화점에 있어요. I am in the department store.

1 은행 bank
2 카페 café
3 회의실 conference room
4 컴퓨터 랩 computer lab

Exercise 5 (CD1; 46)

Your friend is asking where you are going now. Construct dialogues following the model: answer him using each of the following destinations.

Example A: 어디 가세요? Where are you going?
B: 카페에 가요. I am going to a café.
A: 같이 가요. Let's go together.

1 도서관 library
2 공항 airport
3 회사 company
4 식당 restaurant

Exercise 6

Ask your friend whether she has the following items, using ... 있어요?

Example 커피 coffee → 커피 있어요?

1 컴퓨터 computer
2 컵 cup
3 펜 pen
4 서울 지도 Seoul map
5 핸드폰 mobile phone [lit. 'hand phone']

Exercise 7

Following the given example, complete the dialogues by answering the question in the negative.

Example A: 서울에 가세요? Are you going to Seoul?
B: 아니오. 서울에 안 가요. No. I am not going to Seoul.

1 A: 일 하세요? Do you work?
B: 아니오. 일 ___________.

2 A: 요즘 바빠요? Are you busy these days?
B: 아니오. _______________

3 A: 백화점에 자주 가세요? Do you go to the department store often?
B: 자주 _______________ (자주: often)

4 A: 회의에 가세요? Are you going to the meeting?
B: 아니오. 회의에 _______________.

Cultural point

Honorific expressions in Korean

One of the most characteristic features of the Korean language is its developed honorific and deferential expressions. Different speech styles, such as different sentence endings, are used for different types of social relationships between speakers or referents. The two most significant factors that affect the use of honorific expressions are:

1 ***social status and power*** such as one's age and social position
2 ***solidarity*** such as how close a relationship the two people have.

Generally speaking, when talking to or referring to a person who is older or/and whose social status is higher, one is expected to use honorific expressions. That is, by elevating the listener, the speaker shows his/her respect and courtesy to the listener. The speaker can also honor the listener by lowering the speaker him/herself, using humble words or expressions. Both honorific words and humble words will be introduced throughout this course.

Dialogue 2

(CD1; 47)

James is introduced to Minsu at his co-worker Mira's birthday party. Minsu asks James some questions to make conversation.

민수 제임스씨는 미국 분이세요?
제임스 아니오. 영국 사람이에요.
민수 아, 그래요? 영국에 자주 가세요?

제임스 아니오. 자주 안 가요.
민수씨는 학생이세요?
민수 아니오. 일해요.
제임스 무슨 일 하세요?
민수 변호사예요.
제임스 요즘 바쁘세요?
민수 아니오. 별로 안 바빠요.

MINSU Cheimsŭ-ssi-nŭn miguk pu-ni-seyo?
JAMES Anio. Yŏng-guk-saram-ieyo.
MINSU Ah, kŭraeyo? Yŏng-gu-ge chaju ga-seyo?
JAMES Anio. Chaju an kayo.
Minsu ssi-nŭn hak-ssaeng-i-seyo?
MINSU Anio. I-raeyo.
JAMES Musŭn-nil ha-seyo?
MINSU Pyŏ-no-sa-e-yo.
JAMES Yojŭm pappŭ-seyo?
MINSU Anio. Pyŏl-lo an ba-ppa-yo.

MINSU *James, are you an American (person)?*
JAMES *No, I am a British (person).*
MINSU *Oh, is that so? Do you go to the UK often?*
JAMES *No. I don't go often. Minsu, are you a student?*
MINSU *No. I work.*
JAMES *What kind of work do you do?*
MINSU *I am a lawyer.*
JAMES *Are you busy these days?*
MINSU *No. Not that busy.*

Vocabulary

미국	United States of America
분	person (honorific word for 사람 "person")
...이세요?	the honorific polite sentence ending for nouns (the honorific form of 이에요)
아니오	No
영국	United Kingdom
사람	person

영국 사람	British person
...이에요	the polite sentence ending, attached to nouns
그래요?	is that so?, is that right?
...에	location marker
...에 가요	to go to... 서울에 가요. (I) go to Seoul
자주	often, frequently
가세요?	(Do you) go? (honorific form of 가요? "go?")
가요	to go (I go/you go/she goes/he goes/they go)
...는	topic marker
학생	student
일해요	to work (< dic. form: 일하다)
무슨 일	what kind of work [lit. what work]
하세요?	do you do? [lit. do?]
변호사	lawyer
요즘	these days, recently
바쁘세요?	Are you busy? [lit. busy?] 바쁘다 (busy) + 세요 (honorific polite ending)
별로	not really, not (that) much
바빠요	be busy

Note:
사람 and 분 both mean "person." However, 분 is an honorific form of 사람, thus 분 is used to convey respect or deference, or to mark a formal social distance between the speaker and the person referred to. 분 should not be used to refer to the speaker himself or herself.

Grammar points

2.7 The honorific polite sentence ending, "Noun + (이)세요"

...이에요/예요 is the polite sentence ending that is attached to nouns. The honorific form of ...이에요/예요 is ...(이)세요. When the preceding noun ends in a consonant, 이세요 is used, and when the noun ends in a vowel, 세요 is used. The polite form 이세요 is used with human nouns to show courtesy, but not with non-human nouns.

학생이에요.	He is a student. (polite)
학생이세요.	He is a student. (honorific polite)
학생이세요?	Are you a student? (honorific polite)

2.8 별로 + negatives "not really, not that much"

The adverb, 별로 is used always together with a negative word (such as *not* and *can't*) and expresses the meaning "not really."

좋아요.	It is good.	별로 안 좋아요.	It is not that good.
바빠요.	I am busy.	별로 안 바빠요.	I am not that busy.

Exercise 8

Make a polite question using ...(이)세요?

Example	학생	→	학생이세요?
	student	→	Are you a student?

1	변호사	lawyer
2	김미라씨	Ms Mira Kim
3	과장님	manager, section chief
4	선생님	teacher

Exercise 9

You met Michael at a birthday party and would like to get better acquainted. Ask him the following questions.

1 What is your name?
2 Are you American?
3 What kind of work do you do?
4 Are you busy these days?

Exercise 10 **(CD1; 48)**

Answer the following questions using 별로.

Example A: 바쁘세요? Are you busy?
B: 별로 안 바빠요. I'm not really busy.

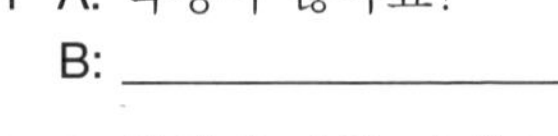

1 A: 학생이 많아요? Are there many students?
B: ________________ There aren't that many students.

2 A: 부산에 자주 가세요? Do you go to Busan often?
B: ________________ I don't go that often.

3 A: 영화 자주 봐요? Do you watch movies often?
B: ________________ I don't watch that often.

Exercise 11

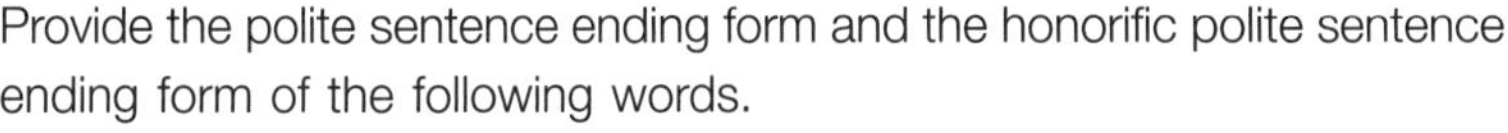

Provide the polite sentence ending form and the honorific polite sentence ending form of the following words.

Example 가다 → 가요 가세요

	dic. form		polite ending	honorific polite ending
1	만나다	to meet	__________	______________
2	시작하다	to start	__________	______________
3	오다	to come	__________	______________
4	보다	to see	__________	______________

Unit Three
사무실에서
At the office

In this unit you will learn about:

- Showing respect using the honorific suffix ...님
- Honorific words for 있다 "to exist, to have"
- Use of the time marker ...에
- Use of the honorific polite sentence ending ...(으)세요
- Providing reasons using ...아서/어서
- How to use the subject marker ...이/가
- How to use the object marker ...을/를
- How to use the topic marker ...은/는
- Expressing "also; too; even" using ...도
- Expressing the starting point of time or place using ...부터

Dialogue 1

(CD1; 49, 50)

James Smith from the Global Printing Company is visiting Mr Han of Hangook Electronics. James is about 10 minutes late for his 2 o'clock appointment.

제임스	한 과장님 계세요?
비서	네. 과장님하고 약속 있으세요?
제임스	예. 2 시에.
비서	성함이 어떻게 되세요?
제임스	제임스 스미스입니다.
비서	잠깐만 기다리세요.
비서	(*after a moment*) 자, 들어가세요.
제임스	감사합니다.
한과장	아, 스미스씨, 어서 오세요. 이리 앉으세요.
제임스	늦어서 죄송합니다.
한과장	아니오, 괜찮습니다.

JAMES	Han kwa-jang-nim Kye-se-yo?
SECRETARY	Ne. Kwa-jang-nim hago yak-ssok i-ssŭ-seyo?
JAMES	Ye. Tu-shi-e.
SECRETARY	Sŏng-a-mi ŏttŏk'e twe-seyo?
JAMES	Che-im-sŭ Sŭmisŭ-im-ni-da.
SECRETARY	Cham-kkan-man Ki-da-ri-seyo.
SECRETARY	(*after a moment*) Cha, dŭrŏ-ga-seyo.
JAMES	Kam-sa-ham-nida.
MR HAN	Ah, Sŭmisŭ-ssi, ŏ-sŏ o-seyo. I-ri an-jŭ-seyo.
JAMES	Nŭ-jŏ-sŏ chwe-song-ham-nida.
MR HAN	Anio, kwaen-ch'an-sŭm-nida.

JAMES	*Is Section Chief, Mr Han here?*
SECRETARY	*Yes. Do you have an appointment with him?*
JAMES	*Yes. At two o'clock.*
SECRETARY	*May I ask your name?*
	[lit. How does your name become?]
JAMES	*I am James Smith.*
SECRETARY	*Wait a moment, please.*
SECRETARY	(after a moment) *Please enter.*

JAMES	*Thank you.*
MR HAN	*Ah, Mr Smith. Welcome. Sit down here.*
JAMES	*Sorry that I am late.*
MR HAN	*No, that is okay.*

Vocabulary

과장님	section chief, manager of a department
계세요	to exist, to be (honorific form of 있어요)
네	yes (= 예)
...하고	with...; ...and (사장님하고 with the president)
약속	appointment
있으세요?	honorific form of 있어요? "Do you have?"
세요 or 으세요	the honorific polite sentence ending
두 시	two o'clock
[time] 에	[time] at (두시에 at two o'clock)
성함이 어떻게 되세요?	What is your name? 성함 (name) + 이 (subject marker) 어떻게 (how) + 되세요 (become)
잠깐만	for a short time, for a minute (= 잠깐)
기다리세요	Please wait. 기다리다 (to wait) + 세요 (honorific polite sentence ending)
자	"자" doesn't have a particular meaning, but it is used, usually at the beginning of a sentence, to draw the listener's attention.
들어가세요.	Please enter. 들어가다 (to go in, to enter) + 세요 (honorific polite sentence ending)
감사합니다.	Thank you.
어서 오세요	Welcome. [lit. Come quickly.] 어서 quickly 오세요 please come (오다 + 세요)
이리	this way, in this direction
앉다	to sit
앉으세요	please sit (honorific polite ending form of 앉다)

늦다	be late
늦어서	be late, so; because I am late 늦다 + 어서 (clausal connective for "reason")
죄송합니다	I am very sorry (idiomatic expression)
괜찮습니다	That is okay; I am okay.

Grammar points

3.1 The honorific suffix ...님

The honorific suffix...님 is attached to a person's name or title to show respect or courtesy.

제임스 스미스	James Smith	→	제임스 스미스님
김미라	Mira Kim	→	김미라님
사장	president of a company	→	사장님
과장	section chief	→	과장님
선생	teacher	→	선생님
교수	professor	→	교수님

3.2 계세요 honorific polite form of 있다 "to exist"

As introduced in Unit 2, 있어요 has two different meanings: (1) to exist (existence) (2) to have (possession), and their honorific forms differ respectively.

dic. form	polite ending		honorific polite ending	
있다	있어요	to exist	계세요?	to exist
	있어요	to have	있으세요?	to have

Look at the following exchanges, paying close attention to different honorific polite endings of 있다.

A: 펜 있으세요? Do you have a pen?
B: 네. 펜 있어요 Yes, I have a pen.

A: 지금 어디 계세요? Where are you now?
B: 카페에 있어요. I am in the café.

The choice between honorific polite forms and polite forms depends on the listener's social status/power (such as age or social position) and the degree of closeness between two speakers. For example, honorific polite forms are used for a person with greater social status/power, such as to one's boss, and/or to a person with whom the speaker has a distant or formal relationship.

3.3 (Time) 에 "at (time)"

In Unit 2, you learned 에's function as a location marker. 에 has another function as a time marker, when attached to [time].

두 시에 at two o'clock

3.4 Providing reasons using ...아서/어서 "because..., since..."

Attached to the base of a verb or an adjective, ...아서/어서 connects two clauses. The clause preceding ...아서/어서 provides reason for the following clause.

늦어서 죄송합니다. I am very sorry that I am late.
because I am late

The choice between 아서 and 어서 follows the same rule as the choice between 아요 and 어요 (refer to Unit 2).

좋다	be good	좋아서	because it is good
늦다	be late	늦어서	because I am late
있다	to exist; to have	있어서	because there is *or* because I have
바쁘다	be busy	바빠서	because I am/he is busy
많다	be a lot	많아서	because there are a lot
일하다	to work	일해서	because I work

바빠서 안 가요. Since I am busy, I don't go.
바빠서 안 가세요? You are not going since you're busy?

Exercise 1

Address people appropriately using the following titles and the honorific suffix 님.

Example 사장 president → 사장님, 안녕하세요?

1 부장 division chief → ________ 계세요?
2 김선생 Teacher Kim or Mr/Ms Kim → ________ 바쁘세요?
3 과장 section chief → ________ 이리 앉으세요.
4 박교수 Professor Park → ________, 안녕하세요?

Exercise 2

Choose the appropriate word from ( ) and circle it.

1 볼펜 (있으세요?/계세요?)
Do you have a ballpoint pen?

2 스미스씨 (있으세요?/계세요?)
Is Mr Smith there?

3 오늘 약속 (있으세요?/계세요?)
Do you have an appointment today?

4 박사장님 지금 (있으세요/계세요.)
President Park is in now.

Exercise 3

Provide reason using the given word in ( ).

Example 늦어서 (늦다) 죄송합니다. Sorry that I am late.

1 일 ______ (많다) 바빠요.
I am busy with a lot of work. [lit. work is a lot so I am busy]

2 일 ______ (있다) 파티에 안 가요.
I have work so I am not going to the party.

3 한국어 ______ (좋다) 한국어 공부해요. (공부하다: to study)
I study Korean since I like it. [lit. Korean good so study Korean]

Cultural point

Hierarchy in the business environment

In the Korean business environment, it is common to observe a strong hierarchy according to one's relative position as well as deference to authority. In the workplace, titles are frequently used with or without surnames as a form of address, such as 한과장님 or 과장님. Here are some commonly used titles:

회장 (chairman), 사장 (president), 부사장 (vice-president), 상무 (senior executive managing director), 전무 (executive managing director), 부장 (division chief), 과장 (section chief), 대리 (assistant section chief), 사원 (employee).

Dialogue 2

(CD1; 51)

James has been assigned to a different office in the company. His co-worker, Mira, is showing James around his new office space.

미라	여기가 제임스씨 자리예요. 어때요?
제임스	책상이 커서 좋아요.
미라	이 컴퓨터를 쓰세요.
제임스	프린터는 어디에 있어요?
미라	저기 있어요.
제임스	팩스기도 있어요?
미라	팩스기는 여기 없어요.
제임스	언제부터 여기서 일을 시작해요?
미라	내일부터 괜찮으세요?
제임스	네. 저는 괜찮아요.

MIRA	Yŏgiga Jaimsŭ-ssi charieyo. Ŏtteyo?
JAMES	Ch'aek-sang-i k'ŏsŏ choayo.
MIRA	I-k'ŏmpyut'ŏ-rŭl ssŭseyo.
JAMES	P'ŭrintŏ-nŭn ŏdi-e issŏyo?
MIRA	Chŏgi issŏyo.
JAMES	P'aeksŭgi-do issŏyo?
MIRA	P'aeksŭgi-nŭn yŏgi ŏp-ssŏyo.

JAMES Ŏnje-but'ŏ yŏgisŏ irŭl shijak-haeyo?
MIRA Naeil-but'ŏ kwaench'anŭseyo?
JAMES Ne, chŏnŭn kwaench'anayo.

MIRA *Here is your seat. How is it?*
JAMES *I like that the desk is big.*
[lit. The desk is big, so it is good.]
MIRA *Use this computer.*
JAMES *Where is the printer?*
MIRA *It's over there.*
JAMES *Is there a fax machine also?*
MIRA *There is no fax machine here.*
JAMES *When do I start work here?*
MIRA *Is it okay (to work here) from tomorrow?*
JAMES *Yes, that is okay for me. [lit. I am okay.]*

Vocabulary

여기	here
가	subject marker
자리	seat
책상	desk
커서	big, so (크다 "big" + 어서 "because")
좋다	be good 좋습니다: deferential (formal polite) form of 좋다
이	this
컴퓨터	computer
를	object marker
쓰세요	Please use. (honorific polite form of 쓰다) (쓰다, 써요, 쓰세요)
팩스기	fax machine (팩스: fax)
도	also
는	topic marker; contrast marker
프린터	printer
없어요	to not exist, to not have
언제	when

...부터	from...
다음	next
주	week
괜찮으세요	honorific polite form of 괜찮다 "be okay" (괜찮다, 괜찮아요, 괜찮으세요)
저	I
월요일	Monday
알겠습니다	understood
한국말	Korean language (= 한국어)
아주	very well
잘	well
배우다	to learn
조금	a little

3.5 Subject marker 이/가

...이 or ...가 is used after a subject noun and shows that the preceding noun is the subject of the sentence. When the preceding noun ends in a consonant, 이 is used, and when the preceding noun ends in a vowel, 가 is used. In colloquial speech, subject markers are often omitted; this is not the case in formal writing, however.

제임스가 바빠요. (=제임스 바빠요.)	James is busy.
김사장님이 바쁘세요. (=김사장님 바쁘세요.)	Mr Kim is busy.

3.6 Object marker 을/를

...을 or ...를 is used after a noun and indicates that the preceding noun is the object of the sentence. After a consonant-ending noun, 을 is used and after a vowel-ending noun, 를 is used. In colloquial speech, 을/를 is frequently deleted.

제임스를 만나요.	I meet James.
김사장님을 만나요.	I meet Mr Kim.
제임스가 김사장님을 만나요.	James meets Mr Kim.
언제 일을 시작해요?	When do I/you start work?
내일 일을 시작해요.	I/You start work tomorrow.

3.7 Topic marker 은/는 "As for…"

은/는 usually follows a noun, but can also follow adverbs or adverb phrases. 은/는 indicates that the preceding word is the topic that the speaker is going to talk about. By using 은/는, the speaker brings the listener's attention to the preceding word/topic. The literal meaning of 은/는 is equivalent to "as for…" or "talking about…" in English. When the preceding word ends in a consonant, 은 is attached, and after a vowel-ending word, 는 is attached. The major functions of 은/는 are as follows:

1 to bring the listener's attention to the topic.

제임스는 영국 사람이에요.

James is a British person. [lit. Talking about James, he is British.]

저는 미국 사람이에요.

I am an American person. [lit. Talking about me, I'm American.]

The speaker introduces "James" or "I" as a topic by attaching …는 to it and brings the listener's attention to the topic.

2 to contrast or compare two things.

아이스크림은 없어요. 아이스커피는 있어요.

I don't have ice cream. (But) I have iced coffee.
[lit. As for ice cream, I don't have. (But) as for iced coffee, I have.]

The speaker contrasts ice cream with iced coffee by attaching 은 and 는 to them.

3 to signal the shift of a topic.

A: 팩스기 어디 있어요?	Where is a fax machine?
B: 저기 있어요.	It's over there.
A: 프린터는 어디 있어요?	Where is a printer?
B: 프린터도 저기 있어요.	It's also over there.

After asking about a fax machine, A turns the listener's attention from a fax machine to a printer. The shift of the topic to the printer is marked by the 는 that is attached to 프린터.

Note:
When the preceding word is the subject or object of the sentence, 은/는 replaces the subject or object marker. The subject marker 이/가 or the object marker 을/를 aren't used together with the topic marker 은/는.

제임스<u>가는</u> 바빠요. (incorrect)
제임스<u>를는</u> 만나요. (incorrect)

3.8 ...도 "also; too; even"

Attached to nouns or adverbs, ...도 emphasizes the preceding word with the meaning of "also; too; even."

제임스는 바빠요. 미라도 바빠요.
James is busy. Mira also is busy.

팩스기 있어요? 프린터도 있어요?
Do you have a fax machine? Do you have a printer too?

제임스는 한국말을 잘 해요. 제임스는 일본말도 잘 해요.
James speaks Korean well. He also speaks Japanese well.
(일본말: Japanese language)

3.9 ...부터 "from..."

Attached to nouns or adverbs, ...부터 indicates the starting point in terms of time or place.

내일부터 from tomorrow
오늘부터 from today
여기부터 from here

두 시부터 회의가 있어요. From two o'clock, there is a meeting.
오늘부터 아주 바빠요. From today on, I am very busy.

Exercise 4

Choose an appropriate subject or object marker from ( ) and circle it.

Example 책상 (이/가/을/를) 커요. The desk is big.

1 언제 일(이/가/을/를) 시작해요? When do I start work?
2 이 컴퓨터(이/가/을/를) 좋아요. This computer is good.
3 오늘 제임스(이/가/을/를) 만나요. I meet James today.
4 핸드폰(이/가/을/를) 없어요. I don't have a mobile phone. [lit. Mobile phone not exist]
5 무슨 일(이/가/을/를) 하세요? What kind of work do you do?
6 고향(이/가/을/를) 서울이에요. My hometown is Seoul.

Exercise 5

You are introducing people at a party. Fill in the blanks using the topic marker 은/는.

1 수잔____ 미국 사람이에요. Susan is an American.
2 민수____ 변호사예요. Minsu is a lawyer.
3 마이클____ 학생이에요. Michael is a student.

Exercise 6

Fill in the blanks using 은/는 to express contrastive meaning.

1 오늘____ 바빠요. 내일____ 안 바빠요.
As for today, I am busy. (But) as for tomorrow, I am not busy.

2 프린터____ 있어요. 팩스기____ 없어요.
I have a printer. (But) I don't have a fax machine.

3 커피____ 안 마셔요. 차____ 마셔요.
I don't drink coffee. (But) I drink tea.

4 마이클____ 학생이에요. 민수____ 학생이 아니에요.
Michael is a student. (But) Minsu is not a student.

Exercise 7

Translate the following into Korean using …부터.

1 When do you start work?
2 I start from today.
3 Come (starting) from tomorrow.
4 I work from two o'clock.

Exercise 8

You met a person from England at a conference. Tell him that you also are British.

Exercise 9

Your colleague is asking what you are doing this afternoon. Tell her that you are meeting Mr Han (한과장님) at two o'clock.

Cultural point

Working days and school days in Korea

It wasn't until 2004 that employees in Korea started to work five days a week, as the government reduced the working hours from 44 hours to 40 hours a week. Public companies and companies with over 1,000 workers are obliged to follow this five-day work system so that workers can enjoy their Saturdays.

The government also changed the number of school days in 2006 from six days every week to having the second and fourth Saturday off each month giving students a five-day week twice a month.

Unit Four

어디 있어요?

Where is it?

In this unit you will learn about:

- Asking for directions
- Useful words and expressions for providing directions
- Asking for the location of something/someone
- Confirming information using [noun] + (이)요?
- How to say "It takes [amount of time]"
- Expressions for riding and getting off a vehicle
- Location markers 에 and 에서
- Connecting two sentences using 그리고
- Expressing the purpose of going using ...(으)러 가다

Dialogue 1

(CD1; 52, 53)

James is looking for the US Embassy. He asks a passer-by for directions.

제임스	실례지만, 미국 대사관이 어디 있어요?
행인	미국 대사관이요?
제임스	예.
행인	이 쪽으로 계속 가세요. 그럼, 세종문화회관이 보여요. 세종문화회관 건너편에 미대사관이 있어요.
제임스	여기서 멀어요?
행인	아니오. 걸어서 한 오분 걸려요.
제임스	감사합니다.
행인	뭘요.

JAMES	Shil-le-ji-man, mi-guk tae-sa-kwa-ni ŏ-di i-ssŏ-yo?
PASSER-BY	Mi-guk tae-sa-kwa-ni-yo?
JAMES	Ye.
PASSER-BY	I-tch-gŭ-ro kye-sok ka-se-yo. Kŭ-rŭm Se-jong Mu-nwa Hwe-gwa-ni bo-yŏ-yo. Se-jong Mu-nwa Hwe-gwan kŏn-nŏ-pyŏ-ne Mi-dae-sa-gwa-ni i-ssŏ-yo.
JAMES	Yŏ-gi-sŏ mŏ-rŏ-yo?
PASSER-BY	Anio. Kŏ-rŏ-sŏ han o-bun kŏl-lyŏ-yo.
JAMES	Kam-sa-ham-nida.
PASSER-BY	Myŏl-yo.

JAMES	*Excuse me, but where is the US Embassy?*
PASSER-BY	*The US Embassy?*
JAMES	*Yes.*
PASSER-BY	*Go straight in this direction. Then you will see the Sejong Culture Center.* *[lit. Then the Sejong Culture Center is seen.]* *Across from the Sejong Culture Center is the US Embassy.*
JAMES	*Is it far away from here?*
PASSER-BY	*No. It takes about five minutes walking.*
JAMES	*Thank you.*
PASSER-BY	*You're welcome.*

Vocabulary

실례지만	Excuse me but
미국	the US
대사관	Embassy
미국 대사관	The US (American) Embassy (= 미대사관)
이 쪽	this way, this direction
계속	continuously 계속 가다: go continuously
그럼	then; if so
세종문화회관	Sejong Culture Center
건너편	the opposite side, the other side
여기	here
여기서	from here; here (= 여기에서)
멀어요	(< dic. form: 멀다) be far (away)
걸어서	by walking, on foot
한	about
오분	five minutes 오 (five) + 분 (minutes)
한 오분	about five minutes
걸려요	(< dic. form: 걸리다) (time) to take
뭘요	You're welcome. [lit. What]

Names of public places (CD1; 54)

은행	[eŭnhaeng or eŭnaeng]	bank
병원	[byŏng-won]	hospital
약국	[yak-gguk]	pharmacy
학교	[hakkyo]	school
도서관	[tosŏkwan]	library
우체국	[uch'eguk]	post office
극장	[kŭk-tchang]	movie theater
공항	[konghang or kongang]	airport
시청	[shi-ch'ŏng]	City Hall
호텔	[hot'el]	hotel
백화점	[paek'wajŏm]	department store

Grammar points

4.1 Asking the location of something/someone "Where is...?"

The following expressions are frequently used to ask for the location of something.

> [place/person] 이/가 어디 있어요?
> [place] 이/가 어디예요?

After a consonant-ending noun, the subject marker 이 is used, and after a vowel-ending noun, the subject marker 가 is used.

맥도날드가 어디 있어요?	Where is McDonald's?
커피숍이 어디예요?	Where is the coffee shop?

Subject markers are frequently omitted in colloquial speech.

맥도날드 어디 있어요?	Where is McDonald's?
커피숍 어디예요?	Where is the coffee shop?
수잔씨 어디 있어요?	Where is Susan?

4.2 Seeking confirmation using (noun) + (이)요? "(noun)?"

When the listener wants to confirm what was said by the speaker, he/she can repeat the noun that was just mentioned. The approximate meaning of *[noun] 이요?* is "*You mean [noun]?*" or "*Did you say [noun]?*"

When the noun ends in a consonant, 이요 is attached, while to a vowel-ending noun, 요 is attached.

1 A: 롯데 호텔이 어디 있어요?	Where is Hotel Lotte?
B: 롯데 호텔이요?	[You mean] Hotel Lotte?
2 A: 수잔씨 어디 있어요?	Where is Susan?
B: 수잔씨요?	[You mean] Susan?

4.3 Providing directions

쪽 literally means "direction." 쪽 is frequently used with pronouns 이, 그, 저 to express direction:

이 쪽	in this direction; this way
그 쪽	in that direction; that way
저 쪽	in that direction; that way over there

The difference between 그 쪽 and 저 쪽 is that 저 쪽 is used when referring to a direction that is much further away from the speaker and the listener.

The following words are also useful when expressing directions.

오른쪽	right direction; right-hand side
왼쪽	left direction; left-hand side
어느 쪽	which direction; which side
오른쪽에 있어요.	It is on (your) right-hand side.

4.4 Expression of direction ...(으)로 가다 "go toward..."

Attached to nouns, ...(으)로 marks direction; its function is similar to "toward(s)" in English.

이 쪽으로 가세요.	Go toward this direction.
왼쪽으로 가세요.	Go to the left.
어느 쪽으로 가세요?	Which way are you going?

Note the difference between ...에 가다 and ...(으)로 가다. While ...에 가다 focuses on the destination, ...(으)로 가다 focuses on the direction.

집에 가요.	I am going home.
집으로 가요.	I am going (toward) home.

4.5 (landmark) 이/가 보여요 "you will see (landmark)"

When providing directions in English, the following construction "*[If you go...], you will see [landmark]*" is frequently used. In Korean, directions are usually provided using the landmark as a subject. That is, the corresponding expression of "*you will see [landmark]*" in Korean is "*[landmark] will be seen.*"

보여요 is a polite sentence-ending form of 보이다 "to be seen":

보이 (verb base) + 어요 → 보이어요 → contracted to 보여요.

은행이 보여요.	You will see a bank. [lit. A bank is seen.]
백화점이 보여요.	You will see a department store.

이쪽으로 계속 가세요. 그럼, 시청이 보여요.
Continue in this direction. Then, you will see City Hall.

"Something/someone 이/가 보여요" is also used to express the meaning "can see something/someone."

A: 저기 은행이 보여요?	Do you see the bank over there? [lit. Over there, is bank seen?]
B: 네. 보여요.	Yes, I can see. [lit. Yes, it is seen.]

4.6 Providing location using a reference place

When providing a specific location of something or someone in reference to a certain place, the following expressions are frequently used.

[place]	옆에	next to [place]
	앞에	in front of [place]
	뒤에	at the back of [place]
	건너편에	on the opposite side of [place]

신라호텔 옆에 있어요.	It is next to Hotel Silla.
커피숍 앞에 있어요.	It is in front of the coffee shop.
서울은행 뒤에 있어요.	It is behind Seoul Bank.

When used with a subject, the following construction is frequently used.

[object] 은/는	[reference place]	옆에	있어요.
		앞에	
		뒤에	
		건너편에	
[object] is	next to	[reference place]	
	in front of		
	at the back of		
	across from		

현대백화점은 서울은행 건너편에 있어요.
Hyundai Department Store is across from Seoul Bank.
제임스는 수잔 앞에 있어요.
James is in front of Susan.

4.7 (amount of time) 걸려요 "It takes (amount of time)"

걸려요 is a polite sentence-ending form (or 아요/어요 form) of 걸리다:

걸리다 + 어요 → 걸리어요 → contracted to 걸려요.

When used with the amount of time, 걸리다 means "(It) takes [amount of time]."

오 분 걸려요.	It takes five minutes.
두 시간 걸려요.	It takes two hours. (두 시간: two hours)

Exercise 1 (CD1; 55)

You are trying to go to the following places. Ask your co-worker where it is.

Example 서울은행 → 서울은행이 어디 있어요?
or 서울 은행이 어디예요?

1 서울대학교 Seoul National University
2 영국문화원 British Culture Center
3 롯데 백화점 Lotte Department Store

Exercise 2

Confirm what you just heard from A using Noun + 이요?

Example A: 세종문화회관이 어디 있어요?
B: 세종문화회관이요?

1 A: 현대백화점이 어디예요?
2 A: 제임스씨 어디 있어요?
3 A: 팩스기가 어디 있어요?
4 A: 우체국이 어디 있어요? (우체국: post office)

Exercise 3

Provide the appropriate directions by filling in the blanks.

1 Go (toward) this way. ________ 으로 가세요.
2 Go (toward) that way. ________ 으로 가세요.
3 Go (toward) that way over there. ________ 으로 가세요.
4 Go to the left. ________ 으로 가세요.
5 Go to the right. ________ 으로 가세요.

Exercise 4

You were asked for directions by a passer-by on the street. Explain that if he goes straight on he will see the following places.

Example [미대사관] 이 쪽으로 가세요. 그럼, 미대사관이 보여요.
[US Embassy] Go this way. Then, you will see the US Embassy.

1 [서울대학교] Seoul National University
2 [한국은행] Korea Bank
3 [시청] City Hall

Exercise 5

Look at the following map and provide the locations of the following places using …옆에/앞에/뒤에/건너편에.

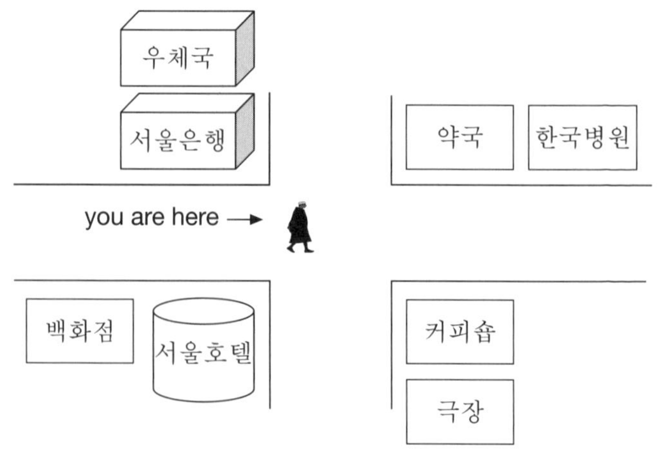

Example A: 약국이 어디 있어요?
B: 한국 병원 옆에 있어요.

1 서울은행 (Seoul Bank) 이 어디 있어요?
2 백화점이 어디 있어요?
3 커피숍이 어디 있어요?
4 우체국이 어디 있어요?
5 서울호텔이 어디 있어요?

Exercise 6

Using the map above, follow the directions provided below, and circle the location that you will encounter.

1 여기서 오른쪽으로 가세요.
그럼 (한국병원/백화점/극장) 이/가 보여요

2 여기서 왼쪽으로 가세요.
그럼 (우체국/커피숍/백화점) 이/가 보여요.

경복궁 Kyŏngbok-gung, the Royal Palace of the Chosŏn Dynasty

Dialogue 2

(CD1; 56)
James is asking Mira for directions to the Daehan Movie Theater.

제임스	미라씨. 대한 극장이 어디 있어요?
미라	대한 극장이요? 지하철 3호선을 타세요. 그리고 충무로 역에서 내리세요.
제임스	충무로역이요?
미라	네. 아, 그리고 지하철 4호선도 가요.
제임스	고마워요.
미라	대한 극장에 영화 보러 가세요?
제임스	네. 내일 친구하고 영화 봐요.

JAMES	Mira-ssi. Tae-han kŭk-tchang-i ŏ-di i-ssŏ-yo?
MIRA	Taehan kŭk-tchang-i-yo? Chi-ha-ch'ŏl sam-ho-sŏ-nŭl t'a-seyo. Kŭ-ri-go Ch'ung-mu-ro yŏ-ge-sŏ nae-ri-seyo.
JAMES	Ch'ung-mu-ro yŏ-giyo?
MIRA	Ne. Ah, kŭ-ri-go chi-ha-ch'ŏl sa-ho-sŏn-do kayo.
JAMES	Ko-ma-wŏ-yo.
MIRA	Taehan-gŭk-tchang-e yŏng-hwa bo-rŏ ga-seyo?
JAMES	Ne. Nae-il ch'in-gu-ha-go yŏng-hwa bwa-yo.

JAMES	*Mira. Where is Daehan Movie Theater?*
MIRA	*Daehan Movie Theater? Take the subway line number 3. And get off at the Choongmuro Station.*
JAMES	*Choongmuro Station?*
MIRA	*Yes. Ah, and the subway line number 4 also gets you there. [lit. The subway line number 4 also goes.]*
JAMES	*Thank you.*
MIRA	*Are you going to Daehan Movie Theater to see a movie?*
JAMES	*Yes. Tomorrow, I am watching a movie with a friend.*

Vocabulary

극장	movie theater (대한 극장: Daehan Movie Theater)
지하철	subway 지하철 일 (1) 호선 Subway Line Number 1 지하철 이 (2) 호선 Subway Line Number 2 지하철 삼 (3) 호선 Subway Line Number 3 지하철 사 (4) 호선 Subway Line Number 4
타세요	(<타다) to ride; to get on (a vehicle) 타요 (polite sentence-ending) 타세요 (honorific polite sentence-ending)
그리고	and
충무로 역	the Choongmuro (subway) Station
...에서	at, on, in, from
내리세요	(<내리다) to get off (a vehicle) 내려요 (polite sentence-ending) 내리세요 (honorific polite sentence-ending)
영화	movie
보다	to see, to watch
보러	in order to see, for the purpose of seeing
내일	tomorrow
친구	friend

Words expressing time (CD1; 57)

그제/그저께 the day before yesterday	어제/어저께 yesterday	오늘 today	내일 tomorrow	모레 the day after tomorrow
지지난 주 the week before last	지난 주 last week	이번 주 this week	다음 주 next week	다다음주 the week after next
지지난달 the month before last	지난 달 last month	이번 달 this month	다음 달 next month	다다음달 the month after next
재작년 the year before last	작년 last year	올해/금년 this year	내년 next year	내후년 the year after next

4.8 Riding and getting off a vehicle

Verbs 타다 and 내리다 are used to express "to ride" and "to get off" a vehicle. The object marker 을/를 is used with 타다 and the source/origin marker 에서 (which means "*from*") is used with 내리다.

[vehicle] 을/를 타다	to ride/get on a vehicle
[vehicle] 에서 내리다	to get off a vehicle

지하철을 타요. I take the subway.
택시를 타요. I take a taxi.
버스를 타세요. Take a bus.

시청 역에서 내리세요. Get off at the City Hall Station. (시청: City Hall)
차에서 내리세요. Get out of the car.
충무로 역에서 내려요. I get off at the Choongmuro Station.

4.9 Location marker ...에서 "at; on; in"

Attached to nouns, ...에서 indicates that the preceding noun is the location of a certain activity.

서울대학교에서 한국어를 배워요.
I learn Korean at Seoul National University.

In Unit 2, another location marker ...에 was introduced as in [location] +에 있어요. The difference between ...에 and ...에서 is that ...에 indicates that the preceding noun is a static location where a certain thing/person exists or stays, while ...에서 marks a dynamic location where a certain activity occurs.

제임스는 서울에 있어요.
James is in Seoul.
제임스는 서울에서 일해요.
James works in Seoul.

마이클은 지금 백화점에 있어요.
Michael is at the department store.
마이클은 지금 백화점에서 쇼핑해요.
Michael is shopping at the department store.

Functions of ...에

1 marks a static location: *at/on/in* (refer to Unit 2.6)
미라씨는 이층에 있어요. Mira is on the second floor.
2 marks destination: *to* (refer to Unit 2.3)
은행에 가요. I go to the bank.
3 marks time: *at* (refer to Unit 3.3)
두 시에 약속이 있어요. I have an appointment at two o'clock.

Functions of ...에서

1 marks a dynamic location: *at/on/in*
미라씨는 서울백화점에서 쇼핑해요.
Mira shops at Seoul Department Store.
2 marks source or origin: *from*
제임스는 영국에서 왔어요. (왔어요: came)
James came from the UK.

4.10 Connecting sentences using 그리고 "and"

그리고 meaning "and" is used to connect sentences.

제임스는 영국 사람이에요. <u>그리고</u> 수잔은 미국 사람이에요.
James is British. <u>And</u> Susan is American.

Note that 하고 is used to connect two nouns.

제임스<u>하고</u> 수잔은 친구예요.
James <u>and</u> Susan are friends.

4.11 Expressing the purpose of going ...(으)러 가다 "go to do..."

...(으)러 가다 is used to indicate the purpose of going somewhere. ...(으)러 is used together with go or come verbs such as 가다 (to go), 오다 (to come) or 다니다 (to attend).

...(으)러 가다	to go for the purpose of...
...(으)러 오다	to come for the purpose of...
...(으)러 다니다	to attend for the purpose of...

When the preceding verb-base ends in a consonant, ...(으)러 is used and when the preceding verb-base ends in a vowel, ...러 is used.

쇼핑하다	to shop	쇼핑하러 가요.	I go to shop.
먹다	to eat	먹으러 가요.	I go to eat.
사다	to buy	사러 가요.	I go to buy.

친구 만나러 가요.	I go to meet my friend.
영화 보러 가요.	I go to see a movie.

To indicate the destination, add [Place]에:

> ...(으)러 [Place]에 가요/와요/다녀요.
> go/come/attend to [Place] for the purpose of...

친구 만나러 카페에 가요.
I go to a café to meet my friend.
쇼핑하러 백화점에 가요.
I go to the department store to shop.
한국어 배우러 연세대학교에 다녀요.
I attend Yonsei University to learn Korean.

Exercise 7

Your friend is visiting your place and asking for directions. Tell her to take the following subway, and to get off at the station given below.

Example [지하철 1 호선—시청]
→ 지하철 1 호선을 타세요. 그리고 시청에서 내리세요.

1 [지하철 2 호선—신촌]
2 [지하철 3 호선—경복궁]
3 [지하철 4 호선—사당]

Exercise 8

Fill in the blanks with either 에 or 에서. Pay attention to whether the place involves static existence or a dynamic activity.

1 연세대학교______ 한국어를 배워요.
I learn Korean at Yonsei University.

2 미라씨는 사무실______ 있어요.
Mira is in the office.

3 미라씨는 사무실______ 일해요.
Mira works in the office.

4 대한극장 앞______ 만나요.
Let's meet in front of the Daehan Movie Theater.

5 대한극장 앞______ 커피숍이 있어요.
There is a coffee shop in front of the Daehan Movie Theater.

Exercise 9

Fill in the blanks with either 그리고 or 하고.

1 오늘 친구를 만나요. ______ 영화를 봐요.
2 마이클______ 수잔은 미국 사람이에요.
3 제임스는 한국말을 잘 해요. ______ 일본어도 잘 해요.
4 제임스는 한국말______ 일본어를 잘 해요.

Exercise 10 **(CD1; 58)**

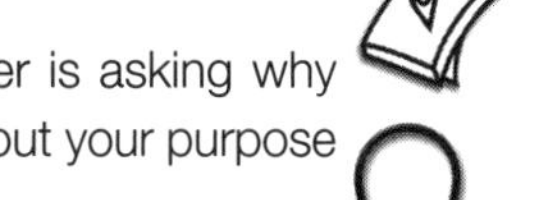

You are going to 신촌 (Shinchon) today. Your co-worker is asking why you are going to Shinchon (신촌에 왜 가요?). Tell him about your purpose for going to Shinchon.

Example [쇼핑하다] to shop → 쇼핑하러 가요.

1 [친구 만나다] to meet a friend
2 [영화 보다] to watch a movie
3 [친구하고 밥 먹다] to eat a meal with a friend
4 [옷 사다] to buy clothes (옷: clothes)

Unit Five

이거 뭐예요?

What is this?

In this unit you will learn about:

- How to say this and that in Korean
- How to say here and there in Korean
- How to say days of the week
- Describing continuing action (be …ing) using …고 있다
- Talking about one's possessions
- How to use ㅂ irregular words
- How to use ㄷ irregular words
- How to use 으 irregular words
- Connecting clauses with the meaning of "but": …지만
- Connecting clauses with the meaning of "and": …고
- How to use the sentence ending …네요

Dialogue 1

(CD1; 59)

James is studying Korean during the lunch break. Mira stops by and asks a few questions.

미라 그거 뭐예요?
제임스 이거요? 한국어 책이에요.
미라 한국어 공부하세요?
제임스 네. 요즘 연세대학교에서 한국어를 배우고 있어요.
미라 그래요? 한국어 공부가 어때요?
어려워요, 쉬워요?
제임스 조금 어렵지만 재미있어요.
미라 매일 한국어 수업 들으세요?
제임스 아니오. 월, 수, 금에 들어요.

MIRA Kŭ-gŏ Mwŏ-e-yo?
JAMES I-gŏ-yo? Han-gu-gŏ ch'ae-gi-e-yo.
MIRA Han-gu-gŏ gong-bu-ha-se-yo?
JAMES Ne. Yo-jŭm Yŏn-se dae-ha-kkyo-e-sŏ han-gu-gŏ-rŭl pae-u-go i-ssŏ-yo.
MIRA Kŭ-rae-yo? Han-gu-gŏ gong-bu-ga ŏ-ttae-yo?
Ŏ-ryŏ-wŏ-yo, shi-wŏ-yo?
JAMES Cho-gŭm ŏ-ryŏp-tchi-man chae-mi-i-ssŏ-yo.
MIRA Mae-il han-gu-gŏ su-ŏp tŭ-rŭ-se-yo?
JAMES Anio. Wŏl, su, gŭ-me tŭ-rŏ-yo.

MIRA *What is that?*
JAMES *This? It's a Korean book.*
MIRA *Do you study Korean?*
JAMES *Yes. These days, I am learning Korean at Yonsei University.*
MIRA *Is that so? How is your Korean study?*
Is it difficult or easy?
JAMES *It is a little difficult, but it is fun.*
MIRA *Do you take the Korean class every day?*
JAMES *No, I take it on Mondays, Wednesdays, and Fridays.*

Vocabulary

그거 — that [lit. that thing] (= 그것)
이거 — this [lit. this thing] (= 이것)
뭐 — what (= 무엇)
뭐예요? — What is it?
한국어 — the Korean language (= 한국말 [han-gung-mal])
책 — book
공부하다 — to study
배우다 — to learn
...고 있다 — be ...ing
배우고 있다: be learning
어려워요 — (< 어렵다) be difficult
쉬워요 — (< 쉽다) be easy
조금 — a little (= 좀)
...지만 — but; although
재미있어요 — (< 재미있다) be interesting, be fun
매일 — every day
수업 — class
수업을 들어요 — (< 수업을 듣다) to take a class
듣다: (1) to hear, to listen (2) to take (a class)
월 — Mon. (shortened form of 월요일 Monday)
수 — Wed. (shortened form of 수요일 Wednesday)
금 — Fri. (shortened form of 금요일 Friday)

Days of the week (CD1; 60)

월요일 [Wŏ-ryo-il] — Monday
화요일 [Hwa-yo-il] — Tuesday
수요일 [Su-yo-il] — Wednesday
목요일 [Mo-gyo-il] — Thursday
금요일 [Kŭm-yo-il] — Friday
토요일 [T'o-yo-il] — Saturday
일요일 [I-ryo-il] — Sunday

무슨 요일 [Musŭn yoil] — What day
오늘 무슨 요일이에요? — What day is it today?

Grammar points

5.1 이거/그거/저거 "this/that/that over there"

이거 (= 이것) this, this thing
(refers to a thing near the speaker)

그거 (= 그것) that, that thing
(refers to a thing near the listener or a thing that was previously mentioned)

저거 (= 저것) that thing over there
(refers to a thing away from both the speaker and the listener)

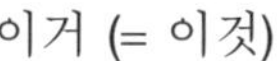
이거 (= 이것)

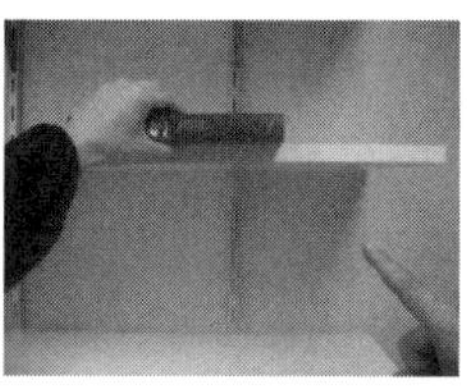

그거 (= 그것)

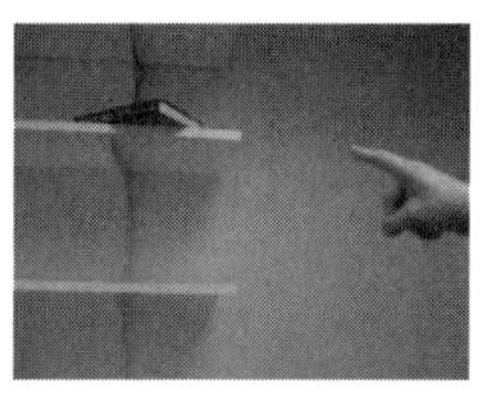

저거 (= 저것)

이거, 그거, and 저거 are combined forms of 이 (this) + 것 (thing), 그 (that) + 것 (thing), and 저 (that over there) + 것 (thing) respectively. 거 is a colloquial form of 것. In colloquial speech, 이거, 그거, 저거 are more frequently used than 이것, 그것, 저것.

이거 주세요.	Give this (to me).	(주다: to give)
이거 얼마예요?	How much is this?	(얼마: how much)
그거 뭐예요?	What is that?	
저거 한국어 책이에요?	Is that thing (over there) a Korean book?	

5.2 Continuing action ...고 있다 "be (am/are/is) ...ing"

Attached to a verb base, ...고 있다 indicates that an action is continuing or in progress.

가고 있어요	is going
일하고 있어요	is working
듣고 있어요	is listening
보고 있어요	is watching
살고 있어요	is living

점심 먹고 있어요.	I am eating lunch.
한국어를 배우고 있어요.	I am learning Korean.
제임스씨는 영어를 가르치고 있어요.	James is teaching English. (가르치다: to teach)

5.3 ㅂ irregulars

Most verb/adjective bases (such as 가 in 가다 or 먹 in 먹다) do not change their forms when followed by auxiliary verbs or functional words. However, there are some verbs or adjectives whose base forms change, influenced by a certain sound in the following word. Such verbs or adjectives are called irregular verbs or adjectives. One of the six types of irregular verbs/adjectives in Korean is the ㅂ irregular word. In the case of ㅂ irregular words, ㅂ in the verb/adjective base changes to 우, when followed by a vowel.

Some of the most commonly used ㅂ irregular words are displayed below. Note the changes in the verb/adjective base when they are combined with ...아요/어요.

dic. form	ㅂ → 우		어요/아요 form
쉽다 (be easy)	쉬 + 우 + 어요	→	쉬워요
어렵다 (be difficult)	어려 + 우 + 어요	→	어려워요
덥다 (be hot)	더 + 우 + 어요	→	더워요
춥다 (be cold)	추 + 우 + 어요	→	추워요
가깝다 (be close)	가까 + 우 + 어요	→	가까워요

Note:

1 Exception: in the case of 돕다 (to help), ㅂ changes to 오 not 우. (돕다: 도 + 오 + 아요 → 도와요.)

2 Regular ㅂ words do not follow this rule: 좁다 (be narrow) → 좁아요.

5.4 ㄷ irregular word 듣다

When ㄷ irregular words are followed by a vowel, ㄷ in the base changes to ㄹ. The two ㄷ irregular words to remember for now are 듣다 (to listen) and 걷다 (to walk).

dic. form	combined with …아요/어요	combined with …(으)세요
듣다 (to listen)	듣 + 어요 → 들어요	들으세요
걷다 (to walk)	걷 + 어요 → 걸어요	걸으세요

5.5 Connecting clauses using …지만 "…but; although…"

지만 is put at the end of a clause to express the meaning "but" or "although."

Clause 1				Clause 2
한국어가 어렵다.	+	지만 but	+	한국어가 재미있다.
Korean is difficult.				Korean is fun.

→ 한국어가 어렵지만 (한국어가) 재미있어요.
Korean is difficult but (it is) fun.

See more examples below:

바쁘지만 한국어를 매일 공부해요.
I am busy but I study Korean every day.
일이 많지만 재미있어요.
Although my workload is heavy [lit. Work is a lot but], it is fun.

Exercise 1

Change the verbs in the following sentences to express that the action of the verb is still in progress so that each sentence would mean "one is doing something."

Example 민호가 친구를 만나요 Minho meets a friend.
→ <u>민호가 친구를 만나고 있어요</u>. Minho is meeting a friend.

1 샤워해요. I take a shower.

____

2 텔레비전을 봐요. I watch T.V.

____

3 김미라씨가 일해요. Ms Kim Mira works.

____

4 저는 점심을 먹어요. I eat lunch.

____

5 저는 한국어를 공부해요. I study Korean.

____

6 지호가 커피를 마셔요. Jiho drinks coffee.

____

Exercise 2

Complete the dialogues by providing the polite sentence ending form (...아요/어요) of the following words in parentheses ( ).

1 A: 한국어가 _______? (쉽다) Is Korean easy?
B: 아니오. 조금 _______ (어렵다) No. It's a little difficult.

2 A: 여기서 _________? (가깝다) Is it close to here?
B: 아니오. 조금 멀어요. No. It's a little far.

3 A: _________? (춥다) Do you feel cold? [lit. Cold?]
B: 네. 조금 ______ (춥다) Yes, a little cold.

4 A: 내일 ________? (덥다) Is tomorrow hot?
B: 아니오. 별로 안 ______ (덥다) No. Not that hot.

Exercise 3

Complete the following dialogues using either ...(으)세요 or ...아요/어요 form of the following ㄷ irregular words.

1 A: 뭐 하세요? What are you doing?
B: 라디오 ________ (듣다) I am listening to the radio.

2 A: 어디서 한국어 ______? (듣다) Where are you taking Korean?
B: 연세대학교에서 들어요. I am taking it at Yonsei University.

3 [Talking about how to get to a place]
A: 지하철 어때요? How about (taking) the subway?
B: 같이 ________ (걷다) Let's walk together.

Exercise 4

Connect the following two clauses using ...지만 (but; although).

Example 한국어가 어려워요 + 재미있어요
Korean is difficult + (it is) fun
→ 한국어가 어렵지만 재미있어요.
Korean is difficult but it's fun.

1 커피 안 마셔요 + 차 마셔요
→ ____________________________
I don't drink coffee but I drink tea.

2 미국 친구 많아요 + 한국 친구 안 많아요
→ ____________________________
I have many American friends but I don't have many Korean friends.

3 일이 재미있어요 + 조금 어려워요
→ ____________________________
My work is fun but it's a little difficult.

4 제임스는 한국말 조금 해요 + 수잔은 한국말 아주 잘 해요
→ ____________________________
James speaks Korean a little but Susan speaks Korean very well.

Exercise 5

Your friend calls to ask what you are doing now. Tell her that you are having coffee.

Exercise 6

Your friend asks how your work is going. Tell him that you are busy but the work is fun.

Dialogue 2

(CD1; 61)

Mira and her roommate, Soojin, have invited James to their apartment. Mira shows James around her place.

미라 여기가 제 아파트예요. 들어오세요.
제임스 아파트가 아주 예뻐요.
미라 이게 제 방이에요.
그리고, 저게 제 룸메이트, 수진씨 방이에요.
제임스 방이 크고 좋은데요.
미라 여기가 거실이고 저기가 부엌이에요.
제임스 와, 부엌이 아주 깨끗한데요.
미라 하하, 제가 요리를 별로 안 해서 깨끗해요.
제임스 화장실은 어디 있어요?
미라 저기 수진씨 방 옆에 있어요.

MIRA Yŏ-gi-ga je a-p'a-t'ŭ-eyo. Tŭ-rŏ-o-se-yo.
JAMES A-pa'-t'ŭ-ga a-ju ye-ppŏ-yo.
MIRA I-ge je bang-i-e-yo.
Kŭ-ri-go, chŏ-ge je rum-mei-tŭ, su-jin-ssi bang-i-e-yo.
JAMES Bang-i K'ŭ-go cho-ŭn-de-yo.
MIRA Yŏ-gi-ga kŏ-shi-ri-go chŏ-gi-ga bu-ŏk-i-eyo.
JAMES Wa, pu-ŏ-gi a-ju kke-ggŭ-t'an-deyo.
MIRA Ha-ha, che-ga yo-ri-rŭl pyŏl-lo an-(h)e-sŏ kke-ggŭ-t'ae-yo.
JAMES Hwa-jang-shi-rŭn ŏ-di-i-ssŏ-yo?
MIRA Chŏ-gi sujin-ssi bang yŏ-p'e-i-ssŏ-yo.

MIRA *This [lit. Here] is my apartment. Come in.*
JAMES *Your apartment is very pretty.*
MIRA *This is my room. And that one over there is my roommate Soojin's room.*
JAMES *The rooms are big and nice.*
MIRA *This is the living room and that is the kitchen.*
JAMES *Wow, your kitchen is very clean.*
MIRA *Haha, it's clean because I don't really cook much.*
JAMES *Where is the bathroom?*
MIRA *It is right next to Soojin's room over there.*

Vocabulary

제	my
아파트	apartment
들어오다	to come in (cf. 들어가다: to go in)
아주	very, very much
예뻐요	(< 예쁘다) be pretty
이게	this (contracted form of 이것이) 이것 (this) + 이 (subject marker)
방	room
저게	that (contracted form of 저것이) 저것 (that) + 이 (subject marker)
룸메이트	roommate
크다	be big
...ㄴ데요	sentence ending
여기	here
거실	living room
저기	over there
부엌	kitchen
깨끗하다	be clean
제가	I 저 (I) + 가 (subject marker) → 제가
요리	cooking
화장실	bathroom

Loanwords (CD1; 62)

There are quite a few Korean words that were borrowed from other languages. Pronunciation of those words is modified to fit into the Korean phonetic system.

바나나	banana	파인애플	pineapple
피아노	piano	바이올린	violin
테니스	tennis	골프	golf
카드	card	코트	coat
빌딩	building	아르바이트	part-time job

Grammar points

5.6 여기/거기/저기 "here/there/over there"

여기 here; this place
(refers to a place near the speaker)

거기 there; that place
(refers to a place near the listener or a place that was previously mentioned)

저기 (place) over there
(refers to a place away from both the speaker and the listener)

여기 있어요.	Here it is/Here I am/Here she is.
거기 잠깐 계세요.	Stay there for a moment.
저기가 제 집이에요.	That place over there is my house.

5.7 Expressing one's possession

제 is equivalent to *my* in English. Note the pronoun *I* in Korean and its possessive form.

I	*my*	example	
나	내	내 컴퓨터	my computer
저 (humble polite)	제	제 컴퓨터	my computer

나 and 저 both mean *I*. 저 is a humble-polite word for 나, thus sounds politer than 나. The possessive forms of 나 and 저 are 내 and 제 respectively.

To express someone else's possession, use the name or title of the person followed by his/her possessed item.

제임스 컴퓨터	James's computer
미라 책	Mira's book
김사장님 이메일 주소	President Kim's e-mail address

5.8 으 irregular words

Some words containing 으 in their base may change their form depending on the following sound. When followed by a vowel, 으 in the base is dropped. When the following sound is a consonant, 으 is retained, as shown below.

으 irregular words		combined with …아요/어요	combined with …(으)세요
바쁘다	busy	바빠요*	바쁘세요
예쁘다	pretty	예뻐요*	예쁘세요
크다	big	커요	크세요
쓰다	write	써요	쓰세요

***Note:**
After 으 is lost, the choice between 아요 and 어요 depends on the preceding vowel.

5.9 Sentence ending …ㄴ데요

While the 아요/어요 form (the polite sentence ending) is probably the most widely used sentence ending in colloquial speech, there is another frequently used sentence ending …ㄴ데요. Although …ㄴ데요 can sometimes be used interchangeably with …아요/어요, its meaning sometimes carries a slightly different nuance from …아요/어요. This ending is frequently used when providing background information or when implying a certain situation without directly mentioning it (for politeness).

A: 오늘 같이 영화 봐요. — Let's watch a movie together today.
B1: 오늘 바빠요. — I am busy today.
B2: 오늘 바쁜데요. — I am busy today (so I probably can't).

A: 김선생님 계세요? — Is Mr Kim there?
B1: 지금 회의실에 계세요. — He is in the conference room.
B2: 지금 회의실에 계신데요. — He is in the conference room (so you might want to wait or come later).

In the first example above, B1 and B2 do not have much difference in terms of meaning, but B2 sounds less direct and implies that the speaker probably cannot make it to the movie. In the latter example also, by using the ... ㄴ데요 ending, the speaker delivers the meaning with a nuance of asking the listener to understand the situation.

The usage of ... ㄴ데요 is as follows:

verb	+ 는데요
adjective	+ (으)ㄴ데요 (after a consonant, 은데요; after a vowel, ㄴ데요)
noun	+ (이)ㄴ데요 (after a consonant, 인데요; after a vowel, it may be shortened to ㄴ데요)
있, 없	+ 는데요

요즘 한국어 공부하는데요. I study Korean these days.
방이 큰데요. The room is big.
수잔은 영국사람인데요. Susan is a British person.
제임스는 학생이 아닌데요. James is not a student.
영화가 재미있는데요. The movie is interesting.

5.10 Connecting two clauses using ... 고 "and"

... 고 meaning "and" is used to connect two or more clauses.

verb or adjective + 고
noun + (이)고

Example 방이 크다 + 방이 좋다 → 방이 크고 좋아요.
The room is big and nice.

아침에 일하고 저녁에 한국어 공부해요.
I work in the morning and study Korean in the evening.
(아침에: in the morning, 저녁에: in the evening)
집이 깨끗하고 예뻐요.
The house is clean and pretty.
수잔은 학생이고 제임스는 회사원이에요.
Susan is a student and James is a company worker.
(회사원: company employee)

Note the distinction between …고 which connects clauses and …하고 which connects nouns.

제임스하고 수잔은 친구예요. James and Susan are friends.

Exercise 7 **(CD1; 63)**

Whose is it? (누구 거예요?) Answer in Korean using the possessive expression.

Example my book → 제 책이에요.

1 my coffee
2 Susan's computer
3 James's bag
4 Mira's watch (watch: 시계)

Exercise 8

Who is it? (누구예요?) Answer in Korean using the possessive expression.

Example Mira's roommate → 미라 룸메이트예요.

1 James's friend
2 my parents (parents: 부모님)
3 my colleague (colleague: 동료)
4 my Korean language teacher (teacher: 선생님)

Exercise 9

Provide polite sentence-ending forms of the underlined words.

1 오늘 바쁘다 I am busy today.
2 미라씨는 예쁘다 Mira is pretty.
3 사무실이 크다 The office is big.
4 제 핸드폰을 쓰다 Use my mobile phone.

Exercise 10

Change the 아요/어요 ending to the …ㄴ데요 ending.

Example 커피가 없어요 → 커피가 없는데요.
There is no coffee.

1 오늘 친구하고 영화 봐요. →
2 지금 백화점에 가요. →

3 내일은 일 안 <u>해요</u>. →
4 오늘은 일이 <u>많아요</u>. →
5 방이 아주 <u>커요</u>. →
6 아파트가 아주 <u>예뻐요</u>. →
7 한국어 공부가 <u>재미있어요</u>. →
8 내일은 좀 <u>바빠요</u>. →

Exercise 11

Connect the following two clauses using . . . 고.

Example 여기가 거실이에요. 저기가 부엌이에요.
→ <u>여기가 거실이고 저기가 부엌이에요</u>.

1 한국어가 쉬워요. 한국어가 재미있어요.
2 사무실이 커요. 사무실이 깨끗해요.
3 영화 봐요. 커피 마셔요.
4 요리를 좋아해요. 요리를 자주 해요. (좋아하다: to like)

Cultural point

Korea is densely populated, and space is limited in urban areas. Thus, houses tend to be small, and you can easily see many high-rise apartments in the cities. High-rise apartments are as expensive as or even more expensive than single-family houses. Apartments in Korea usually have two or three bedrooms, one or two bathrooms, a kitchen with dinette, and a living room. For young single adults, a popular living arrangement is the “One Room (원룸),” equivalent to a studio apartment. An “Officetel (오피스텔)” is another form of apartment in Korea that combines the functions of office and house as implied in its name, “office + hotel.” Most houses in Korea have *ondol* (온돌) floors, a heating system underneath the floor that keeps the house warm during the winter.

Unit Six

몇 시예요?

What time is it?

In this unit you will learn about:

- Numbers in Korean
- Asking or telling the time in Korean
- The expression for "before doing..." in Korean: ...기 전에
- Asking the listener's opinion using ...(으)ㄹ까요?
- Expressing one's intention in a casual setting using ...(으)ㄹ래요
- Describing past events using the past tense sentence ending ...았어요/...었어요
- Providing reason using ...거든요
- How to use the sentence ending ...네요
- Expressing a date
- Days of the month

Dialogue 1

(CD2; 1)

James and Mira are going to see a movie. They have bought their tickets and talk about what to do before the movie starts.

제임스 지금 몇 시예요?
미라 두 시 십오 분(2 시 15 분)이에요.
제임스 영화 몇 시에 시작해요?
미라 세 시 삼십 분(3 시 30 분)에요.
제임스 그럼, 영화 보기 전에 뭐 할까요?
미라 커피 마시러 갈래요?
제임스 좋아요. 이 근처에 카페가 있어요?
미라 네. 저기 많이 있어요.

JAMES Chi-gŭm myŏt-ssi-e-yo?
MIRA Tu-shi shi-bo-bun-i-e-yo.
JAMES Yŏng-hwa myŏt-ssi-e shi-ja-k'ae-yo?
MIRA Se-shi sam-ship-ppu-ne-yo.
JAMES Kŭ-rŏm, yŏng-hwa bogi-jŏ-ne myŏ hal-kka-yo?
MIRA K'ŏ-p'i ma-shi-rŏ gal-lae-yo?
JAMES Chŏ-a-yo. I gŭn-ch'ŏ-e k'a-p'e-ga i-ssŏ-yo?
MIRA Ne. Chŏ-gi ma-ni i-ssŏ-yo.

JAMES *What time is it now?*
MIRA *It's two fifteen.*
JAMES *What time does the movie start?*
MIRA *At three thirty.*
JAMES *Then, what shall we do before watching the movie?*
MIRA *Do you want to go have a cup of coffee?*
JAMES *Sure. [lit. Good.] Is there a café around here?*
MIRA *Yes. There are a lot over there.*

Vocabulary

지금	now
몇 시	what time
시작하다	to start

세 시 삼십 분에요	세 시 삼십 분 (3:30) + 에 (at) + 요 (polite ending)
아직	still, not yet
시간	hour (한 시간: one hour)
...정도	about..., approximately...
남다	to remain
...기 전에	before...
...(으)ㄹ까요?	Shall we...?; Shall I...?; Do you think...?
마시다	to drink
...(으)ㄹ래요?	Do you want to...?; Will you...?
...(으)ㄹ래요.	will...; want to...
근처	vicinity, nearby place

Telling the time in Korean **(CD2; 2)**

오전: a.m., 오후: p.m.

Example 오전 아홉 시: 9:00 a.m., 오후 두 시: 2:00 p.m.

아침: morning; morning meal
점심: lunch time; lunch meal
저녁: evening; evening meal

...시	**...o'clock**	...분	**...minute(s)**
한 시	1 o'clock	오 분	5 minutes
두 시	2 o'clock	십 분	10 minutes
세 시	3 o'clock	십오 분	15 minutes
네 시	4 o'clock	이십 분	20 minutes
다섯 시	5 o'clock	이십오 분	25 minutes
여섯 시	6 o'clock	삼십 분	30 minutes
일곱 시	7 o'clock	삼십오 분	35 minutes
여덟 시	8 o'clock	사십 분	40 minutes
아홉 시	9 o'clock	사십오 분	45 minutes
열 시	10 o'clock	오십 분	50 minutes
열한 시	11 o'clock	오십오 분	55 minutes
열두 시	12 o'clock		

Grammar points

6.1 Numbers in Korean (CD2; 3; 4)

There are two sets of numbers in Korean:

	Native Korean numbers	Sino-Korean numbers
1	하나 (→ 한)*	일
2	둘 (→ 두)*	이
3	셋 (→ 세)*	삼
4	넷 (→ 네)*	사
5	다섯	오
6	여섯	육
7	일곱	칠
8	여덟	팔
9	아홉	구
10	열	십
11	열하나	십일
12	열둘	십이
20	스물 (→ 스무)*	이십
30	서른	삼십
40	마흔	사십
50	쉰	오십
60	예순	육십
70	일흔	칠십
80	여든	팔십
90	아흔	구십

	Native Korean numbers	Sino-Korean numbers
100		백
1,000		천
10,000		만
100,000		십만
1,000,000		백만
10,000,000		천만
100,000,000		억

Note:

*1 When followed by a noun, the forms change to 한, 두, 세, 네, 스무.

2 From 100 above, only Sino-Korean numbers are used.

Which set of numbers to use depends on the object that you count (namely, the counter that you use), as shown in the following table. For example, when counting *hours*, native Korean numbers are used, whereas when counting *minutes*, Sino-Korean numbers are used.

	Counters	Example	
Native Korean numbers	시 (o'clock)	한 시	one o'clock
	개 (piece, object)	두 개	two pieces
	사람 or 명 (person)	세 사람	three people
	번 (times, occurrences)	네 번	four times
	달 (months)	다섯 달	five months
	잔 (cup, glass)	여섯 잔	six cups/glasses
	병 (bottle)	일곱 병	seven bottles
	마리 (counter for animals)	여덟 마리	eight animals
	가지 (kinds, sorts)	아홉 가지	nine kinds
	시간 (hour)	열 시간	ten hours
	장 (sheets)	열한 장	eleven sheets
	권 (volumes)	열두 권	twelve volumes

	Counters	Example	
Sino-Korean numbers	분 (minutes)	일 분	one minute
	월 (name of the month)	이 월	February
	일 (days)	삼 일	the third day or three days
	년 (years)	사 년	four years
	개월 (months)	오 개월	five months
	층 (floors)	육 층	sixth floor/six stories
	원 (won)	백 원	100 won
	불 (dollar)	십 불	10 dollars

Particularly when counting people or things using native Korean numbers, note that the following word order is frequently used:

[name of the object] + [number] + [counter]

Example	학생 두 명	two students [lit. student + 2 + person-counter]
	맥주 세 병	three bottles of beer [lit. beer + 3 + bottle]
	도우넛 다섯 개	five doughnuts [lit. doughnut 5 pieces]
	개 네 마리	four dogs [lit. dog + four + animal-counter]
	책 여섯 권	six books [lit. book six volumes]
	종이 한 장	one sheet of paper [lit. paper one sheet]

6.2 Asking numbers using 몇 "how many"

One can ask the number or quantity of something/someone by using 몇 [**myŏt**] followed by a counter.

지금 몇 시예요?	What time is it now?
사람이 몇 명 있어요?	How many people are there?
책이 몇 권 있어요?	How many books are there?
사무실이 몇 층에 있어요?	On what floor is your office located?

6.3 ...기 전에 "before doing..."

Used after a verb, ...기 전에 means "before doing something."

가기 전에	before going
자기 전에	before sleeping

영화 보기 전에 저녁을 먹었어요.
Before watching the movie, we ate dinner. (먹었어요: ate)
오기 전에 먼저 전화하세요.
Before you come, please call first. (먼저: first; ahead of)

6.4 Asking the listener's opinion ...(으)ㄹ까요? "Shall I/we...?; Do you think...?"

You can suggest something or ask the listener's opinion by using... (으)ㄹ까요? after a verb.

갈까요?	Shall I go?; Shall we go?
영화 볼까요?	Shall we watch a movie?
몇 시에 만날까요?	What time shall we meet?
회의 시작할까요?	Shall we start the meeting?
사장님 오실까요?	Do you think the president will come?

6.5 Expressing one's intention ...(으)ㄹ래요 "will...; want to..."

When attached to a verb base, (으)ㄹ래요 is used to express the speaker's intention or to ask for the listener's intention. It is used more in a casual setting than in a formal setting.

A: 뭐 마실래요?	What would you like to drink?
B: 차 마실래요.	I will have tea.
A: 영화 보러 같이 갈래요?	Would you like to go to see a movie together?
B: 좋아요.	That's good/fine.

Exercise 1

Look at the following pictures and tell the time in Korean.

1

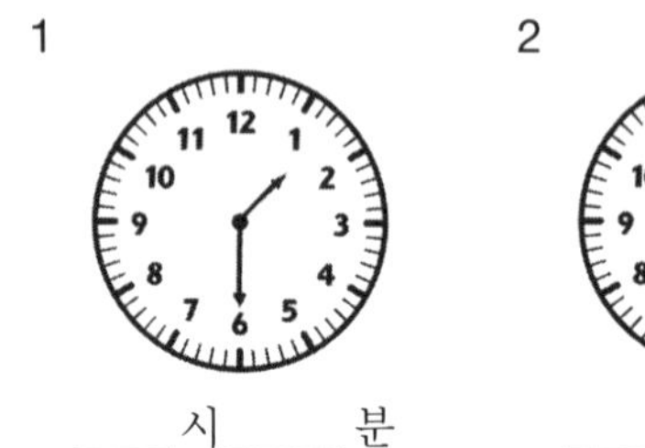

___ 시 ___ 분

2

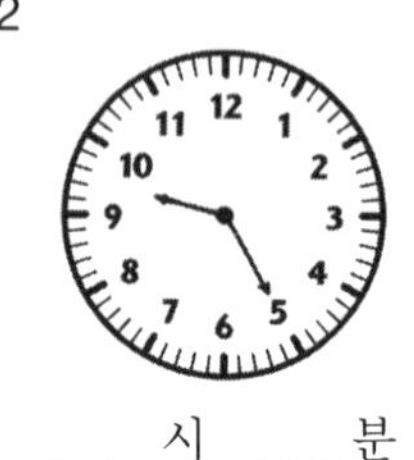

___ 시 ___ 분

3

___ 시 ___ 분

Exercise 2

Look at the pictures and fill in the blanks with the appropriate number words in Korean.

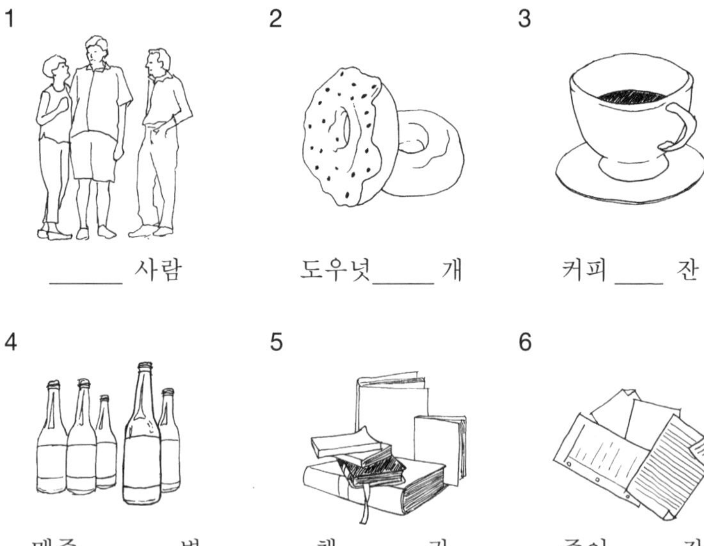

1 ___ 사람

2 도우넛 ___ 개

3 커피 ___ 잔

4 맥주 ___ 병

5 책 ___ 권

6 종이 ___ 장

Exercise 3

The following two sentences are sequentially displayed. Connect the two sentences using ...기 전에.

Example 밥 먹다 (to eat a meal) → 영화 보다 (to watch a movie)
→ 영화 보기 전에 밥 먹어요.

1 팝콘을 사다 → 영화를 보다 (팝콘: popcorn)
2 전화하다 → 가다
3 표를 사다 → 지하철 타다 (표: ticket)
4 커피를 마시다 → 일을 시작하다

Exercise 4 **(CD2; 5)**

Ask your co-worker's opinion using ...(으)ㄹ까요?

Example 같이 영화 보다 → 같이 영화 볼까요?
Shall we watch movies?

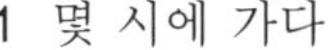

1 몇 시에 가다 What time shall I go?
2 회사 앞에서 만나다 Shall we meet in front of the company?
3 언제부터 일을 시작하다 When shall I start the work?
4 내일 날씨가 좋다 Do you think the weather tomorrow will be good? (날씨: weather)

Exercise 5

Ask your friend if he wants to do the following activities.

Example 커피 마시다 → 커피 마실래요?

1 텔레비전 보다
2 한국 음식 먹다 (한국 음식: Korean food)
3 백화점에 쇼핑하러 가다
4 같이 한국어 배우다 (배우다: to learn)

Cultural point

Korean holidays

Korean families celebrate holidays and festive days with food and events. Some of the holidays are based on the lunar calendar that was used for so long in the old days. The two most popular holidays in Korea are Sŏllal (설날) and Chusŏk (추석). On Sŏllal and Chusŏk, many people wear Hanbok (한복), the traditional Korean costume.

New Year's Day (설날), January 1

Families get together and eat 떡국, rice cake soup, to celebrate the new year. Children bow to family elders and receive good luck money. Lunar New Year's Day (usually late January or early February) is also popularly celebrated as a big holiday when people play various folk games. In effect, there are two annual New Year's Day celebrations in Korea.

Harvest Festival Day (추석), August 15 (by lunar calendar)

Chusŏk is Korean Thanksgiving, when people celebrate the autumn harvest. Families get together and eat a meal, including rice cake, called songpyon (송편). Families honor their ancestors and visit ancestral gravesites.

Hanbok, the traditional Korean costume

Dialogue 2

(CD2; 6, 7)

Mira, James, and Soojin are meeting at a coffee shop. Mira brought a birthday cake to the coffee shop to celebrate her roommate Soojin's birthday. While waiting for Soojin, James and Mira chat about the cake and their birthdays.

제임스 이거 뭐예요?
미라 케이크예요. 오늘 수진씨 생일이거든요.
제임스 아, 그래요? 미라씨가 만들었어요?
미라 아니오. 빵집에서 샀어요.
제임스 미라씨는 생일이 언제예요?
미라 팔월이에요. 제임스씨는요?
제임스 저는 겨울이에요. 일월 오일이요.
미라 그럼, 다음 달이네요.
제임스 어, 저기 수진씨가 와요.
미라 수진씨, 생일 축하해요.

JAMES I-gŏ mwŏ-e-yo?
MIRA K'e-i-k'ŭ-e-yo. Ŏ-nŭl Su-jin-ssi saeng-i-ri-gŏ-dŭn-yo.
JAMES Ah, kŭ-rae-yo? Mira-ssi-ga man-dŭ-rŏ-ssŏ-yo?
MIRA Anio. Ppang-tchi-be-sŏ ssat-ssŏ-yo.
JAMES Mira-ssi-nŭn saeng-i-ri ŏn-je-e-yo?
MIRA P'a-rwŏ-ri-e-yo. Che-im-sŭ-ssi-nŭn-yo?
JAMES Chŏ-nŭn kyŏ-u-ri-e-yo. I-rwŏl-o-i-ri-yo.
MIRA Kŭ-rŏm, ta-ŭm-tta-ri-ne-yo.
JAMES Ŏ, chŏ-gi su-jin-ssi-ga wa-yo.
MIRA Su-jin-ssi, saeng-il ch'u-k'a-hae-yo.

JAMES *What is this?*
MIRA *It is a cake. You see, today is Soojin's birthday.*
JAMES *Oh, really? Did you make the cake?*
MIRA *No. I bought it at a bakery.*
JAMES *When is your birthday, Mira?*
MIRA *It's August. What about you, James?*
JAMES *Mine is (in the) winter. It's January fifth.*
MIRA *It's next month then.*
JAMES *Oh, Soojin is coming over there.*
MIRA *Soojin, happy birthday.*

Vocabulary

케이크	cake
생일	birthday
...거든요	It's because; you see; you know
만들다	to make
...았어요/었어요	past-tense sentence ending
빵집	bakery (= 제과점)
사다	to buy (샀어요: bought)
언제	when (언제예요?: When is it?)
팔월	August
겨울	winter
다음	next
달	month
...네요	the emphatic sentence ending
축하하다	to congratulate 생일 축하해요 (Happy birthday)

The months (CD2; 8, 9)

일월	[i-rwŏl]	January
이월	[i-wŏl]	February
삼월	[sa-mwŏl]	March
사월	[sa-wŏl]	April
오월	[o-wŏl]	May
*유월	[yu-wŏl]	June
칠월	[ch'i-rwŏl]	July
팔월	[p'a-rwŏl]	August
구월	[ku-wŏl]	September
*시월	[shi-wŏl]	October
십일월	[shi-bi-rwŏl]	November
십이월	[shi-bi-wŏl]	December

*Note the spelling of 유월 (not 육월) and 시월 (not 십월)

The four seasons

봄	[bom]	spring	여름	[yŏ-rŭm]	summer
가을	[ka-ŭl]	autumn	겨울	[kyŏ-ul]	winter

Grammar points

6.6 Expressing past events …았어요/었어요 The past-tense sentence ending

…았어요 and …었어요 are the past-tense forms of …아요 and …어요 respectively. The choice between …았어요 and …었어요 follows the same rule as the choice between …아요 and …어요.

1 When the last vowel of the verb or adjective base ends in a bright vowel, ㅏ [a] or ㅗ [o], 았어요 is used.

앉다	to sit	앉았어요	sat
좋다	be good	좋았어요	was good
가다	to go	*가 + 았어요 → 갔어요	went
자다	to sleep	*자 + 았어요 → 잤어요	slept
오다	to come	*오 + 았어요 → 왔어요	came
		(* vowel contraction)	

2 When the last vowel of the verb or adjective base ends in a vowel other than ㅏ [a] or ㅗ [o], 었어요 is used.

먹다	to eat	먹었어요	ate
읽다	to read	읽었어요	read
있다	to exist; to have	있었어요	was there; had

3 When the verb or adjective ends in…하다, 했어요 is used.

공부하다	to study	공부했어요	studied
일하다	to work	일했어요	worked
시작하다	to start	시작했어요	started
운동하다	to exercise	운동했어요	exercised

6.7 Providing explanation using …거든요 "it's because…; you see"

…거든요 is a sentence ending that is attached to verbs, adjectives, and nouns and provides explanation or reason. After nouns, …(이)거든요 is used.

내일 모임에 못 가요. 요즘 바쁘거든요.
I can't go to tomorrow's gathering. Because I am busy these days.

지하철을 타세요. 지하철이 빠르거든요.
Take the subway. The subway is fast. (빠르다: be fast)

그 영화를 보세요. 아주 재미있거든요.
Watch that movie. It's really interesting.

In colloquial Korean, ...거든요 is frequently used as a sentence ending that approximately means *you know* or *you see* in English.

요즘 영어를 가르치거든요. 재미있어요.
I teach English these days, you know. It's fun.

마이클은 한국어를 삼년 배웠거든요. 한국어를 잘 해요.
You know, Michael learned Korean (for) three years. He speaks Korean well.

핸드폰이 없거든요. 집으로 전화하세요. (핸드폰: cell phone)
I don't have a cellular phone. Call me at home [lit. Call to home].

내일 제 아파트에서 파티를 하거든요. 오실래요?
Tomorrow we are having a party at my apartment. Would you like to come?

6.8 ...네요 sentence ending

...네요 is the sentence ending that shows the speaker's reaction to or realization of what was just heard or presented. It often involves the speaker's surprise or realization.

Look at the following example of the ...네요 ending in (2) and compare it with (1).

(After hearing a foreigner speaking Korean fluently)
1 한국말 잘 하세요. You speak Korean very well.
2 한국말 잘 하시네요. You speak Korean very well.

Both (1) and (2) have the same meaning, but (2) shows the speaker's surprise and spontaneous reaction to what he/she just heard or saw, by using the ...네요 ending. Look at some more examples of ...네요 below.

A: 이 케이크 제가 만들었어요. 좀 드세요.
I made this cake. Please try some.
B: (after tasting the cake) 와, 정말 맛있네요.
Wow, it is really delicious. (정말: really)

A: 고향이 어디세요?
Where is your hometown?
B: 대전이에요.
It's Daejeon.
A: 아, 그래요? 저하고 같네요.
Ah, is that right? It's the same with me (with surprise).
(같다: be the same; ...하고 같다: be the same as...)
저도 고향이 대전이에요.
My hometown is also Daejeon.
[lit. Me too hometown is Daejeon.]

6.9 Expressing a date

A date is expressed in the following order in Korean:
the year → the month → the day of the month.

2010 년 3 월 5 일 (이천십년 삼월 오일)
1987 년 4 월 21 일 (천구백팔십칠년 사월 이십일일)

■ Days of the month

Sun. 일요일	Mon. 월요일	Tue. 화요일	Wed. 수요일	Thur. 목요일	Fri. 금요일	Sat. 토요일
			1 일일	2 이일	3 삼일	4 사일
5 오일	6 육일	7 칠일	8 팔일	9 구일	10 십일	11 십일일
12 십이일	13 십삼일	14 십사일	15 십오일	16 십육일	17 십칠일	18 십팔일
19 십구일	20 이십일	21 이십일일	22 이십이일	23 이십삼일	24 이십사일	25 이십오일
26 이십육일	27 이십칠일	28 이십팔일	29 이십구일	30 삼십일	31 삼십일일	

Exercise 6

Provide the past tense form (았어요/었어요) of the following words.

Example 가요 go → 갔어요 went

1 와요 come
2 시작해요 start
3 없어요 not have
4 만나요 meet
5 좋아요 good
6 봐요 see
7 먹어요 eat
8 바빠요 busy

Exercise 7

The following is a list of what you did yesterday. Complete each sentence by providing the past form of the word given in ( ).

1 어제 한국어 수업을 (듣다) ________
2 수업을 듣기 전에 한국어를 (공부하다) ________
3 한국어 수업이 (재미있다) ________
4 세 시에 친구를 (만나다) ________
5 친구하고 같이 (운동하다) ________ (운동하다: to work out)
6 친구하고 같이 저녁 (먹다) ________ (저녁: dinner; evening)

Exercise 8

Your co-worker is asking the following questions. Answer the following questions using ...거든요.

Example A: 케이크 왜 샀어요? (왜: why)
B: 오늘이 수진씨 생일이거든요.

1 A: 왜 집에 안 가세요?
B: (일이 많다) ____________

2 A: 어제 왜 안 왔어요?
B: (아팠다) ____________ (아프다: be sick; 아팠다: was sick)

3 A: 왜 주말에 일하세요? (주말: weekend)
B: (요즘 바쁘다) ____________

4 A: 왜 한국어를 배우세요?
B: (한국 회사에서 일하다) ______________ (한국 회사: Korean company)

Exercise 9

Provide the following dates in Korean.

Example January 1 → 일월 일일

1 August 15
2 October 9
3 March 21
4 May 30
5 December 24
6 June 8

Exercise 10

Change the following ...아요/어요 sentence ending into the ...네요 ending.

Example 한국말 잘 하세요. → 한국말 잘 하시네요.

1 커피가 맛있어요.
2 음식이 아주 많아요.
3 방이 아주 깨끗해요.
4 장미꽃이 아주 예뻐요. (장미꽃: rose)

Unit Seven
밖에서 식사하기
Dining out

In this unit you will learn about:

- Describing one's experience using ...아/어 보다
- Expressing one's wish or someone else's wish
- Expressing one's volition using ...(으)ㄹ게요
- How to use the honorific marker ...(으)시
- Expressing one's intention or inference using ...겠
- How to politely ask the listener's intention
- Use of the formal polite sentence ending ...ㅂ니다/습니다
- Two different ways to express "only" in Korean
- Politely asking someone to give you something
- Ordering food at a restaurant
- Popular Korean dishes

Dialogue 1

(CD2; 10, 11)

Mira has taken James to a Korean restaurant. They are talking about what to order.

미라	제임스씨, 여기 와 봤어요?
제임스	아니오. 처음이에요.
미라	여기 음식이 아주 맛있어요.
제임스	그래요?
미라	뭐 드시고 싶으세요?
제임스	저는 갈비요.
미라	그럼, 저도 같이 갈비 먹을게요.
종업원	주문하시겠어요?
미라	네. 갈비 2 인분 주세요.
종업원	알겠습니다.

MIRA	Che-im-sŭ-ssi, yŏ-gi wa-pwa-ssŏ-yo?
JAMES	Anio. Ch'ŏ-ŭm-i-e-yo.
MIRA	Yŏ-gi ŭm-shi-gi a-ju ma-shi-ssŏ-yo.
JAMES	Kŭ-rae-yo?
MIRA	Mwŏ tŭ-shi-go shi-p'ŭ-se-yo?
JAMES	Chŏ-nŭn Kal-bi-yo.
MIRA	Kŭ-rŏm, chŏ-do ka-ch'i kal-bi mŏ-gŭl-kke-yo.
WAITER	Chu-mun-ha-shi-ge-ssŏ-yo?
MIRA	Ne. Kal-bi i-in-bun chu-se-yo.
WAITER	Al-ge-ssŭm-nida.

MIRA	*James, have you been here?*
JAMES	*No. This is the first time [lit. first time].*
MIRA	*The food here is very delicious.*
JAMES	*Is that so?*
MIRA	*What do you want to eat?*
JAMES	*As for me,* Kalbi.
MIRA	*Then, I will also have* Kalbi. *[lit. Then, I also together will have* Kalbi.*]*
WAITER	*Would you like to order? [lit. Will you order?]*
MIRA	*Yes. Give us* Kalbi *for two people.*
WAITER	*Understood.*

Vocabulary

...아/어 보다	try to... 와 보다 try to come (오다 + 아/어 보다)
처음	first time
맛있다	delicious (pronounced [마시따] or [마디따])
드시다	to eat; to drink (honorific word for 들다 "*to eat*," 먹다 "*to eat*," and 마시다 "*to drink*")
...고 싶다	want to..., would like to...
갈비	Korean barbecued short-rib dish
...(으)ㄹ게요	I will...
주문하다	to order (food)
2 인분	two-people portion 이 (two) + 인 (person) + 분 (portion)
주다	to give 주세요: please give
알겠습니다	I understood; I got it [lit. I will understand.]

Meals (CD2; 12, 13)
아침: breakfast, 점심: lunch, 저녁: dinner

Names of some Korean dishes

불고기(*Bulgogi*): Thinly sliced beef, marinated with soy sauce and other ingredients

김밥(*Kimbap*): Rice and assorted vegetables with or without meat rolled in seaweed

냉면(*Nangmyon*): Cold buckwheat noodles with pickled turnip and beef

비빔밥(*Bibimbap*): Rice topped with an assortment of vegetables, egg, and beef served with spicy sauce 돌솥비빔밥: 비빔밥 in a hot stone pot

된장찌개 (*Twenjangjjigae*): Soybean paste stew

김치찌개 (*Kimchijjigae*): Kimchi stew

잡채 (*Chapchae*): Potato noodles stir-fried with vegetables and beef

Grammar points

7.1 Describing one's experience ...아/어 보다 "try to...; have been to..."

보다 (the dictionary form of 봐요) means *to see.* When it is preceded by ...아/어 form, it conveys a different meaning. A verb base plus ...아/어 보다 means "try something and find out how you like it."

...아/어 보세요 is frequently used as a suggestion to try something.

...아/어 보세요. Try ...ing

김치를 먹어 보세요.
Try *Kimchi* and see how it is. [lit. Try to eat Kimchi.]
노래방에 가 보세요. (노래방: karaoke [lit. singing room])
Try karaoke and see how it is.
그 책을 한번 읽어 보세요. (한번: once, one time; 읽다: to read)
Read that book and see if you like it.
김선생님을 한번 만나 보세요.
Won't you meet Mr Kim? (선생님: teacher; Mr/Ms)

When used with the past tense, it often expresses one's past experience.

...아/어 봤어요	have tried ...
가 봤어요.	I have been there.
해 봤어요.	I have tried it.
불고기 먹어 봤어요.	I have tried *Bulgogi.*
영국에 가 봤어요?	Have you been to the UK?

7.2 Expressing one's desire ...고 싶다 "want to...; would like to..."

Attached to verbs, ...고 싶다 is used to express one's desire.

한국어를 배우고 싶어요.	I want to learn Korean.
런던에 가고 싶어요.	I want to go to London.
김선생님을 뵙고 싶어요.	I would like to see Mr Kim.

(뵙다: humble polite word of 보다 *to see*)

테니스를 치고 싶어요.	I want to play tennis.
핸드폰을 사고 싶어요.	I would like to buy a cell phone.

...고 싶다 is used to express the speaker (first person)'s wish or to ask the listener (second person)'s wish. However, when expressing a third person's wish, ...고 싶다 cannot be used but instead ...고 싶어하다 should be used.

런던에 가고 싶어요.	I want to go to London.
런던에 가고 싶어요?	Do you want to go to London?

김선생님은 런던에 가고 싶어해요.
Mr Kim wants to go to London.
마이클은 한국에서 영어를 가르치고 싶어해요.
Michael wants to teach English in Korea.

7.3 Expressing one's intention ...(으)ㄹ게요 "I will..."

Attached to a verb base, ...(으)ㄹ게요 expresses the speaker's voluntary will or intention. It is only used with the first person (I) and never used with the second person (you) or the third person (he/she/they). ...(으)ㄹ게요 sounds rather casual, so it is not likely to be used in a formal setting. It is usually pronounced [...(으)ㄹ께요, ...(ŭl)kkeyo] in colloquial speech.

갈게요.	I am going to go.
열심히 할게요.	I will do it diligently. (열심히: diligently, hard)
잘 먹을게요.	I will enjoy the food. [lit. I will eat well.]

7.4 The honorific marker ...(으)시

...(으)시 is the honorific marker that is attached to the base of a verb or an adjective to express respect or esteem for a certain person. That is, the speaker elevates the respected person by attaching ...(으)시 to the verb or adjective that describes the action or state of the respected person. ...(으)시 is frequently used to a person who is older than the speaker, higher than the speaker in terms of social status, or distant from the speaker in terms of social relationships.

The honorific sentence ending ...(으)세요 is the combination of the honorific marker and the polite sentence ending: ...(으)시+어요.

After a verb/adjective base that ends in a vowel, 시 is used, and after a verb/adjective base that ends in a consonant, 으시 is used.

verb/adjective base		verb/adjective honorific base	honorific polite sentence ending
가...	to go	가시	가세요
오...	to come	오시	오세요
보...	to see	보시	보세요
좋아하...	to like	좋아하시	좋아하세요
만나...	to meet	만나시	만나세요
듣...	to hear	들으시	들으세요
먹...	to eat	*드시 (or 잡수시...)	드세요 (or 잡수세요)
마시...	to drink	*드시	드세요
자...	to sleep	*주무시	주무세요
바쁘...	be busy	바쁘시	바쁘세요
좋...	be good	좋으시	좋으세요

*There is a limited number of words whose honorific forms are very different from their dictionary forms. For example, the honorific base of 먹다 is not 먹으시 but 드시 (or 잡수시).

After nouns, ...(이)시 is used.

선생님	teacher	선생님이시	선생님이세요.
의사	doctor	의사시	의사세요.

7.5 Intention or supposition marker ...겠 "will..."

1 Attached to a word base, ...겠 expresses the subject's intention.

가...	to go	가겠어요	I will go.
		가겠어요?	Will you go?
하...	to do	하겠어요	I will do.
읽...	to read	읽겠어요	I will read.

Note that ...겠 *can* is used with the second person (*you*) as in 가겠어요? *Will you go?* In comparison, ...(으)ㄹ게요 (grammar point 7.3

in this unit) which also expresses one's intention, cannot be used with the second person.

주문하시겠어요? was constructed by the combination of:

주문하...	+ 시	+ 겠	+ 어요?
verb base	+ honor. marker	+ intention	+ sentence ending

Combined with the honorific marker ...(으)시, ...겠 is frequently used in the form of ...시겠어요? when politely asking the listener's intention.

...(으)시겠어요?	***Will you...or Would you like to...?***
가시겠어요?	Will you go?/Would you like to go?
뭐 드시겠어요?	What would you like to have?
몇 시에 시작하시겠어요?	At what time will you start (it)?
언제 오시겠어요?	When will you come?

2 ...겠 is also used to express the speaker's guess or inference, meaning "I suppose; I will bet; it must be that..."

내일은 날씨가 좋겠어요.	I'll bet that the weather tomorrow is good.
기분 좋으시겠어요.	You must be happy. (기분: feeling) [lit. Your feeling must be good.]

Exercise 1

Your friend is new to Korea. Suggest the following activities to her using...아/어 보세요.

1 갈비를 먹다 eat *Kalbi*
2 노래방에 가다 go to Karaoke
3 부산을 여행하다 travel to Busan
4 제 친구를 만나다 meet my friend

Exercise 2 (CD2; 14)

Talk about your past experience using...아/어 봤어요.

1 유럽을 여행하다 tour Europe
2 소주 마시다 drink *Soju* (or Korean hard liquor)
3 민수씨 집에 가다 go to Minsu's house
4 맥도날드에서 일하다 work at McDonald's

Exercise 3

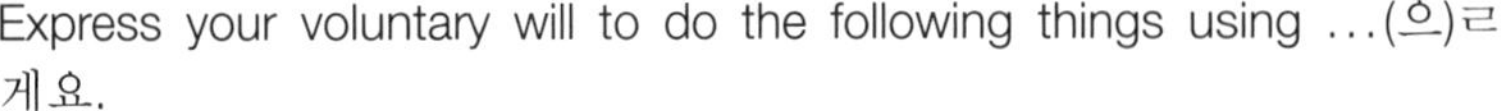

Express your voluntary will to do the following things using ...(으)ㄹ 게요.

1 내일 다시 전화하다 will call again tomorrow
2 다음 주에 이메일하다 will e-mail next week
3 김민수씨를 만나 보다 will meet Minsu Kim (and see how he is)
4 부산으로 출장가다 go on a business trip to Busan (출장가다: to go on a business trip)

Exercise 4

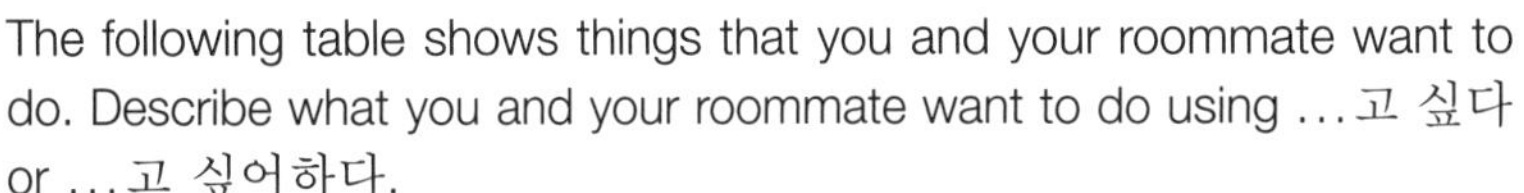

The following table shows things that you and your roommate want to do. Describe what you and your roommate want to do using ...고 싶다 or ...고 싶어하다.

Example 저는 한국어를 배우고 싶어요.
제 룸메이트는 중국어를 배우고 싶어해요.
I want to learn Korean.
My roommate wants to learn Chinese.

What I want to do	What my roommate wants to do
Example 한국어를 배우다	중국어를 배우다
1 주말에 영화 보다	주말에 집에서 쉬다
2 한국에서 일하다	미국에 돌아가다
3 한국 음식을 주문하다	이태리 음식을 주문하다
4 아침에 밥을 먹다	아침에 빵을 먹다

(주말: weekend, 쉬다: to rest, ...에 돌아가다: return to..., 주문하다: to order, 이태리: Italy, 밥: rice; meal, 빵: bread)

1 ______________________________
2 ______________________________
3 ______________________________
4 ______________________________

Exercise 5

Provide the honorific base forms of the following words by attaching ...으시 or ...시 to the word base.

Example 좋아하다 → 좋아하시

1 싫어하다 [shirŏhada] to dislike
2 약속하다 to promise; to make an appointment
3 말씀하다 to speak, to tell
4 먹다 to eat
5 전공하다 to major in, to specialize in

Exercise 6

Politely ask the listener's intention by using ...(으)시겠어요?

Example 주문하다 to order
→ 주문하시겠어요? Would you like to order?

1 말씀하다 to speak, to tell
2 먼저 하다 to do (something) first, to do (something) ahead of someone
3 한국말로 하다 to speak in Korean [lit. to do in Korean]
4 이 컴퓨터를 쓰다 to use this computer

Cultural point

The traditional Korean diet consists of rice, soup, and a main entrée along with various side dishes.

Among side dishes (or 반찬 *Banchan* in Korean), *Kimchi* is almost always served at a Korean meal. *Kimchi* is a fermented vegetable dish containing high levels of vitamins and nutrients. There are over 100 kinds of Kimchi that are made with a variety of vegetables. The most common Kimchi is the one made of Korean cabbage seasoned with salt, garlic, fish sauce and red pepper.

Rice is eaten at every meal, although bread or cereal are also breakfast items, especially with the younger generation.

Dialogue 2

(CD2; 15)

James and Mr Han are in a restaurant that serves both food and alcohol. Mr Han asks James to have a drink.

한과장	제임스씨, 술 한 잔 하시겠어요?
제임스	네, 좋습니다.
	근데 술 조금 밖에 못 마셔요.
한과장	그래요? 그럼, 조금만 드세요.
	맥주 마실까요, 소주 마실까요?
제임스	저는 맥주 좋아하는데요.
한과장	그럼, 저도 맥주 마시겠습니다.
	(to the waiter) 저기요.
	여기 맥주 두 병 좀 주세요.

MR HAN	Che-im-sŭ-ssi, su-ran-jan ha-shi-ge-ssŏ-yo?
JAMES	Ne, cho-ssŭm-nida.
	Kŭn-de sul cho-gŭm ba-kke mon-ma-syŏ-yo.
MR HAN	Kŭ-rae-yo? Kŭ-rŏm, cho-gŭm-man tŭ-se-yo.
	Maek-tchu ma-shil-kka-yo, so-ju ma-shil-kka-yo?
JAMES	Chŏ-nŭn maek-tchu jo-a-ha-nŭn-de-yo.
MR HAN	Kŭ-rŏm chŏ-do maek-tchu ma-shi-ge-ssŭm-nida.
	(*to the waiter*) Chŏ-gi-yo.
	Yŏ-gi maek-tchu du-byŏng chom chu-se-yo.

MR HAN	*James, would you like to have alcohol?*
JAMES	*Yes, that is fine. But I can only drink a little bit of alcohol.*
MR HAN	*Really? Then, have only a little bit.*
	Shall we have beer or soju?
JAMES	*I like beer. [lit. As for me, I like beer so…]*
MR HAN	*Then, I will have beer, too.*
	(to the waiter) *Excuse me. [lit. (Hello), there.]*
	Please give (us) two bottles of beer here.

Vocabulary

술	alcoholic drink, liquor 술 한 잔: a glass of alcohol
…겠	will
…습니다	the formal polite sentence ending
…겠습니다	will…(formal polite) = …겠어요 (polite)
…밖에	only, nothing but (always followed by a negative word such as 안 and 못)

못...	cannot... 못 마시다 [몬 마시다 mon mashida]: can't drink Note: The pronunciation of 못 [mot] becomes [mon] when followed by a nasal sound such as [n] and [m].
...만	only 조금만 only a little
드시다	to eat; to drink the honorific word for 들다, 먹다 or 마시다
맥주	beer
소주	Korean hard liquor
좋아하다	to like (cf. 싫어하다: to dislike)
저기	over there
좀	(1) please (2) a little
주다	to give

...(이/가) 좋다 **vs.** ...(을/를) 좋아하다

좋다 is an adjective, meaning "be good." It can be used with the subject marker ...이/가. Although the literal meaning of ...이/가 좋다 is "some thing/one is good," it also equates to "I like...."

> 이 컴퓨터가 좋아요.
> This computer is good. (*or* I like this computer.)

좋아하다 is a verb, meaning "to like." As a verb, it can take an object which can be marked with the object marker ...을/를.

> 제임스는 이 컴퓨터를 좋아해요.
> James likes this computer.

Grammar points

7.6 The formal polite sentence ending ...ㅂ니다/습니다

Like ...아요/어요, ...ㅂ니다/습니다 functions as a polite sentence ending. However, the ...ㅂ니다/습니다 ending sounds more formal than the ...아요/어요 ending, thus it is more frequently used in a formal setting such as at a conference, at work, or on a TV news show. After a vowel base, ...ㅂ니다 is used and after a consonant base, 습니다 is used. Note that 습니다 is pronounced [**sŭm-ni-da**] because the sound 습 [**sŭb**] becomes nasalized to [**sŭm**] because of the following nasal sound 니 [**ni**].

verb/adjective base		formal polite ending
가...	to go	갑니다
오...	to come	옵니다
먹...	to eat	먹습니다
만나...	to meet	만납니다
시작하...	to start	시작합니다
일하...	to work	일합니다
좋...	be good	좋습니다
괜찮...	be all right	괜찮습니다
바쁘...	be busy	바쁩니다

verb/adjective honorific base		honorific formal polite ending
가시...	to go	가십니다
오시...	to come	오십니다
드시...	to eat	드십니다
만나시...	to meet	만나십니다
시작하시...	to start	시작하십니다
일하시...	to work	일하십니다
좋으시...	be good	좋으십니다
괜찮으시...	be all right	괜찮으십니다
바쁘시...	to be busy	바쁘십니다

The formal polite sentence ending for nouns is 입니다 [**imnida**]. ...이십니다 [**ishimnida**] is the honorific ending form of 입니다.

선생님입니다.	(I am/He is/She is) a teacher.
선생님이십니다.	(He is/She is) a teacher.

The polite sentence ending ...아요/어요 can be used for questions in addition to statements by simply attaching the question mark ? and raising the ending tone. However, ...ㅂ니다/습니다 is used only for statements. To change the sentence to a question, ...ㅂ니까?/습니까? is used.

	Polite ending		Formal polite ending	
	statement	question	statement	question
Verb Adjective	...아요/어요 먹어요. 바빠요.	...아요/ 어요? 먹어요? 바빠요?	...ㅂ니다/ 습니다 먹습니다. 바쁩니다.	...ㅂ니까?/ 습니까? 먹습니까? 바쁩니까?
Noun	...이에요/ 예요 학생이에요.	...이에요/ 예요? 학생이에요?	...입니다 학생입니다.	입니까? 학생입니까?

7.7 Expressing "only" using ...밖에 + a negative word

밖에 is attached to nouns or adverbs, and is always followed by a negative word such as 안 *not*, 못 *cannot*, 없다 *to not exist* and 모르다 *to not know*. 밖에 literally means "outside" and the 밖에 + negative construction expresses the meaning "only" or "nothing but."

미라씨 밖에 안 왔어요.
Only Mira came (Nobody came except Mira)
[lit. Outside of Mira, nobody came.]

한국음식 밖에 못 만들어요.
Other than Korean food, I can't make anything.

민수 밖에 몰라요.
Except Minsu, I don't know (anybody). (몰라요: to not know)

Note that ...만 also expresses the meaning "only" which is also introduced in this lesson. However, as compared to ...만, ...밖에 + negative gives the nuance that the preceding noun is less than what the speaker wishes to have.

A: 한국말 하세요?	Do you speak Korean? [lit. Do you do Korean?]
B: 조금 밖에 못 해요.	I can speak only a little. [lit. I do only a little.]
A: 콜라 있어요?	Do you have cola?
B: 물밖에 없어요.	I have nothing but water.

7.8 Expressing "only" using ...만

Attached to nouns or adverbs, ...만 means "only" or "just."

미라씨만 왔어요.	Only Mira came.
조금만 마셔요.	Drink just a little.
물만 있어요.	I only have water.
잠깐만 기다리세요.	Wait just a second. (잠깐: a short moment)

7.9 Request for giving ...좀 주세요 "Please give me..."

...좀 주세요 is a useful expression for asking someone to give you something. 좀 which is a contracted form of 조금 literally means *a little*. However, it can also mean *please* in the context of a request.

...좀 주세요	Please give...
...좀 주십시오	Please give... (in a more formal setting)
...좀 주시겠어요?	Would you give...?
물 좀 주세요.	Please give me water.
설탕하고 크림 좀 주세요.	Please give me sugar and cream.
전화번호 좀 주세요.	Please give me your phone number.
이메일 주소 좀 주시겠어요?	Would you give me your e-mail address?

Exercises 7

Change the polite sentence ending to the formal polite sentence ending.

Example 사람이 많아요. → 사람이 많습니다.

1 어제 김선생님을 만났어요.
2 회의를 시작하겠어요. (회의: meeting, conference)
3 한국말을 몇 년 배웠어요? (몇년: how many years)
4 학생이에요?
5 어디서 일해요? (어디서: at where)

Exercise 8

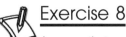

Assume that you are speaking to people at a formal setting. Change the honorific polite sentence ending to the honorific formal polite sentence ending.

Example 지금 어디세요? → 지금 어디십니까?
Where are you now?

1 어디 가세요?
2 요즘 많이 바쁘세요?
3 골프 치세요? (골프 치다: to play golf)
4 김사장님은 지금 안 계세요.
5 박교수님이세요? (교수: professor)

Exercise 9

Complete the sentence using 밖에 or 만.

1 십 불 ______ 없어요. I have nothing but ten dollars.
2 하나 ______ 주세요. Give me just one.
3 다섯 개 ______ 없어요. I have only five pieces.
4 주말에 ____ 한국어 공부해요. I study Korean only on weekends.

Exercise 10

Politely ask someone to provide you with the following item(s).

1 소금 salt
2 연락처 [yŏl-lak-ch'ŏ] contact number [lit. contact place]
3 한국말 사전 Korean dictionary
4 숟가락하고 젓가락 spoon and chopsticks
(숟가락 [su-kka-rak]: spoon
젓가락 [chŏ-kka-rak]: chopsticks)

Unit Eight
사람 만나기
Meeting people

In this unit you will learn about:

- Expressing past events or states using the formal polite sentence ending
- Providing reasons using 때문에
- Expressing duration of time using ...동안
- Expressing one's guess or intention using ...(으)ㄹ 거예요
- Verbs of giving: 주다, 주시다, 드리다
- Responding to compliments
- Seeking agreement using ...죠?
- How to say "If..." in Korean
- Expressing "when" using ...(으)ㄹ 때
- Providing background information using ...(으)ㄴ데/는데
- Making a suggestion using ...(으)ㅂ시다
- Talking about one's major and future occupation

Dialogue 1

(CD2; 16)

After having a business meeting, James and Mr Kim, an assistant section chief at Hangook Electronics, are talking together casually.

김대리 한국에 언제 오셨습니까?
제임스 지난 1 월에 왔습니다.
김대리 무슨 일로 오셨어요?
제임스 일 때문에 왔습니다.
김대리 그래요? 한국에 얼마 동안 계실 거예요?
제임스 아마 4 년이나 5 년동안 있을 거예요.
김대리 한국말을 아주 잘 하십니다.
제임스 아닙니다. 아직 잘 못합니다.
김대리 나중에 다시 연락 드리겠습니다.
제임스 네. 저한테 전화나 이메일 주세요.

MR KIM Han-gu-ge ŏn-je o-ssyŏ-ssŭm-ni-kka?
JAMES Chi-nan i-rwŏ-re wa-ssŭm-nida.
MR KIM Mu-sŭn il-lo o-ssyŏ-ssŏ-yo?
JAMES Il ttae-mŭ-ne wa-ssŭm-nida.
MR KIM Kŭ-rae-yo? Han-gu-ge ŏl-ma-ddong-an kye-shil-kkŏ-e-yo?
JAMES A-ma sa-nyŏn-i-na o-nyŏn ttong-an i-ssŭl-kkŏ-e-yo.
MR KIM Han-gung-ma-rŭl a-ju chal ha-shim-nida.
JAMES A-nim-nida. A-jik chal mo-t'am-nida.
MR KIM Na-jung-e ta-shi yŏl-lak tŭ-ri-ge-ssŭm-nida.
JAMES Ne. Chŏ han-t'e chŏ-nwa-na i-me-il chu-se-yo.

MR KIM *When did you come to Korea?*
JAMES *I came last January.*
MR KIM *What brought you to Korea?*
[lit. For what business, you came to Korea?]
JAMES *Because of business, I came (to Korea).*
MR KIM *I see [lit. Is that so?].*
How long are you going to be in Korea?
JAMES *I will be (here) probably for four or five years.*
MR KIM *You speak Korean very well.*

JAMES	*No. Still not that good [lit. I still don't do well].*
MR KIM	*I will contact you again later.*
JAMES	*Okay [lit. Yes]. Give me a call or e-mail.*

Vocabulary

대리	assistant section chief, assistant manager
언제	when
오셨습니까?	came? 오시 (to come, honorific) + 었습니까? (formal polite question past)
지난	last
무슨 일로	for what business
... 때문에	because of ...; due to ...
얼마 동안	for how long
얼마	how much
동안	for, during
계시다	to be, to exist, to stay (honorific form of 있다)
아마	probably
...이나	...or
아닙니다	formal polite form of 아니다 (to be not) 아니에요 (polite form), 아닙니다 (formal polite form)
아직	yet, still
못하다	cannot do
드리다	to give (humble polite word of 주다, "to give")

Cultural point

Responding to compliments

In English, the most common way to respond to compliments is probably accepting the compliment by saying "thank you." In Korean, the cultural norm is to say "no" and deprecate the compliment, even if it's highly deserved. Rejection of compliments is showing one's humbleness and is thus considered a virtue in Korea.

One possible result of western cultural influence is that younger speakers in Korea nowadays sometimes say “thank you” in response to a compliment. However, in general, Koreans still tend to reject a compliment rather than accept it.

Grammar points

8.1 Formal polite sentence ending past ...았습니다/었습니다

In Unit 6, the past-tense ending ...았어요/었어요 was introduced. ...았습니다/었습니다 serves the same function as ...았어요/었어요. The only difference is that the ...았습니다/었습니다 ending is more formal than ...았어요/었어요, and therefore used more in formal settings. The choice between ...았습니다 and ...었습니다 follows the same rule as the choice between ...았어요 and ...었어요:

1 When the last vowel of the verb/adjective base ends in a bright vowel, ㅏ [a] or ㅗ [o], ...았습니다 is used.

앉다	to sit	앉았습니다	sat
좋다	be good	좋았습니다	was good
가다	to go	갔습니다	went

2 When the last vowel of the verb/adjective base ends in a vowel other than ㅏ [a] or ㅗ [o], ...었습니다 is used.

먹다	to eat	먹었습니다	ate
읽다	to read	읽었습니다	read
있다	to exist; to have	있었습니다	was there; had

3 When the verb/adjective ends in ...하다, 했습니다 is used.

일하다	to work	일했습니다	worked
공부하다	to study	공부했습니다	studied
운동하다	to exercise	운동했습니다	exercised

4 After a noun, ...이었습니다/였습니다 is used.

학생	student	학생이었습니다	was a student
변호사	lawyer	변호사였습니다	was a lawyer

The honorific form of ...았습니다/었습니다 is ...(으)셨습니다.

verb/adjective honorific base		honorific formal polite ending	
가시...	to go	가셨습니다	went
드시...	to eat	드셨습니다	ate
만나시...	to meet	만나셨습니다	met
시작하시...	to start	시작하셨습니다	started
바쁘시...	be busy	바쁘셨습니다	was busy

8.2 Expressing reason using 때문에 "because of...; due to..."

때문에 is attached to nouns and expresses reason.

일 때문에 바빠요.
Because of work, I am busy.
시험 때문에 스트레스가 많아요.
Because of the exam, I have a lot of stress [lit. stress is a lot].
다른 약속 때문에 못 갔습니다.
I couldn't go due to another appointment. (다른: other; another)

In colloquial speech, 때문에 is often pronounced 땜에 [ttae-me].

8.3 Expressing duration of time using ...동안 "for...; during..."

동안 is attached to nouns in order to express the duration of time.

일 주일동안	for one week
한 달 동안	for one month
일 년 동안	for one year
얼마 동안	for how long

영국에서 일 년 동안 살았어요.
I lived in the UK for one year.
IBM 에서 삼 년 동안 일했습니다.
I worked at IBM for three years.

8.4 Speaker's conjecture or intention …(으)ㄹ 거예요 "will…; be going to…"

…(으)ㄹ 거예요 used after a verb or an adjective base expresses the speaker's conjecture or intention.

verb/adjective base ending in a vowel + ㄹ 거예요
verb/adjective base ending in a consonant + 을 거예요
noun + (이)ㄹ 거예요.

가… + ㄹ 거예요 will go
먹… + 을 거예요 will eat
좋… + 을 거예요 will be good
하… + ㄹ 거예요 will do

내일 비가 올 거예요.
It will rain tomorrow.

다음 주에 아마 많이 바쁠 거예요.
I will probably be very busy next week.

일요일이라서 백화점에 사람이 많을 거예요.
Since it is Sunday, there will be many people in the department store.
(Noun + (이)라서: because it is Noun)

영호씨가 미국에 오래 살아서 영어를 잘 할 거예요.
Since Youngho has lived in the US for so long, he probably speaks English very well. (살다: to live, 오래: for long)

프랑스 사람일 거예요.
He is probably French. (프랑스: France)

내년에 유럽에 갈 거예요.
I am going to go to Europe (or I will probably go to Europe) next year.

내일까지 그 일을 끝낼 거예요.
I am going to finish (or I will probably finish) that work by tomorrow.

다음 주에 차를 살 거예요.
I am going to buy (or I will probably buy) a car next week.

재미없을 거예요.
It will probably not be fun.

8.5 Verbs of giving 주다, 주시다, 드리다 "to give"

주다 ("to give") has two other different forms: 주시다 and 드리다.

When a senior person is giving something to you, use the verb 주시다—the combination of 주 "to give" and the honorific marker ...(으)시.

When someone is giving something to one's senior, the humble polite word 드리다 is used.

when giving to close equals or juniors: 주다 (plain)
when giving to distant equals or seniors: 드리다 (humble polite)
when a senior gives something: 주시다 (honorific polite)

For example:

1 [to your friend] 내일 줄게요	I will give it to you tomorrow.
2 [to your boss] 내일 드리겠습니다.	I will give it to you tomorrow.
3 이거 선생님이 주셨어요.	The teacher gave it to me.

Exercise 1

The following sentences describe past events or states. Change the underlined part into the formal polite sentence ending form.

Example 어제 김민호씨를 만났어요. I met Kim Minho yesterday.
→ 어제 김민호씨를 만났습니다.

1 어제 영화보러 갔어요.	I went to see a movie yesterday.
2 전에 한국은행에서 일했어요.	I worked at Korea Bank previously. (전에: before)
3 다섯 시에 회의가 끝났어요.	The meeting ended at five. (끝나다: to end)
4 사람이 별로 없었어요.	There weren't many people.
5 어제 아주 더웠어요.	It was very hot yesterday.
6 영국에서 한국어를 배웠어요.	I learned Korean in the UK.
7 저는 몰랐어요.	I didn't know.
8 음식이 아주 맛있었어요.	The food was very delicious.
9 많이 먹었어요.	I ate a lot.
10 담배를 끊었어요.	I quit smoking. (끊다: to quit, to cut off)

Exercise 2

Your colleague is asking what you did last weekend. Answer the question using the formal polite past tense form.

Example A: 주말에 뭐 했습니까?
What did you do at the weekend?
B: (친구를 만나다) <u>친구를 만났습니다</u>. I met a friend.

1 (헬스센터에서 운동하다)
to work out at a fitness center [lit. a health center]
2 (골프를 치다)
to play golf
3 (부산에 놀러가다)
to go to Busan to have fun [lit. go to Busan to play]
4 (친구하고 같이 영화를 보다)
to watch a movie with a friend

Exercise 3

You are asked the following questions from a person that you met at a party. Answer the following questions using . . . 동안.

Example A: 한국어를 얼마 동안 배웠어요?
For how long did you learn Korean?
B: (for one year) <u>일년 동안 배웠어요</u>.
I learned for one year.

1 A: 얼마 동안 출장을 가세요?
For how long are you going on a business trip?
B: (for five days) ______________________

2 A: 한국에 얼마동안 있을 거예요?
How long will you be in Korea?
B: (for three months) ______________________

3 A: 그 일을 얼마 동안 하셨어요? How long did you do that job?
B: (for two years) ______________________

4 A: 얼마 동안 미국에서 유학하셨어요?
How long did you study abroad in the US?
B: (for four years) ______________________

Exercise 4

Express your guess/conjecture using ...(으)ㄹ 거예요.

Example 내일 날씨가 (좋다) <u>좋을 거예요</u>.
The weather tomorrow will (probably) be good.

1 김선생님도 내일 모임에 (오다/오시다) ________________
Mr Kim also will probably come to tomorrow's gathering.

2 스티브는 한국말을 (잘 못하다) __________________
Steve probably cannot speak Korean well.

3 내일도 날씨가 아주 (춥다) ____________________
It will be very cold tomorrow, too.

4 지하철이 (빠르다) __________________________
The subway will probably be fast.

Exercise 5

You are going on a trip to Busan next week. The following is a list of what you are planning to do. Tell your co-worker about your plans and intentions using ...(으)ㄹ 거예요.

Your plan:

— 다음 주에 부산에 가다	to go to Busan next week
— 기차를 타고 가다	to take a train
— 부산에 3(삼)일동안 있다	to stay in Busan for three days
— 바다를 구경하다	to look around the coast
— 수영하다	to swim
— 회를 먹다	to eat raw fish
— 호텔에서 지내다	to stay at a hotel

다음 주에 부산에 갈 거예요. ____________________________________

____

____

____

____

Dialogue 2

(CD2; 17, 18)

James is at a gathering hosted by his co-worker, Mira. He is talking to Soyoung, a graduate student whom he met once before through Mira.

제임스 소영씨는 대학원생이죠?
소영 네. 맞아요.
제임스 뭐 공부하세요?
소영 경영학을 전공해요.
제임스 졸업하면 뭐 하고 싶으세요?
소영 컨설턴트가 되고 싶어요.
제임스 소영씨는 시간 있을 때 보통 뭐 하세요?
소영 저는 골프를 자주 쳐요.
제임스 그래요? 저도 골프를 아주 좋아하는데
언제 저랑 같이 칩시다.

JAMES So-yŏng-ssi-nŭn tae-ha-gwŏn-saeng-i-jyo?
SOYOUNG Ne. Ma-ja-yo.
JAMES Mwŏ gong-bu ha-se-yo?
SOYOUNG Kyŏng-yŏng-ha-gŭl chŏn-gong-hae-yo.
JAMES Cho-rŏ-p'a-myŏn Mwŏ ha-go-shi-p'ŭ-se-yo?
SOYOUNG K'ŏn-sŏl-t'ŏn-t'ŭ-ga twe-go-shi-p'ŏ-yo.
JAMES So-yŏng-ssi-nŭn shi-gan i-ssŭl-ttae bo-t'ong mwŏ ha-se-yo?
SOYOUNG Chŏ-nŭn gol-p'ŭ-rŭl cha-ju ch'yŏ-yo.
JAMES Kŭ-rae-yo? Chŏ-do gol-p'ŭ-rŭl a-ju cho-a-ha-nŭn-de
ŏn-je chŏ-rang ka-ch'i chi'p-shi-da.

JAMES *Soyoung, you are a graduate student, right?*
SOYOUNG *Yes, that is correct.*
JAMES *What are you studying?*
SOYOUNG *I'm majoring in business management.*
JAMES *After graduation [lit. if you graduate], what do you want to do?*
SOYOUNG *I want to be a consultant.*
JAMES *What do you usually do when you have time?*
SOYOUNG *I often play golf.*
JAMES *Really? I also like playing golf very much.*
Let's play together some time.

Vocabulary

대학원	graduate school
대학원생	graduate student
맞다	be correct, be right
경영학	studies of business management
전공하다	to major 전공: major 부전공: minor ...을/를 전공하다: to major in...
졸업하다	to graduate
컨설턴트	consultant
시간	time
보통	usually; the average
골프	golf
치다	to hit 골프를 치다: to play golf
자주	frequently, often
언제	when, some time
...(이)랑	with, and (= 하고) 저랑: with me 오늘이랑 내일: today and tomorrow
같이	together
...(으)ㅂ시다	let's do... 칩시다: let's play

Academic majors (CD2; 19)

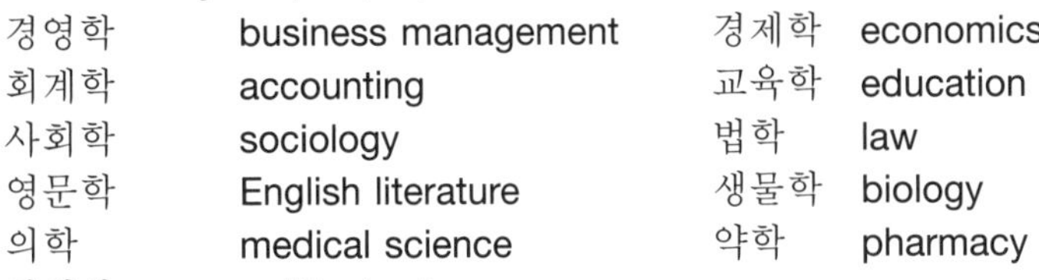

경영학	business management	경제학	economics
회계학	accounting	교육학	education
사회학	sociology	법학	law
영문학	English literature	생물학	biology
의학	medical science	약학	pharmacy
정치학	political science		
기계공학	mechanical engineering		
컴퓨터 공학	computer science		

8.6 Seeking agreement using ...죠? "isn't it?; isn't that right?"

...지요? or 죠? (contracted form of 지요?) is attached to verbs, adjectives or nouns to seek the listener's agreement or confirmation.

오늘 날씨가 좋지요?	The weather is good today, isn't it?
요즘 바쁘시죠?	You are busy these days, aren't you?
잘 지내시죠?	You are doing well, right?
내일 모임에 오시죠?	You are coming to tomorrow's gathering, right?
김선생님이지요?	You are Mr Kim, right?
전에 한번 만났지요?	We met once before, didn't we?
많이 기다렸죠?	You waited for a long time, right? (기다리다: to wait)

8.7 Expression of condition ...(으)면 "if ..."

Attached to a clause, ...(으)면 provides the condition for the following clause. That is, the clause that precedes ...(으)면 is the condition of the following clause. After a vowel-ending word, ...면 is used, and after a consonant-ending word (except the consonant ㄹ) ...으면 is used.

이번 주말에 날씨가 좋으면 여행을 갈 거예요.
If the weather is good this weekend, I will go on a trip.
(이번 주말: this weekend, 날씨: weather,
여행을 가다: to go on a trip)
비싸지 않으면 살 거예요.
If it is not expensive, I will buy it.
(비싸다: be expensive, cf. 싸다: be cheap)
바쁘지 않으시면 오세요.
If you are not busy, please come.
늦으면 전화하세요.
If you will be late, please call (me). (늦다: be late, 전화하다: to call)

In Korean, ...(으)면 is often used as an equivalent to English "When."

도착하면 연락하세요.
When you arrive [lit. If you arrive], please contact me.
일이 다 끝나면 전화하세요.
When you finish the work [lit. If the work all ends], call me.
시간이 있으면 보통 뭐 해요?
When you have time [lit. If you have time], what do you usually do?

The past tense conditional form, ...았으면/었으면 is frequently used to express one's strong wish.

았/었으면 좋겠다	**I wish...**
한국말을 잘 했으면 좋겠어요.	I wish I could speak Korean well.
시험에 합격했으면 좋겠어요.	I wish I would pass the exam.

(시험: exam, 시험에 합격하다: to pass the exam)

일찍 퇴근했으면 좋겠어요.	I wish I could leave my work early.

(일찍: early, 퇴근하다: to leave the office, to go home from work)

8.8 Expressing "when" using ...(으)ㄹ 때 "when..."

...(으)ㄹ 때 connects two clauses and is used to mark the time of the preceding clause. When the preceding word ends in a vowel, ㄹ때 is used, and after a consonant-ending word, 을때 is used.

공부할 때	when studying
갈 때	when going
바쁠 때	when one is busy

시간 있을 때 보통 뭐 하세요?
When you have time, what do you usually do?

한국어 공부할 때 친구들이 도와줘요. (친구.들: friends)
When I study Korean, my friends help me. (도와주다: to help)

부산에 갈때 기차 타고 가세요. (기차 타고 가다: to go by train)
When you go to Busan, take a train.

시간이 없을 때 샌드위치를 먹어요.
When I don't have time, I eat a sandwich.

어렸을 때, 가수가 되고 싶었어요. (어리다: be young, 가수: singer)
When I was young, I wanted to be a singer. (되다: to become)

한국에 처음 왔을 때, 한국말을 못 했어요.
When I first came to Korea, I couldn't speak Korean.

8.9 Providing background information using ...(으)ㄴ데/는데

...(으)ㄴ데/는데 is a sentence-connective form that connects two clauses. The clause before ...(으)ㄴ데/는데 is background information for the second clause. ...(으)ㄴ데/는데 can be translated into English as "and," "so," "but," "although" depending on the content and context of the second clause.

After an adjective base that ends in a vowel, ...ㄴ데 is used, and after an adjective base that ends in a consonant, ...은데 is used. After a verb base, ...는데 is used. Note that adjectives that end in 있다/없다 take 는데, not ...은데.

an adjective base (except ...있다/없다 adjectives) + ...(으)ㄴ데
a verb base, ...있다/없다 adjective base + 는데 noun + (이)ㄴ데

내일 파티에 가는데 같이 갈래요?
I am going to a party tomorrow, and do you want us to go together?

오늘은 시간이 없는데 내일 의논할까요? (의논하다: to discuss)
I don't have time today, so shall we discuss it tomorrow?

아들이 하나 있는데, 지금 대학생이에요.
I have a son, and he is a college student now. (아들: son, 하나: one)

그 식당은 싼데 음식이 맛없어요.
[Food at] that restaurant is inexpensive, but the food is not delicious.

한국 사람인데 영어를 아주 잘 해요.
He is Korean, but he speaks English very well.

미국 사람인데 한국말을 너무 잘 해요. (너무: very; too much)
She is an American, but she speaks Korean very well.

동생은 선생님인데 지금 부산에 살아요. (동생: younger sibling)
My sister is a teacher, and she lives in Busan now.

After …았/었 the past tense marker, …는데 is used.

한국에서 오래 살았는데 아직 한국어를 잘 못해요.
I lived in Korea for a long time, but I still don't speak Korean well.

공부를 열심히 했는데 아직 잘 모르겠어요. (모르겠다: to not know)
I studied hard, but I still don't understand [lit. know] it well.

최선을 다 했는데 안 됐어요. (최선을 다하다: to do one's best)
I did my best, but I failed [lit. but it didn't become].

박선생님을 만났는데 아주 친절하셨어요.
I met Ms Park, and she was very kind. (친절하다: be kind, be nice)

8.10 Making a suggestion using …(으)ㅂ시다 "Let's do …"

Attached to a verb base, …(으)ㅂ시다 is used when proposing or suggesting something. After a vowel, …ㅂ시다 and after a consonant, …읍시다 are used.

가…	to go	갑시다	Let's go.
하…	to do	합시다	Let's do.
먹…	to eat	먹읍시다	Let's eat.

다음 주에 모두 같이 만납시다 (모두: all)
Let's all meet next week.
내일까지 그 일을 모두 끝냅시다.
Let's finish up that work by tomorrow. (끝내다: to finish)

Exercise 6

Change the underlined part using …죠? to seek the listener's agreement or confirmation.

Example 요즘 <u>바쁘세요</u>? Are you busy these days?
→ 요즘 바쁘시죠? You are busy these days, aren't you?

1 한국은행에서 <u>근무하세요</u>?
Are you working for Korea Bank? (...에서 근무하다: to work at...)

2 영국에 비가 자주 <u>와요</u>?
Does it rain often in the UK?

3 서울은 크고 <u>복잡해요</u>?
Is Seoul big and crowded?

4 김민호씨는 <u>학생이에요</u>?
Is Kim Minho a student?

Exercise 7

Ask your friend what he/she wants to do when the following condition is given. Use ...(으)면 in your question.

Example 시간이 있다 (to have time)
→ <u>시간이 있으면 뭐 하고 싶어요</u>?

1 월급을 받다 to receive a salary
2 대학교를 졸업하다 to graduate from a college
3 돈이 많다 to have lots of money
4 유럽에 여행가다 to go on a trip to Europe

Exercise 8

Complete the sentence by filling in the blank using ...(으)ㄹ 때.

Example (시간 있다) <u>시간 있을 때</u>, 같이 테니스 칩시다.
When you have time, let's play tennis together.

1 (이사하다) ______________, 도와 주세요. (도와주다: to help)
When I move, please help me.

2 (한국어 공부하다) ______________, 이 사전을 쓰세요.
When studying Korean, use this dictionary.

3 (밤에 운전하다) ______________, 조심하세요.
When driving at night, be careful.
(밤: night, 운전하다: to drive, 조심하다: be careful, to watch out)

4 (세일하다) ____________, 사세요.
When it is on sale, buy it.

Exercise 9

Connect the two clauses using ...는데/은데. The first clause provides the background information for the following clause.

Example 내일 등산가다/ 같이 갈래요?
I am going hiking tomorrow./Do you want us to go together?
→ <u>내일 등산 가는데 같이 갈래요</u>?

1 여동생이 한 명 있어요./ 대학생이에요.
I have a younger sister./She is a college student.

2 지금 바빠요./ 나중에 얘기해요 (얘기하다: to talk, 나중에: later)
I am busy now./Let's talk later.

3 날씨가 좋아요./ 어디 놀러 갈까요?
The weather is good./Where shall we go to have fun?

4 마이클은 키가 작아요./ 농구를 잘 해요. (농구: basketball)
Michael is short./He plays basketball very well.

5 한국어를 공부해요/ 조금 어려워요.
I am studying Korean./It is a little difficult.

6 어제 백화점에 갔어요/ 사람들이 아주 많았어요.
I went to a department store yesterday./There were so many people.

Exercise 10

Suggest the following activities to your friend using ...(으)ㅂ시다.

Example 내일 같이 영화 보다
watch a movie together tomorrow
→ <u>내일 같이 영화 봅시다</u>.
Let's watch a movie together tomorrow.

1 남대문 시장에 쇼핑하러 가다
go to the Namdaemoon Market to shop

2 공원에서 같이 조깅하다
jog together in a park

3 다음 주 토요일에 모이다 (모이다: to get together)
get together next Saturday

4 한선생님도 초대하다 (초대하다: to invite)
invite Mr Han, too

5 11(열한) 시에 떠나다 leave at 11 o'clock

6 주말에 등산가다 go hiking at the weekend

Exercise 11 (Listening) **(CD2; 20)**

James has met Mr Kim, the assistant section chief of Hanguk Electronics for business. Mr Kim and James are talking after a meeting. Listen to the conversation and answer the following questions in English.

1 What is Mr Kim suggesting to James?
2 How is the food at the Korean restaurant in front of the office?
3 Is James still taking Korean class? And why?
4 How are James's Korean studies going these days?

(점심식사: lunch, 아직: still, not yet, 못하다 [mo-t'a-da]: can't do, 시간: time, 식사하다: to eat, to have a meal, 어디로: to where, 한식: Korean food, 어떠세요?: How is it?, the honorific form of 어때요?, 한식집: Korean restaurant [lit. Korean food house], 값: price, 싸다: be cheap, be inexpensive, 그렇지만: but, however, 혼자서: alone, by oneself)

Unit Nine
교통 수단
Transportation

In this unit you will learn about:

- Expressing condition …(으)려면
- How to say "Don't do …"
- Expressing one's obligation using …아/어야 되다
- Making comparisons using 보다 (더)
- Expressing means of transportation
- Taking a taxi and providing a destination
- Making a polite request
- Expressing the duration of travel time
- The public transportation system in Korea

Dialogue 1

(CD2; 21, 22)
James wants to go to Shinchŏn this afternoon. He asks Mira how to get there.

제임스 미라씨, 여기서 신촌에 가려면 몇 번 버스를 타야 돼요?
미라 오(5)번 버스요. 근데 버스 타지 마세요.
지금 이 시간에는 차가 많이 막혀요.
제임스 그래요?
미라 네. 지하철을 타세요. 지하철이 버스보다 더 빨라요.
제임스 여기서 지하철을 타면 신촌까지 바로 가요?
미라 아니오, 중간에 한번 갈아타야 돼요.
제임스 지하철 몇 호선을 타야 돼요?
미라 여기서 일호선을 타세요.
그리고 시청에서 이호선으로 갈아타세요.
제임스 고마워요.

JAMES Mira ssi, yŏ-gi-sŏ Shin-ch'o-ne ga-ryŏ-myŏn myŏ-ppŏn ppŏ-sŭ-rŭl t'a-ya-dwae-yo?
MIRA O-bŭn ppŏ-sŭ-yo. Kŭn-de ppŏ-sŭ t'a-ji-ma-se-yo. Chi-gŭm i-shi-ga-ne-nŭn ch'a-ga ma-ni ma-k'yŏ-yo.
JAMES Kŭ-rae-yo?
MIRA Ne. chi-ha-ch'ŏ-rŭl t'a-se-yo. chi-ha-ch'ŏ-ri ppŏ-sŭ-bo-da tŏ ppal-la-yo.
JAMES Yŏ-gi-sŏ chi-ha-ch'ŏ-rŭl t'a-myŏn shin-ch'on-kka-ji ba-ro ga-yo?
MIRA A-ni-o. chung-ga-ne han-bŏn ka-ra-t'a-ya twae-yo.
JAMES Chi-ha-ch'ŏl myo-t'o-sŏ-nŭl t'a-ya-twae-yo?
MIRA Yŏ-gi-sŏ i-ro-sŏ-nŭl t'a-se-yo. Kŭ-ri-go shi-ch'ŏng-e-sŏ i-ho-sŏ-nŭ-ro ga-ra-t'a-se-yo.
JAMES Ko-ma-wŏ-yo.

JAMES *Mira, what number bus should I take here to go to Shinchon?*
MIRA *The number five bus. But don't take a bus. At this time, the traffic is very congested.*
JAMES *Really?*
MIRA *Yes. Take the subway. The subway is faster than the bus.*

JAMES *If I take the subway here, does it go straight to Shinchon?*
MIRA *No. You have to transfer once in the middle.*
JAMES *Which subway line should I take?*
MIRA *Take line one from here. And at the City Hall, transfer to line two.*
JAMES *Thank you.*

Vocabulary

신촌	Shinchon (name of place in Seoul)
...아/어야 되다	to have to, must, should (= ...아/어야 하다)
...(으)려면	if one wants/intends to...
몇 번	what number 몇: how many; 번: number
타다	to ride (a vehicle) 버스를 타다: to ride/take a bus
...지 마세요	Don't...
차	car
막히다	to be blocked (pronounced [ma-k'i-da]) 차가 막히다: traffic is heavy [lit. cars are blocked]
훨씬	much (more), even (more)
빨라요	(<빠르다) be fast
...까지	up to..., until...
바로	straight; directly
중간	the middle 중간에 in the middle
갈아타다	to change (a vehicle) ...에서 -(으)로 갈아타다: change [a vehicle] at...into...
...보다	than...
더	more
지하철	subway
몇 호선	what line
일 호선	line one
이 호선	line two
고마워요	(<고맙다 be thankful) Thank you.

Seoul subway

Grammar points

9.1 Expressing condition ...(으)려면 "if one wants/intends to do..."

Attached to a verb base, ...(으)려면 expresses the meaning "If one intends to..."

verb ending in a vowel or ㄹ + 려면
verb ending in a consonant + 으려면

한국말을 잘 하려면 한국사람을 자주 만나세요.
If you intend to speak Korean well, meet Koreans often.

미국에 가려면 비자가 필요해요? (...이/가 필요하다: ...is necessary)
To go to the US, do I need a visa?

불고기를 만들려면 소고기가 필요해요.
To make *Bulgogi* [lit. If you intend to make *Bulgogi*], you need beef.

한국에 살려면 한국 문화를 배우세요.
If you want to live in Korea, learn Korean culture.

춘천에 가시려면 기차를 타세요.
If you intend to go to Chunchon, take a train.

In colloquial speech, ...(으) ㄹ려면 instead of ...(으) 려면 is frequently used, such as 갈려면 (=가려면) and 먹을려면 (=먹으려면).

신촌에 갈려면 5 번 버스를 타세요.
To go to Shinchon, take the Number Five bus.

한국어를 잘 배울려면 수업을 들으세요.
If you want to learn Korean well, take a class.

9.2 Negative command or request ...지 마세요 "Don't do..."

...지 마세요 is used when telling someone not to do something. Attached to a verb base, it means "Don't..."

가지 마세요.	Don't go.
하지 마세요.	Don't do it.
술을 많이 마시지 마세요.	Don't drink alcohol too much.
걱정하지 마세요.	Don't worry. (걱정하다: to worry)
버스 타지 마세요.	Don't take a bus.
농담하지 마세요.	Don't kid me. (농담하다: to joke)
울지 마세요.	Don't cry. (울다: to cry)
웃지 마세요.	Don't laugh./Don't smile. (웃다: to laugh, to smile)
화내지 마세요.	Don't get angry. (화내다: to show one's anger)

9.3 Expressing obligation ...아/어야 되다 "have to...; must..."

...아/어야 돼요 or ...아/어야 해요 corresponds to *have to*, *should* or *must* in English and is attached to a verb or an adjective.

지금 가야 돼요.	I have to go now.
회의에 참석해야 합니다.	You have to attend the meeting.
신발을 벗어야 돼요.	(신발을 벗다: to take off one's shoes) You have to take off your shoes.

꼭 A를 받아야 해요. I have to get an A without fail.
먼저 허락을 받아야 해요. (허락: permission; approval)
We have to get approval first.
예약해야 돼요? Do I have to make a reservation?
처음부터 다시 시작해야 합니까?
Do I have to start it over again from the beginning?
지금 출발해야 해요? Do we have to depart now?
언제까지 그 일을 끝내야 됩니까?
When should we finish the work?

9.4 Making comparisons using ...보다 (더) "(more) than..."

...보다 (더) is used when comparing two nouns. To express [A] is more...than [B] ([A]>[B]), use the following construction:

	[A] 이/가 **[B]** 보다 더...:	A is more...than B
or	**[B]** 보다 **[A]** 이/가 더...:	than B, A is more...

The use of 더 "more" is optional, so it can be deleted.

서울이 부산보다 더 복잡해요.
Seoul is more crowded than Busan.
이게 저거보다 더 비싸요.
This is more expensive than that. (이게=이것이)
어제보다 오늘이 더 추워요.
Today is colder than yesterday.
금요일보다 토요일이 좋아요.
Saturday is better than Friday.
지하철이 버스보다 빨라요.
The subway is faster than the bus.
저보다 제 동생 키가 더 커요. (키가 크다: be tall)
My sister is taller than me. (제 동생: my younger sibling)

Exercise 1

Your friend wants to do the following things. Advise him that if he intends to do that, he should then do...

Example 한국어를 잘 하다/ 열심히 공부하다
speak Korean well/study hard
→ 한국어를 잘 하려면, 열심히 공부해야 돼요.
If you intend to speak Korean well, you have to study hard.

1 골프를 잘 치다/ 연습을 많이 하다
play golf well/practice a lot (연습을 하다: to practice)

2 미국에서 살다/ 영어를 알다
live in the US/know English

3 일찍 일어나다/ 일찍 자다
get up early/go to bed early [lit. sleep early]

4 내일까지 이 일을 끝내다/ 오늘 밤을 새다
finish this work by tomorrow/stay up tonight
(밤을 새다: to stay up all night)

Exercise 2

You are providing an orientation session to new employees at work. Tell new employees not to do the following things at work using . . . 지 마세요.

Example 늦다 be late → 늦지 마세요. Don't be late.

1 건물 안에서 담배를 피우다 (건물: building)
smoke inside the building

2 사무실에서 식사하다
eat a meal in the office

3 회의중에 핸드폰을 쓰다 (회의중에: during the meeting)
use a cell phone in the middle of the meeting (쓰다: to use; to write)

4 회사에서 술을 마시다
drink alcohol in the building [lit. in the company]

Exercise 3

The following is the list of what you have to do this week and next. Tell your friend about it using 아/어야 돼요 or 아/어야 해요.

김선생님을 만나다	meet Mr Kim
제주도로 출장을 가다	go on a business trip to Cheju island
백화점에서 쇼핑하다	shop at a department store
보고서를 쓰다	write a report
친구한테 이메일을 보내다	send an e-mail to a friend

Example 김선생님을 만나야 해요.

1 ____________________

2 ____________________

3 ____________________

4 ____________________

Exercise 4

Compare each of the two noun pairs using 보다 (더).

Example 마크 175 cm / 마이클 180 cm

→ 마크가 마이클보다 키가 더 작아요.

Mark is shorter than Michael. (키가 작다: (height) to be short)

1 햄버거 1000 won/샌드위치 1200 won
2 이 아파트 600 sq. ft./저 아파트 900 sq. ft.
3 오늘 75°F/어제 56°F

(싸다: be cheap, 비싸다: be expensive, 크다: be big, 작다: be small, 춥다: be cold, 따뜻하다: be warm)

Dialogue 2

(CD2; 23)

James takes a taxi to go to Seoul Station. The following is the conversation between him and the taxi driver.

기사 손님, 어디로 가세요?
제임스 서울역으로 가 주세요.
기사 알겠습니다.
제임스 여기서 서울역까지 얼마나 걸려요?
기사 차가 안 막히면, 한 20(이십) 분쯤 걸립니다.
(*after a while*)

기사 서울역에 거의 다 왔는데요.
제임스 저기 신호등 앞에서 내려 주세요.
얼마예요?
기사 팔천구백 원입니다.
제임스 여기 있습니다.

DRIVER Son-nim, ŏ-di-ro ka-se-yo?
JAMES Sŏ-ul-yŏ-gŭ-ro ga-ju-se-yo.
DRIVER al-gge-ssŭm-nida.
JAMES Yŏ-gi-sŏ sŏ-ul-yŏk-kka-ji ŏl-ma-na kŏl-lyŏ-yo?
DRIVER Ch'a-ga an-ma-k'i-myŏn han i-shi-ppun-tchŭm kŏl-lim-nida.
(*after a while*)
DRIVER Sŏ-ul-yŏ-ge kŏ-i da wan-nŭn-de-yo.
JAMES Chŏ-gi shi-no-dŭng a-p'e-sŏ nae-ryŏ ju-se-yo. ŏl-ma-e-yo?
DRIVER P'al-ch'ŏn gu-bae-kwŏn im-ni-da.
JAMES Yŏ-gi i-ssŭm-ni-da.

DRIVER *Mr [lit. Customer], where are you going?*
JAMES *Seoul Station, please.*
[lit. Please go to Seoul Station for me.]
DRIVER *Okay [lit. Understood].*
JAMES *From here to Seoul Station, how long does it take?*
DRIVER *If the traffic is not congested, it takes about 20 minutes.*
(after a while)
DRIVER *We are almost at Seoul Station.*
JAMES *Please let me off in front of the traffic light over there.*
How much is it?
DRIVER *It's 8,900 won.*
JAMES *Here it is.*

Vocabulary

기사	driver
손님	customer, guest
...(으)로	toward, to
서울역	Seoul Station

역	station
여기서	from here (= 여기에서)
...까지	up to..., until...
얼마나	how much, how many, how long
걸리다	[time] to take
차가 막히다	traffic is heavy [lit. cars are blocked]
한...	about, approximately, around (followed by a number) (= 약...)
...쯤	about, approximately, around (preceded by a number) (= ...정도)
거의	almost
다	all
왔는데요	왔다 (came) + 는데요 (sentence ending)
신호등	traffic light
앞	front (앞에서: in front)
내리다	to get off; to off-load (내려 주세요: 내리다 + 아/어 주다, please let me off)

Grammar points

9.5 Polite request ...아/어 주세요 "Please do... (for me)"

A way to make a polite request is to attach ...아/어 주세요 to a verb base. While 주다 means "give," ...아/어 주다 means "to do something (for someone)."

verb base		아/어 주세요	
가	to go	가 주세요.	Please go (for me).
오	to come	와 주세요.	Please come (for me).
앉	to sit down	앉아 주세요.	Please sit down (for me).
하	to do	해 주세요.	Please do it (for me).
기다리	to wait	기다려 주세요.	Please wait (for me).
사	to buy	사 주세요.	Please buy it (for me).
돕	to help	도와 주세요.	Please help me.

The formal form of ...아/어 주세요 is ...아/어 주십시오.

잠깐 기다려 주십시오.	Please wait for a second.
모두 일어서 주십시오.	Please all stand up. (일어서다: to stand up)

9.6 A 에서 B 까지 (time) 걸려요 "It takes (time) from A to B"

...에서 -까지 "from...to..." is used to express the starting location and the ending location.

서울에서 광주까지	from Seoul to Gwangju
엘에이에서 뉴욕까지	from L.A. to New York

The verb 걸리다 "(time) to take" expresses duration.

십 분 걸려요.	It takes ten minutes.
일 년 걸렸어요.	It took one year.
한 일주일 걸립니다.	It takes about one week.

To express how much time it takes to get from one location to another location, ...에서 -까지 [time] 걸려요 construction is frequently used.

서울에서 대전까지 얼마나 걸려요?
How long does it take from Seoul to Daejeon?
여기서 거기까지 세 시간쯤 걸려요. (여기서=여기에서)
It takes about three hours from here to there.

Exercise 5 (CD2; 24)

Make a polite request using ...아/어 주세요, "Please do it (for me)."

Example (잠깐만 기다리다) wait a second
→ 잠깐만 기다려 주세요. Please wait a second (for me).

1 (문을 좀 닫다)	please close the door
2 (문을 좀 열다)	please open the door
3 (일곱 시까지 오다)	come by seven o'clock
4 (이메일 주소를 말씀하다)	give (one's) e-mail address

Exercise 6

Make a polite request in formal settings using . . . 아/어 주십시오 "Please do it (for me)."

Example Please teach me. (가르치다)
→ 가르쳐 주십시오

1 Everybody, please be seated. (모두 앉다)
2 Please be quiet. (조용히 하다)
3 Please write your address here. (여기에 주소를 쓰다)
4 Everybody, please stand up. (모두 일어서다)

Exercise 7

Tell us how long it takes from location A to location B. Also indicate the means of transportation.

Example 집 . . . 학교 10 minutes on foot
→ 집에서 학교까지 걸어서 십 분 걸려요. (걸어서: on foot)

1 회사 . . . 서울역 — 20 minutes by car (차로: by car)
2 대전 . . . 부산 — 3 hours by train (기차로: by train)
3 집 . . . 지하철역 — 5 minutes on foot (걸어서: on foot)
4 서울대학교 . . . 시청 — 40 minutes by subway (지하철로: by subway)

Exercise 8 (Listening) **(CD2; 25)**

Listen to the conversation between James and Mira and answer the following questions.

1 What does James need to do next week?
2 What transportation does Mira suggest and why?
3 How long does it take?
(대전: Daejeon, 시간: time, 서울역: Seoul Station)

Cultural point

Public transportation in Korea is highly developed and very inexpensive. A large proportion of the Korean population depends on public transportation for their daily commute. In cities, it is actually more convenient to use public transportation than one's own car due to the shortage of parking space.

The subway

Major cities in Korea such as Seoul, Busan, Daegu, Daejeon, and Gwangju have a subway system. Since traffic in the cities is usually very heavy, subways are preferable for their convenience and fast speed. The Seoul subway currently has eight lines and serves about four million passengers per day. A one-way subway fare is approximately one dollar (1,000 won as of 2008).

Buses

There are regular buses that run within the city or district as well as long-distance express buses that connect major cities in Korea. In Seoul, buses are colored blue, green, red, and yellow according to route type: blue buses connect suburbs to Seoul city, green buses connect subway stations to bus stations, red buses connect the greater metropolitan area to downtown Seoul, and yellow buses circulate within the Seoul downtown area.

Taxies

The taxi fare in Korea is relatively cheap compared to the fares in many other cities throughout the world. In Korea, there are regular taxies and deluxe taxies. Deluxe taxies are called 모범택시. 모범 literally means "exemplary." 모범 taxies are black and provide quality service. The 모범 taxi can be twice as expensive as the regular taxi.

Unit Ten

쇼핑

Shopping

In this unit you will learn about:

- How to use pronouns with subject/object/topic markers
- How to use noun modifiers
- Asking for permission
- Giving permission
- Purchasing items at stores
- Asking for prices
- How to say "It seems"
- Naming articles of clothing

Dialogue 1

(CD2; 26)

James is at a clothing store shopping for a pair of blue jeans. The following is a conversation between the store clerk and James.

점원 어서 오세요. 뭐 찾으세요?
제임스 청바지를 좀 보고 싶은데요.
점원 네. 구경하세요.
제임스 이게 마음에 드는데, 입어 봐도 돼요?
점원 네, 물론이에요. 입어 보세요.
(*after James has tried it on*)
점원 어떠세요?
제임스 좀 작아요. 이것보다 좀 더 큰 사이즈 있어요?
점원 네. 이 쪽에 많이 있어요.

CLERK Ŏ-sŏ o-se-yo. Mwŏ ch'a-jŭ-se-yo?
JAMES Ch'ŏng-ba-ji-rŭl chom bo-go shi-p'ŭn-de-yo.
CLERK Ne. Ku-gyŏng-ha-se-yo.
JAMES I-ge ma-ŭ-me tŭ-nŭn-de, i-bŏ-bwa-do dwae-yo?
CLERK Ne. Mul-lo-ni-e-yo. I-bŏ-bo-se-yo.
(*after James has tried it on*)
CLERK Ŏ-ttŏ-se-yo?
JAMES Chom ja-ga-yo. i-gŏ-ppo-da chom dŏ k'ŭn sa-i-jŭ i-ssŏ-yo?
CLERK Ne. I-tcho-ge ma-ni i-ssŏ-yo.

CLERK *Welcome. [lit. Come quickly]. What are you looking for?*
JAMES *I would like to see some blue jeans.*
CLERK *I see. Look around.*
JAMES *I like this: can I try this on?*
CLERK *Yes, of course. Try it on, please.*
(after James has tried it on)
CLERK *How is it?*
JAMES *It is a little small. Do you have a slightly bigger size?*
CLERK *Yes. There are many this side.*

Vocabulary

점원	clerk
어서	quickly 어서 오세요: Welcome. [lit. Come quickly.]
뭐	what (= 무엇)
찾다	to look for, to find
청바지	blue jeans
보고 싶은데요	보다 (to see) + ...고 싶다 (want to...) + ...은데요 (sentence ending)
구경하다	to look around
이게	this, 이것 (this) + 이 (subject marker)
마음	heart, mind
마음에 들다	be to one's liking [lit. enter one's heart] ...이/가 마음에 들어요: ...is to one's liking; to like... 이 옷이 마음에 들어요. I like this clothing item.
입다	to wear, to put on 입어 보다: to try on
...아/어도 되다	be okay to do...
물론	of course, for sure
...아/어 보다	try to..., give...a try
어떠세요?	how is it? (honorific form of 어때요?)
작다	be small
좀 더	a little more
크다	be big
사이즈	size (더 큰 사이즈: the bigger size)
이 쪽	this way, this direction

Names of clothes (CD2; 27)

바지	pants
셔츠	shirt (티셔츠: T-shirt)
정장	formal suit
원피스	(female's) one-piece dress
투피스	(female's) two-piece suit
치마 or 스커트	skirt
스웨터	sweater
코트 or 외투	coat
재킷 or 자켓	jacket
속옷	underwear

Grammar points

10.1 Pronouns with the subject, object or topic marker

In Unit 5, you learned the pronouns 이거, 그거 and 저거. When they are followed by a subject marker, object marker, or topic marker, contracted forms are frequently used:

이것 (=이거) this
- 이것 + 이 (subject marker) → 이것이 or contracted to 이게
- 이것 + 을 (object marker) → 이것을 or contracted to 이걸
- 이것 + 은 (topic marker) → 이것은 or contracted to 이건

그것 (=그거) that
- 그것이(=그게), 그것을(=그걸), 그것은(=그건)

저것 (=저거) that over there
- 저것이(=저게), 저것을(=저걸), 저것은(=저건)

이게 뭐예요?	What is this?
이걸 주세요.	Give this to me.
이건 어때요?	What about this?
저건 얼마예요?	How much is that one?
저게 더 좋아요.	That one is better.

누구 who
- 누구 + 가 (subject marker) → 누가 (not 누구가)
- 누구 + 를 (object marker) → 누구를 or contracted to 누굴

누가 가요?	Who is going?
누구를 좋아해요?	Who do you like?
누구세요?	Who are you?; Who is he/she?

나 I (저: the humble polite word of 나)
- 나 + 가 (subject marker) → 내가 I
- 저 + 가 (subject marker) → 제가 I
- 나 + 의 (possession marker) → 나의 or 내 my
- 저 + 의 (possession marker) → 저의 or 제 my

제가 할게요.	I will do it.
제 거예요.	It's mine [lit. (It's) my thing].

10.2 Asking permission using ...아/어도 돼요? "Is it okay to do...?"

Attached to a verb base, ...아/어도 돼요 or ...아/어도 괜찮아요 is used to ask for or grant permission.

The literal meaning of ...아/어도 돼요? is "Is it okay even though one does...?" and it is translated as "Is it all right to...?," "Can I...?," "Am I allowed to...?"

가도 돼요?	Can I go?
들어가도 돼요?	May I enter?
이거 먹어도 돼요?	Is it all right for me to eat this?
일찍 퇴근해도 됩니까?	Is it all right if I leave my office early?

To give permission, use ...아/어도 돼요 or ...아/어도 괜찮아요.

가도 돼요.	It is all right for you to go.
안 가도 돼요.	It is all right for you not to go.
들어오셔도 됩니다.	You can come in.
늦게 오셔도 돼요.	It is okay for you to come late.
정장을 안 입어도 됩니다.	It is all right not to wear a formal suit.
앉으셔도 됩니다.	You can sit down.

To deny permission, use ...(으)면 안 돼요, literally "It is not all right if you do...."

가면 안 돼요.	You are not allowed to go. [lit. It is not all right if you go.]
들어오시면 안 돼요.	You can't come in.

10.3 The noun modifier for adjectives ...(으)ㄴ

When an adjective modifies the following noun, a noun modifier ...(으)ㄴ is attached to the adjective base. After a consonant, the modifier 은 is used and after a vowel, the modifier ㄴ is used.

adjective base		adjective + noun	
바쁘	be busy	바쁜 사람	a busy person or a person who is busy
좋	be good	좋은 책	a good book or a book that is good
작	be small	작은 집	a small house or a house that is small
유명하	be famous	유명한 배우	a famous actor or an actor who is famous

Note:
Adjectives that end in ... 있다/없다 take the noun modifier ... 는.

재미있	be fun	재미있는 영화	an interesting movie
맛있	be delicious	맛있는 음식	delicious food

Note the noun modifying form of ㅂ irregular words as shown below.

춥	be cold	추운 날씨	cold weather
덥	be hot	더운 곳	hot place
맵	be spicy	매운 음식	spicy food
가깝	be close	가까운 곳	place nearby

Here are some more examples:

저는 추운 날씨를 싫어해요.
I don't like cold weather.
작년에 큰 집을 샀어요.
I bought a big house last year.
여기서 가까운 곳에 갑시다.
Let's go to a place that is close to here [lit. close from here].
마이클은 예쁜 여자를 좋아합니다.
Michael likes a pretty woman.
바쁘신 분은 지금 가셔도 됩니다.
Those who are busy may leave [lit. go] now.

Exercise 1

You are at your friend's house. Ask for your friend's permission to do the following things.

Example 텔레비전을 보다 to watch TV
→ 텔레비전을 봐도 돼요? Is it okay to watch TV?

1	화장실을 쓰다	to use the bathroom
2	구경하다	to look around
3	물 좀 마시다	to drink some water
4	담배를 피우다	to smoke a cigarette
5	전화를 쓰다	to use the phone
6	여기 앉다	to sit here

Exercise 2

Give or deny permission for (1) to (6) above.

Example 네. 텔레비전을 봐도 돼요.
Yes. You can watch T.V.
or 아니오. 텔레비전을 보면 안 돼요.
No. You can't watch T.V.

1 ______________________________
2 ______________________________
3 ______________________________
4 ______________________________
5 ______________________________
6 ______________________________

Exercise 3

Complete a phrase by attaching the noun modifier ...(으)ㄴ to the following adjective bases.

Example 크다 / 건물 → <u>큰 건물</u>
big / building a big building

1 키가 크다 / 사람
tall / person
2 예쁘다 / 딸
pretty / daughter
3 잘 생기다 / 남자
handsome / man
4 멋있다 / 옷
stylish / clothes

Exercise 4

Complete the sentence by filling in the blank using the noun modifier.

Example 어제 아주 (재미있다) <u>재미있는</u> 영화를 봤어요.
I saw a very interesting movie yesterday.

1 저는 (춥다) ______ 날씨를 싫어해요.
I don't like cold weather.

2 (좋다) ______ 한국어 사전을 추천해 주세요.
Please recommend a good Korean dictionary to me.

3 저는 (복잡하다) ______ 도시를 좋아합니다.
I like crowded cities.

4 수진씨는 아주 (부지런하다) ________ 사람이에요.
Soojin is a very diligent person.

Cultural point

There are many shopping districts in Seoul. For clothing and accessories, Namdaemoon Market, Dongdaemoon Market, Itaewon, and Shinchon are popular places. Insa-dong is known for pottery, celadon, antiques, and paintings. You can find all kinds of electronic goods at a discounted price at Yongsan Electronics Market. In places like Namdaemoon and Dongdaemoon, you might be able to get a better deal by haggling over the price. However, when shopping at department stores, do not haggle as the prices are firmly fixed. Most department stores have sale periods on a regular basis during which you can get bigger bargains.

Namdaemoon Market

Dialogue 2

(CD2; 28)

James is shopping for shoes at a department store. The following conversation between James and the clerk takes place at the shoe store.

제임스 이 구두, 까만색도 있어요?
점원 네. 있어요. 사이즈가 어떻게 되세요?
제임스 270 (이백 칠십)입니다.
점원 잠깐만 기다리세요.
손님, 여기 있습니다. 신어 보세요.
제임스 잘 맞는 것 같은데요. 이거 가격이 어떻게 돼요?
점원 십이만오천 원입니다.
제임스 조금 비싸네요.
점원 세일하는 구두도 있는데 보시겠어요?
이거보다 가격이 많이 싸거든요.
제임스 예. 보여 주세요.

JAMES I-gu-du, kka-man-saek-do i-ssŏ-yo?
CLERK Ne. i-ssŏ-yo. sa-i-jŭ-ga ŏ-ttŏ-k'e dwae-se-yo?
JAMES I-baek-ch'il-ship imnida.
CLERK Cham-kkan-man ki-ta-ri-se-yo.
Son-nim, yŏ-gi i-ssŭm-nida. shi-nŏ-bo-se-yo.
JAMES Chal man-nŭn kŏt ka-t'ŭn-deyo. i-gŏ ga-gyŏ-gi ŏ-ttŏ-k'e dwae-yo?
CLERK Ship-i-man o-ch'ŏn-won im-ni-da.
JAMES Cho-gŭm bi-ssa-ne-yo.
CLERK Se-il-ha-nŭn ku-du-do in-nŭn-de po-shi-gge-ssŏ-yo?
I-gŏ-bo-da ga-gyŏ-gi ma-ni ssa-gŏ-dŭn-yo.
JAMES Ye. Po-yŏ ju-se-yo.

JAMES *Do you have these shoes in black?*
CLERK *Yes, we do. What is your size?*
JAMES *It's 270.*
CLERK *Wait for a second.*
Here they are, sir. Try them on, please.
JAMES *It seems they fit well. What is the price for these?*
CLERK *It is 125,000 won.*

JAMES *It is a little expensive.*
CLERK *We have shoes on sale. Would you like to see? They are a lot cheaper than these.*
JAMES *Yes. Please show me.*

Vocabulary

구두	dress shoes
까만색	black (color)
...도	also, too
사이즈	size
...가 어떻게 되세요?	a polite way of saying "What is...?"
잠깐	for a moment
만	only
기다리다	to wait
손님	customer, guest
여기 있습니다	Here it is. (= 여기 있어요.)
신다	to put on (shoes)
신어 보다	to try (shoes) on
맞다	to fit 잘 맞다 to fit well
...는 것 같은데요	...는 것 같다 (it seems...) + 은데요 (sentence ending)
가격	price
비싸다	be expensive
세일하다	to be on sale [lit. to do sale]
세일하는 구두	shoes that are on sale
많이	a lot
싸다	be cheap
...거든요	it's because...; you see (refer to Unit 6)
보여 주다	to show

...이/가 어떻게 되세요? **What is...? (CD2; 29)**

이메일 주소가 어떻게 되세요?	What is your e-mail address?
전화번호가 어떻게 되세요?	What is your telephone number?
성함이 어떻게 되세요?	What is your name?
주소가 어떻게 되세요?	What is your address?
전공이 어떻게 되세요?	What is your major?

(전공: major)

10.4 The noun modifier for verbs

Early in this unit, you learned the noun modifier ...(으)ㄴ for adjective-noun formations. For a verb-noun formation, the following modifiers are used.

tense	modifier	examples (verb + noun)
Present	...는	지금 먹는 음식 the food that I eat now 지금 보는 영화 the movie that I watch now
Past	...(으)ㄴ	어제 먹은 음식 the food that I ate yesterday 어제 본 영화 the movie that I saw yesterday
Future	...(으)ㄹ	내일 먹을 음식 the food that I will eat tomorrow 내일 볼 영화 the movie that I will watch tomorrow

Here are some more examples:

여기가 제가 자주 오는 커피숍이에요.
This is the coffee shop that I often come to.

미라가 좋아하는 영화는 코미디 영화예요.
The movies that Mira likes are comedy movies.

제가 받은 선물은 꽃이에요. (받다: to receive)
The gift that I received is flowers.

지난 주에 만난 분은 최선생님입니다.
The person that I met last week is Mr Choi.

내일 만날 분은 이사장님이에요.
The person that I will meet tomorrow is President Yi.

다음 주에 방문할 곳은 경주입니다. (방문하다: to visit)
The place that we will visit next week is Kyeongju.

10.5 Noun modifier + 것 같다 "seems...; appears...; I think..."

A noun modifying form followed by 것 같다 expresses the meaning "seems" or "appears as if." It is also used when the speaker expresses his/her opinion in a humble way, saying "I think/It seems...." In colloquial speech 거 instead of 것 is frequently used. Also, 같아요 is often pronounced 같애요 **[ka-t'ae-yo]** in colloquial speech.

Noun modifier ...(으)ㄴ/는/(으)ㄹ + 것 같아요.
바쁘신 거 같아요.
You seem to be busy.
아픈 거 같아요.
You seem to be sick.
서울 교통이 아주 복잡한 거 같아요. (복잡하다: be crowded)
Seoul traffic seems to be very busy.
음식이 조금 매운 거 같아요. (맵다: be spicy, ㅂirregular word)
The food seems to be a little spicy.
미라는 요리를 잘 하는 것 같아요. (요리를 하다: to cook)
Mira seems to cook well.
아이들을 아주 좋아하시는 거 같아요. (아이들: children)
You seem to like kids very much.
친구가 밖에서 기다리는 것 같아요. (밖: outside)
It seems your friend is waiting outside.
마이클이 벌써 떠난 것 같아요. (떠나다: to leave)
It seems that Michael has already left.
살이 빠진 거 같아요. (살이 빠지다: to lose weight [lit. weight drains])
You seem to have lost weight.
지갑을 잃어버린 것 같아요. (지갑: wallet, 잃어버리다: to lose)
I think I lost my wallet.
차가 많이 막힐 거 같아요.
I think/It seems that the traffic will be very congested.
일요일보다 토요일이 더 좋을 거 같아요.
I think/It seems that Saturday will be better than Sunday.

Exercise 5

Complete the following phrases using the noun modifier ...(으)ㄴ/는/(으)ㄹ.

Example 지금 일하다 + 곳 work now + place
→ 지금 일하는 곳 the place where I work now

1 지금 다니다 + 학교 attend now + school
2 저기 가다 + 사람 go over there + person
3 좋아하다 + 꽃 like + flower
4 어제 받다 + 선물 received yesterday + gift
5 지난 주에 만나다 + 분 met last week + person
6 내일 해야 하다 + 일 must do tomorrow + work
7 내일 보다 + 영화 watch tomorrow + movie

Exercise 6

Complete the following sentence using the noun modifier ...(으)ㄴ/는/(으)ㄹ.

Example 지금 (일하다)일하는 곳은 한국은행이에요.
The place where I work now is Korea Bank.

1 제가 (찾다) _______ 책이 서점에 없어요.
The book that I am looking for is not at a bookstore.

2 제가 (좋아하다) _______ 음악은 클래식 음악이에요.
The music that I like is classical music.

3 미라씨가 어제 (입다) _______ 옷이 아주 예뻤어요.
The clothes Mira was wearing yesterday were very pretty.

4 어제 (먹다) _______ 음식 이름이 뭐예요?
What is the name of the dish that we had yesterday?

5 다음 학기에 (가르치다) _______ 과목은 한국문화예요.
The subject that I will teach next school term is Korean culture.

Exercise 7

Change the following sentences into "It seems…"

Example 비가 와요. It is raining.
→ <u>비가 오는 것 같아요</u>. It seems it's raining.

1 마이클은 번역을 아주 잘 해요.
Michael is good at translation.

2 존은 매운 음식을 잘 먹어요.
John eats spicy food well.

3 메리는 돈을 잘 벌어요. (돈을 벌다: to earn money)
Mary makes money well.

4 미라는 책을 많이 읽어요.
Mira reads many books.

Exercise 8 (Listening) **(CD2; 30)**

Listen to the dialogue between James and Mira and answer the questions in English.

1 Whose pen is it?
2 Who is the person that James is pointing at?
3 Is Mr Kim tall or short?

(펜: pen, 쓰다: to use, 한국 전자: Korea Electronics)

Exercise 9 (Listening) **(CD2; 31)**

James is talking to Minsu Choi on the phone. Answer the following questions after listening to their conversation.

1 Why is James apologizing to Minsu?
2 When is James suggesting they meet?
3 When is the project likely to be completed?

(내일: tomorrow, 약속: appointment; promise, 약속을 지키다: to keep one's promise, 정말: really, 미안하다: be sorry, 프로젝트: project, 끝나다: to end)

Unit Eleven

여행

Travel

In this unit you will learn about:

- Expressing one's tentative plan
- Talking about one's scheduled plan or decision
- Talking about your travel plan
- How to say "or" in Korean
- Talking about one's past experience
- Expressing means of transportation

KTX (Korea Train eXpress), the high-speed rail train

Dialogue 1

(CD2; 32)

Mira and James are talking about their plans for the weekend.

제임스	이번 주말에 뭐 하세요?
미라	요즘 너무 피곤해서 그냥 집에서 쉴까 해요. 제임스씨는 특별한 계획 있어요?
제임스	네. 부산에 여행가기로 했어요.
미라	부산에요? 혼자 가세요?
제임스	아니오. 제 친구 마이클이랑 같이 가기로 했어요. 미라씨는 부산에 가 보셨어요?
미라	아뇨. 아직 못 가 봤어요. 뭐 타고 가실 거예요?
제임스	기차나 버스를 탈까 해요. 부산까지 얼마나 걸려요?
미라	KTX 로 두시간 반정도 걸릴 거예요.

JAMES	I-bŏn juma-re mwŏ haseyo?
MIRA	Yojŭm nŏmu p'igon-hae-sŏ kŭ-nyang ji-be-sŏ shil-kka-hae-yo. Cheimsŭ ssi-nŭn t'ŭk-ppyŏ-ran kye-hwek issŏyo?
JAMES	Ne. Busan-e yŏhaeng-ga-gi-ro hae-ssŏ-yo.
MIRA	Busan-eyo? Hon-ja kaseyo?
JAMES	Anio. Che ch'ingu ma-i-kŭ-ri-rang ka-ch'i gagiro hae-ssŏ-yo. Mira-ssi-nŭn busan-e ga bo-ssyŏ-ssŏ-yo?
MIRA	Anyo. Ajik mo kka bwa-ssŏ-yo. Mwŏ t'a-go ka-shil-kkŏ-e-yo?
JAMES	Kich'a-na ppŏsŭ-rŭl t'al-kka-hae-yo. Busan-kka-ji ŏl-ma-na kŏl-ryŏ-yo?
MIRA	KTX-ro tu-shi-gan-ban jŏng-do kŏl-lil-kkŏ-e-yo.

JAMES	*What will you do this weekend?*
MIRA	*I am so tired these days, so I am thinking about just resting at home. Do you have a special plan?*
JAMES	*Yes. I decided to go on a trip to Busan.*
MIRA	*To Busan? Are you going alone?*
JAMES	*No. I am going with my friend, Michael.* *Have you been to Busan before, Mira?*
MIRA	*No. I haven't been there. How are you going there?*
JAMES	*I am thinking about taking a train or a bus.* *How long does it take to get to Busan?*
MIRA	*It will probably take about two and half hours by KTX.*

Vocabulary

이번 주말	this weekend (지난 주말 last weekend; 다음 주말 next weekend)
너무	very much; too much
피곤하다	be tired
그냥	just
쉬다	to rest
특별하다	be special
계획	plan
여행가다	to go on a trip (= 여행하다, 여행을 가다) to go on a trip to [place]: [place]에 여행가다 or [place](으)로 여행가다
혼자	alone
제	my
...(이)랑	and, with (= 하고)
...기로 하다	to decide to do...
...타고 가다	to go by [vehicle] [lit. to go riding...]
기차	train
...(이)나	or
버스	bus
KTX	KTX, a high-speed train
...(으)로	by [vehicle]
...정도	approximately...(= ...쯤)

Means of transportation (CD2; 33)

The following expressions are frequently used to indicate means of transportation.

차로	by car
기차로	by train
버스로	by bus
지하철로	by subway
비행기로	by airplane
걸어서	on foot

버스로 가다 =버스(를) 타고 가다 to go by bus

Grammar points

11.1 Tentative plan ...(으)ㄹ까 하다 "to think of doing..."

A verb base plus ...(으)ㄹ까 하다 is used when the speaker is thinking about doing something. It indicates that the speaker has not made a firm decision yet but is considering doing it. Instead of 하다, 생각하다 "to think" can also be used.

대학원에 갈까 합니다.
I am thinking of going to graduate school.
이사를 할까 생각해요. (이사하다, 이사가다: to move house)
I am thinking of moving.
디지털 카메라를 살까 해요.
I am thinking of buying a digital camera.

11.2 Expressing one's decision ...기로 하다 "decide to..."

...기로 하다 expresses one's scheduled plan or decision. It is attached to a verb base.

가...	to go	가기로 했어요.	decided to go
하...	to do	하기로 했어요.	decided to do
팔...	to sell	팔기로 했어요.	decided to sell

내년에 프랑스로 유학가기로 했어요.
I decided to study abroad in France next year.

그 프로젝트를 맡기로 했습니다. (맡다: to take charge)
We decided to take charge of the project.

여섯 시에 김과장님을 만나기로 했습니다.
I am scheduled to meet manager Kim at six.

내일 친구 생일 파티에 가기로 했어요.
I am going to my friend's birthday party tomorrow.

미팅을 취소하기로 했습니다. (미팅: meeting, 취소하다: to cancel)
We decided to cancel the meeting.

To express one's decision not to do something, 안…기로 하다 or …지 않기로 하다 "decide not to…" is used.

그 일을 하지 않기로 했어요. (=그 일을 안 하기로 했어요.)
We decided not to do that job.

이사가지 않기로 했어요. (=이사 안 가기로 했어요.)
I decided not to move.

그 회사하고 거래하지 않기로 했어요.
(=그 회사하고 거래 안 하기로 했어요.)
We decided not to do business with the company.
(거래하다: to do business with…; to deal with…)

11.3 Expressing "or" using …(이)나 "Noun 1 or Noun 2"

Attached to nouns, …(이)나 means "or." After consonants, 이나 is used and after vowels 나 is used.

한 시간이나 두 시간	one hour or two hours
커피나 차	coffee or tea
금요일이나 토요일이 좋겠어요.	Friday or Saturday will be good.
전화나 이메일 하세요.	Call or e-mail me.
가위나 칼 있어요?	Do you have scissors or a knife?

In colloquial speech, …(이)나 can be used twice attached to both Noun 1 and Noun 2.

전화나 이메일이나 주세요.
Give me a call or e-mail.
이번 주나 다음 주나 다 좋아요. (다: all)
Either this week or next week is fine.

아니면 "or (else)" is another expression meaning "or" that is frequently used in colloquial speech.

이메일 아니면 팩스로 보내겠습니다.
I will send it to you either by e-mail or fax.
한식 아니면 중식을 주문합시다.
Let's order Korean food or Chinese food.

Exercise 1

Express your tentative plan using ...(으)ㄹ까 하다.

Example 골프를 배우다 — to learn golf
→ 골프를 배울까 해요. — I am thinking of learning golf.

1 더 큰 집으로 이사가다 — to move to a bigger house
2 새 차를 사다 — to buy a new car (새 차: a new car)
3 내년에 결혼하다 — to get married next year
4 사업을 그만두다 — to quit one's business

(사업: business, 그만두다: to quit)

Exercise 2

The following is your New Year's resolution. Express your resolution using ...기로 하다.

—태권도를 배우다 — to learn Taekwondo
—살을 빼다 — to lose weight
—담배를 끊다 — to quit smoking
—술을 안 마시다 — to not drink alcohol
—아침에 조깅하다 — to jog in the morning
—돈을 많이 안 쓰다 — to not spend much money

1 태권도를 배우기로 했어요.
2 ______________________
3 ______________________
4 ______________________
5 ______________________
6 ______________________

Exercise 3

Complete the following dialogues using ...(이)나.

Example A: 어디로 여행가고 싶어요?
B: (유럽/미국) 유럽이나 미국으로 여행가고 싶어요.

1 A: 서울에서 부산까지 얼마나 걸려요?
B: (다섯 시간 five hours/여섯 시간 six hours) ______________

2 A: 뭐 먹고 싶어요?
   B: (김밥/비빔밥) ______________________________

3 A: 쇼핑하러 보통 어디 가세요? (쇼핑하러: in order to shop)
   B: (서울백화점/한국백화점) ______________________

4 A: 어디서 보통 공부하세요?
   B: (도서관/집) ________________________

Exercise 4 (Listening) (CD2; 34)

Listen to Mira's schedule this weekend and answer the following questions in English.

1 When and where is Mira going to meet Manager Han?
2 What is she planning to do on Saturday morning?
3 What is she going to do on Saturday evening?
4 What is she planning to do on Sunday afternoon?

(과장: section chief; manager, 헬스클럽: fitness center [lit. health club], 오전: a.m., 요리를 하다: to cook, 서점: bookstore, 책: book, 읽다: to read, 연극: play)

Unit Twelve

전화

On the phone

In this unit you will learn about:

- Honorific words and humble words
- How to say “about…” in Korean
- How to say “whenever,” “whatever,” “whoever,” etc.
- Talking about possibility
- Expressing one’s ability
- Making phone calls
- How to say phone numbers
- Idiomatic expressions for telephone conversation
- Asking a favor
- Polite suggestions and requests using …지요

Dialogue 1

(CD2; 35, 36)

James calls Mr Han at home to disucss business matters.

제임스	여보세요. 한과장님 댁입니까?
한과장	네, 그런데요.
제임스	저는 제임스 스미스인데요. 한과장님 계세요?
한과장	아, 네. 저예요, 제임스씨.
제임스	아, 안녕하세요? 과장님께 부탁이 있어서 전화드렸습니다.
한과장	그래요? 뭔데요?
제임스	상품 소개 전략에 대해서 의논하고 싶은데, 언제 뵐 수 있을까요?
한과장	네. 좋습니다. 이번 주는 좀 바쁜데, 다음 주는 언제든지 괜찮습니다.

JAMES	Yŏboseyo. Han kwa-jang-nim tae-gim-ni-kka?
MR HAN	Ne, kŭrŭn-deyo.
JAMES	Chŏnŭn Cheimsŭ Sŭmisŭ-indeyo. Han kwa-jang-nim kye-se-yo?
MR HAN	A, ne. chŏ-e-yo. Cheimsŭ-ssi.
JAMES	A, annyŏng-haseyo? Kwa-jang-nim-kke put'a-gi issŏsŏ chŏ-nwa tŭryŏ-ssŭm-nida.
MR HAN	Kŭraeyo? Mwŏn-deyo?
JAMES	Sang-p'um sogae chŏl-rya-ge dae-hae-sŏ ŭi-non-ha-go ship'ŭnde, ŏnje pwel-su issŭl-kka-yo?
MR HAN	Ne. Chŏ-ssŭm-ni-da. i-bŏn-ju-nŭn chom pa-ppŭn-de taŭm-ju-nŭn ŏnje-dŭnji kwaen-ch'an-ssŭm-nida.

JAMES	*Hello. Is this Mr Han's house?*
MR HAN	*Yes, it is.*
JAMES	*I am James Smith. Is Mr Han there?*
MR HAN	*Oh, yes. It's me, James.*
JAMES	*Ah, how are you? I am calling [lit. I gave a call] to ask a favor from you.*
MR HAN	*Is that right? What is it?*
JAMES	*Regarding product marketing strategies [lit. Regarding product introduction strategy], I would like to discuss this (with you). Can I see you sometime?*

MR HAN *Yes, that is fine. I am a little busy this week, but for next week, any time is fine.*

Vocabulary

여보세요	hello (on the phone)
댁	house (honorific word for 집)
그런데요	It is so. (= 그래요) 그렇다 (be so) + ㄴ데요 (sentence ending)
[person] + 께	to [person] (honorific word for 한테)
부탁	favor
드리다	to give (humble word for 주다)
전화 드리다	to call [lit. to give a call] (humble expression of 전화 주다/하다)
뭔데요?	what is it? (= 뭐예요?) 뭐/(what) + ㄴ데요 (sentence ending)
상품 소개 전략	product marketing strategies (상품: product, 소개: introduction, 전략: strategy)
...에 대해서	about..., concerning...
의논하다	to discuss
뵈다	to see (humble word for 보다)
...(으)ㄹ 수 있어요	can..., be able to...
언제든지	whenever

Useful expressions for telephone conversations (CD2; 37)

전화를 걸다	to call, to dial the phone
... 있어요?	Is...there?
... 계세요?	Is...there? (honorific polite)
...좀 바꿔 주세요.	Please let me talk to... [lit. please switch (the phone) to...]
전화 몇 번에 거셨어요?	What number did you dial?
전화 잘못 거셨어요.	You have the wrong number.
지역 번호	area code [lit. area number]

Reading telephone numbers

Example (614) 295–3871 육일사 이구오 에 삼팔칠일

12.1 Honorific or humble words

In Unit 2, you learned the honorific polite sentence ending ...(으)세요, which is used to convey respect or mark social distance. In addition to the honorific sentence ending, there is a limited number of words that have their own honorific forms. These words are either the honorific polite form (which is used to elevate the respected person) or the humble polite form (which is used to lower the speaker) as shown in the following table

meaning	plain	honorific	humble
person	사람	분	
house	집	댁	
name	이름	성함	
eat	먹다	드시다	
sleep	자다	주무시다	
die	죽다	돌아가시다	
see	보다		뵙다/뵈다
ask	묻다		여쭈다
give	주다		드리다
I I + subject marker I + topic marker	나 내가 나는 (= 난)		저 제가 저는 (= 전)
my	내		제
we	우리		저희
subject marker	...이/가	...께서	
topic marker	...은/는	...께서는	
to	...한테 (= 에게)	...께	

For example, when you ask your boss where his house is, you may use 댁 instead of 집 to show courtesy to him.

집이 어디세요?	Where is your house?
댁이 어디세요?	Where is your house? (honorific polite)

Also, when you talk to your boss, you should use the humble word for "I" 저 instead of 나 to be polite and humble.

나는 제임스입니다.	I am James.
저는 제임스입니다.	I am James. (humble polite)

12.2 ...에 대해서 "about..., regarding..."

...에 대해서 is attached to nouns and means "about...," "regarding...," or "concerning...." 서 can be omitted in both speech and writing. ...에 관해 or ...에 관해서 has the same meaning as ...에 대해(서).

한국 역사에 대해서 잘 몰라요.
I don't know much about Korean history.
이 통계 프로그램에 대해서 잘 아세요?
Do you know much about this statistics program?

When this phrase modifies the following noun, the noun modifying form ...에 대한 is used.

한국에 대한 책	a book about Korea
북한에 대한 최근 뉴스	recent news about North Korea

12.3 언제든지 "whenever"

When question words 누구, 언제, 어디, 뭐, 어떻게 (*who*, *when*, *where*, *what*, *how*) are combined with ...든지, their meanings become:

누구든지	anybody; whoever
언제든지	anytime; whenever
어디든지	anywhere; wherever
뭐든지	whatever (= 무엇이든지)
어떻게든지	no matter how
어디서든지	at any place

누구든지 할 수 있는 아주 쉬운 일이에요.
It is such an easy thing that anybody can do it.
언제든지 놀러 오세요.
Come visit me (to have fun) any time.
뭐든지 물어 보세요. (물어 보다: to ask)
Whatever it is, ask me.
어떻게든지 이 일을 내일까지 끝내야합니다.
No matter how we do it, we have to finish this by tomorrow.

12.4 Ability and possibility ...(으)ㄹ 수 있다/없다 "can.../cannot..."

Attached to verb bases, ...(으)ㄹ 수 있다/없다 expresses possibility or one's ability. After a consonant, 을 수 있다/없다 is used and after a vowel, ㄹ 수 있다/없다 is used.

가...	to go	갈 수 있다/없다	can go/ cannot go
먹...	to eat	먹을 수 있다/없다	can eat/ cannot eat

Note that when the verb base ends in ㄹ, 수 있다/없다 is attached.

만들...	to make	만들 수 있어요	can make
팔...	to sell	팔 수 없어요	can't sell

내일까지 끝낼 수 없어요.
I can't finish it by tomorrow.
불고기를 만들 수 있어요.
I can make Bulgogi.
내일 모임에 올 수 있어요?
Can you come to tomorrow's gathering?
한글을 읽을 수 있으세요?
Can you read the Korean alphabet, Hangŭl?
아파서 출장을 갈 수 없어요.
I am sick, so I can't go on the business trip.
지난 주는 바빠서 만날 수가 없었어요.
I was busy last week, so I couldn't meet you.

Exercise 1

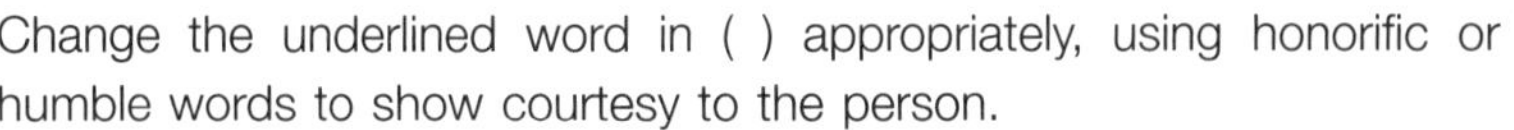

Change the underlined word in ( ) appropriately, using honorific or humble words to show courtesy to the person.

Example 김선생님 (집) __댁__ 은 어디입니까?
Where is Mr Kim's house?

1 (이름) _____이 어떻게 되세요?
What is your name?

2 사장님(이) _____ 오십니다.
The president is coming.

3 선생님(한테) ______ 이메일을 보냈습니다.
I sent an e-mail message to the teacher.

4 저 (사람) _____ 은 누구세요?
Who is that person?

5 할아버지께서 삼년 전에 (죽었습니다) ____________
My grandfather passed away three years ago.

Exercise 2

Are you able to do the following things? Provide your own answer.

Example (피아노를 치다) to play the piano
→ 피아노를 칠 수 있어요. or 피아노를 칠 수 없어요.

1 (스키를 타다) to ski
2 (한국요리를 하다) to cook Korean food
3 (케이크를 만들다) to bake a cake
4 (테니스를 치다) to play tennis

Exercise 3

At work, you are wondering if you could possibly do the following things. Ask your colleague whether you could by using . . .(으)ㄹ 수 있을까요?

Example 컴퓨터를 잠깐 쓰다 use the computer for a moment
→ 컴퓨터를 잠깐 쓸 수 있을까요?
Can I use (your) computer for a moment?

1 미팅을 취소하다 cancel the meeting
2 사장님을 뵈다 meet the president
3 자료를 좀 보다 see the data
4 전화를 좀 빌리다 borrow the phone

Exercise 4

Complete the following dialogues using ... 든지.

1 A: 무슨 음식을 좋아하세요?
B: 저는 ________ 잘 먹어요.

2 A: 백화점에 갈까요? 남대문 시장에 갈까요?
B: __________ 좋아요.

3 A: 그 모임에 한국 사람만 갈 수 있어요?
B: 아니오. _______ 올 수 있어요.

4 A: 여섯 시에 갈까요? 일곱 시에 갈까요?
B: _____________ 괜찮아요.

Dialogue 2

(CD2; 38)
James calls Mr Choi who is a division chief at Korea Bank. The secretary answers the phone.

비서	여보세요. 한국은행입니다.
제임스	여보세요. 거기 최부장님 좀 부탁합니다.
비서	부장님께서 지금 자리에 안 계신데요. 회의중이세요.
제임스	아, 그래요? 언제 회의가 끝나지요?
비서	두시 반쯤에 끝날 거예요.
제임스	그럼, 제가 나중에 다시 전화 드리겠습니다.

SECRETARY	Yŏboseyo. Hanguk-ŭnaeng-imnida.
JAMES	Yŏboseyo. Kŏgi ch'we-bu-jang-nim chom put'ak–hamnida.

SECRETARY	Pujang-nim chigŭm chari-e an kye-shin-deyo. Hwe-i jung-i-se-yo.
JAMES	A, kŭraeyo? Ŏnje hwe-i-ga kŭn-na-ji-yo?
SECRETARY	Tushi ban-tchŭm-e kŭn-nal-kkŏ-e-yo.
JAMES	Kŭrŭm, che-ga na-jung-e tashi chŏnwa-tŭri-get-ssŭm-nida.

SECRETARY	*Hello. This is Korea Bank.*
JAMES	*Hello. May I speak to Mr Choi there?* *[lit. May I speak to the department head, Mr Choi there.]*
SECRETARY	*Mr Choi is not here now.* *[lit. The department head is not at his seat.]* *He is in a meeting.*
JAMES	*Oh, is that so?* *I wonder when the meeting will be over.*
SECRETARY	*It will be over around 2:30.*
JAMES	*If so, I will call again later.*

Vocabulary

한국 은행	Korea Bank
거기	there
부장님	division chief
부탁	favor
부탁하다	to ask a favor
께서	the honorific subject marker
자리	seat
계신데요	계시다 (to exist) + ㄴ데요 (sentence ending)
회의중	meeting in progress
...이/가 끝나다	(something) to end, to be over cf. ...을/를 끝내다: to finish something
반	half
그럼	if so, then
나중에	later (= 이따가)
다시	again

Cultural point

Changing lifestyles in the digital era

South Korea is one of the most connected and digitalized societies in the world. Since the early 1990s, the government has invested aggressively in science and technology to transform the nation into an information-technology-based society and economy. Korea is particularly interested in futuristic technologies including robotics, and the Korean government is aiming to put an information service robot in every household between 2015 and 2020.

The cellular phone has become an indispensable part of one's daily life in Korea. According to a 2006 news item, about 80 percent of the population owns cell phones or 핸드폰 ("hand phone") in Korea. People use cell phones not only to talk or to send a text message but also to listen to music, to watch TV or films, to do internet searches, to purchase items, and so on.

Grammar points

12.5 Asking a favor using ...좀 부탁합니다

...좀 부탁하다 is a useful expression that you can use in various situations. "좀" literally means "little" but it is often used as a word that is equivalent to English "please." By adding "좀" you can make your request or command politer and softer. 부탁 means "favor" and 부탁하다 means "to ask a favor." The humble polite form 부탁 드립니다/부탁 드려요 is also frequently used.

Look at the various contexts where ...좀 부탁합니다 can be used:

On the phone

[person] 좀 부탁합니다.

김미라씨 좀 부탁합니다.	May I talk to Mira Kim?
박과장님 좀 부탁드립니다.	Can I talk to Manager Park?

Taking a taxi

[place] 좀 부탁합니다.

시청 좀 부탁합니다.	To the City Hall, please.
제일병원 좀 부탁합니다.	To the Chaeil Hospital, please.

When requesting something

[thing] 좀 부탁합니다.

커피 좀 부탁해요.	Coffee, please.
이거 복사 좀 부탁합니다.	Please make copies of this.

12.6 ...중 "in the middle of...; under...; ...in progress"

중 literally means "the middle." Combined with nouns, ...중 expresses that something is in progress. This expression is also often used when posting signs. Commonly used phrases are as follows:

회의	meeting	회의중	meeting in progress
수업	class	수업중	class in progress
공사	construction	공사중	under construction
준비	preparation	준비중	preparation in progress
시험	exam	시험중	exam in progress
통화	phone communication	통화중	the line is busy

지금은 회의중입니다. 들어가지 마세요.
The meeting is in progress. Do not enter.
시험중이에요. 조용히 해 주세요. (조용히 하다: to keep quiet)
The exam is in progress. Please be quiet.
공사중이에요. 조심하세요.
It is under construction. Please be careful.

12.7 The sentence ending ...지요

In Unit 8, ...죠 (or 지요?) meaning "isn't it?" was introduced, which is used when seeking the listener's agreement or confirmation. There are other functions of the sentence ending ...지요.

1 Question words + 지요?

When ...지요? is combined with question words such as 누구, 언제, 어디 and 뭐, it expresses the meaning "I wonder who...," "I wonder when...," "I wonder where...," "I wonder what...," etc. This often makes the question politer and softer. For example, 누구시지요? sounds milder and politer than 누구세요? although they both mean the same thing.

누구시지요?	Who are you? (*or* I wonder who you are.)
생일이 언제지요?	When is your birthday? (*or* I wonder when your birthday is.)
뭐지요?	What is it? (*or* I wonder what that is.)

2 Soft suggestion or request

By attaching ...지요 to a verb base, you can make your suggestion or request softer and politer. When making a soft request, ...지요 is often combined with the honorific marker ...(으)시.

가지요.	Let's go.
모두 앉지요.	Let's all sit down.
가시지요.	Please go, *or* Let's go.
이리 오시지요.	Please come this way.
여기 앉으시지요.	Please sit here.

Exercise 5

Ask a favor from someone regarding the following things:

Example 복사 — making copies
→ <u>복사 좀 부탁합니다</u>. — Please make copies (for me).

1 번역 translation
2 통역 interpretation
3 타이핑 typing
4 배달 delivery

Exercise 6

Make the following questions politer using ...지요?

1 이거 얼마예요? How much is it?
2 누구세요? Who are you?
3 지금 어디예요? Where are you now?
4 오늘이 무슨 요일이에요? What day is it today?

Exercise 7

Make the following requests politer using ...시지요.

Example 여기 앉으세요. Sit down here, please.
→ <ins>여기 앉으시지요</ins>.

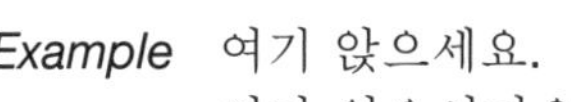

1 여기서 기다리세요. Wait here, please.
2 안으로 들어가세요. Go inside, please.
3 나오세요. Come out, please.
4 드세요. Eat, please.

Exercise 8 (Listening) **(CD2; 39)**

Listen to the following phone conversation between James and someone else, and answer the questions in English.

1 Who is James trying to reach?
2 Where is the person?
3 What time will the person return?
4 When is James going to call again?

(나가다: to go out, 들어오다: to come in, 아마: probably)

Unit Thirteen

날씨

Weather

In this unit you will learn about:

- Talking about and describing weather
- Expressing change of state using ...아/어지다
- Expressing one's dislikes
- Polite suggestions using ...지 그러세요?
- How to use ㅎ irregular words
- How to transform adjectives to adverbs
- The intimate speech style
- Expressing reason using ...(으)니까
- Expressing indefinite selection using ...(이)나
- How to use ...잖아요 ending

Dialogue 1

(CD2; 40)

At work, James is coughing and seems to be feeling unwell. Mira asks James if he has caught a cold.

미라	제임스씨, 감기 걸렸어요?
제임스	네. 그런 것 같아요.
미라	요즘 날씨가 갑자기 추워졌어요.
제임스	저는 겨울이 싫어요. 겨울에 감기에 잘 걸리거든요.
미라	그래요? 옷을 따뜻하게 입으세요.
제임스	서울에는 눈이 자주 와요?
미라	겨울에 가끔 와요. 작년에는 눈이 아주 많이 왔어요.
제임스	그래요?
미라	제임스씨, 아픈데 일찍 퇴근하지 그러세요?
제임스	아니에요. 머리가 좀 아프지만, 괜찮아요.

MIRA	Cheimsŭ ssi, kamgi kŏl-ryŏ-ssŏ-yo?
JAMES	Ne. Kŭrŏn-gŏt kat'a-yo.
MIRA	Yojŭm nal-ssi-ga kap-tcha-gi chu-wŏ-jŏ-ssŏ-yo.
JAMES	Chŏnŭn kyŏ-u-ri shi-rŏ-yo. Kyŏ-u-re kam-gi-e jal kŏl-ri-gŏ-tŭn-yo.
MIRA	Kŭ-rae-yo? O-sŭl tta-ddŭ-t'a-ge i-bŭ-se-yo.
JAMES	Sŏ-u-re-nŭn nu-ni cha-ju wa-yo?
MIRA	Kyŏ-u-re ka-ggŭm wa-yo. Chang-nyŏ-ne-nŭn nu-ni a-ju ma-ni wa-ssŏ-yo.
JAMES	Kŭraeyo?
MIRA	Cheimsŭ-ssi, ap'ŭn-de il-tchik t'we-gŭ-na-ji gŭ-ryŏ-se-yo?
JAMES	Anieyo. Mŏri-ga chom ap'ŭ-ji-man, kwaen-ch'a-na-yo.

MIRA	*James, did you catch a cold?*
JAMES	*Yes. I think so. [lit. It seems so.]*
MIRA	*Recently the weather became cold all of a sudden.*
JAMES	*I don't like winter because I easily catch colds.*
MIRA	*Really? Wear warm clothes.*
JAMES	*Does it snow often in Seoul?*
MIRA	*In the winter, it snows from time to time. Last year, we had lots of snow. [lit. snow came a lot.]*

JAMES *Oh, really?*
MIRA *James, since you are sick, why don't you leave work early?*
JAMES *No. My head aches a little but I am okay.*

Vocabulary

감기	cold
걸리다	to be caught, to be hooked ...에 걸리다: be caught by 감기에 걸리다: to catch a cold [lit. to be caught by cold] 감기에 잘 걸리다: to easily catch a cold
그런 것 같다	it seems so 그렇다 (be so) + ㄴ 것 같다 (it seems)
갑자기	suddenly
날씨	weather
춥다	be cold 추워요: It's cold. 추워 지다: to become cold
...아/어 지다	to become...
싫다	be hateful, be dislikable ...이/가 싫다: something/one is dislikable ...을/를 싫어하다: to dislike/hate something/one
옷	clothes
따뜻하다	be warm 따뜻하게 warmly
눈	snow 눈이 오다 to snow [lit. snow comes]
가끔	from time to time
작년	last year [pronounced 장년]
아프다	be sick, be ill
일찍	early
퇴근하다	to leave one's office, to go home from work (cf. 출근하다: to go to one's work/office)
...지 그러세요?	why don't you...?
머리	head; brain; hair

Grammar points

13.1 ㅎ irregular words

There are a limited number of irregular adjectives whose bases end in ㅎ. When followed by a vowel such as in ...아요/어요, ...(으)ㄴ, ...(으)세요 and ...(으)면, ㅎ in the base is dropped as shown in the following examples.

dic. form	...아요/어요 ending	noun-modifying form
이렇다 be this way	이래요	이런
그렇다 be that way	그래요	그런
저렇다 be that way (there)	저래요	저런
어떻다 be a certain way	어때요	어떤

한국 겨울 날씨가 어때요?	How is the winter weather in Korea?
제 사정이 그래요.	My situation is like that.
이런 거	this kind of thing
그런 거	that kind of thing, such a thing
그런 일이 있었어요?	Was there such an incident?
어떤 선물이 좋을까요?	What kind of gift will be good?
이런 문제를 해결해야 됩니다.	We have to solve this kind of problem.

Note:
In colloquial speech, you may hear 요렇다 (요래요, 요런) which has the same meaning as 이렇다 (이래요, 이런).

13.2 Expressing change of state using ...아/어지다 "become..."

...아/어 지다 is attached to adjectives and expresses a change of state, meaning "to become..."

좋다	be good	좋아지다	become good
예쁘다	be pretty	예뻐지다	become pretty
바쁘다	be busy	바빠지다	become busy

날씨가 추워졌어요.	The weather has become cold.
집 값이 싸졌어요.	The price of housing has become cheap.
옷이 작아졌어요.	The clothes became small.
내일부터 따뜻해질 거예요.	It will become warm starting from tomorrow.

영수하고 친해졌어요. (친하다: be close in terms of relationship)
I became close to Youngsoo.

경기가 요즘 많이 나빠졌어요. (경기: economic conditions)
The economic conditions became worse recently.
(나쁘다: be bad)

13.3 Expressing one's dislikes using ...이/가 싫어요

싫다 is an adjective meaning "hateful" or "dislikable." Used with a subject marker, ...이/가 싫다 literally means "something/one is hateful/dislikable," but it is best translated as "to dislike/hate something/one." You can also express the same meaning using the verb, 싫어하다 "to dislike/hate" together with an object marker ...을/를.

...이/가 싫다 **vs.** ...을/를 싫어하다

매운 음식이 싫어요.	I don't like spicy food. [lit. Spicy food is dislikable.]
매운 음식을 싫어해요.	I don't like spicy food.

...이/가 좋다 **vs.** ...을/를 좋아하다

좋다 is an adjective, meaning "be good." It can be used with the subject marker ...이/가. Although the literal meaning of ...이/가 좋다 is "some thing/one is good," it can also be translated in English as "I like..."

이 컴퓨터가 좋아요. This computer is good. (*or* I like this computer.)

좋아하다 is a verb that means "to like." As a verb, it can take an object word which can be marked with the object marker ...을/를.

제임스는 이 컴퓨터를 좋아해요. James likes this computer.

13.4 Adjective + 게 "...ly"

Attached to adjectives, ...게 transforms adjectives into adverbs, with a function equivalent to the English ...*ly*.

늦다	be late	늦게	late
쉽다	be easy	쉽게	easily
좋다	be good	좋게	nicely
나쁘다	be bad	나쁘게	badly
예쁘다	be pretty	예쁘게	prettily
재미있다	be fun	재미있게	in a fun way
맛있다	be delicious	맛있게	deliciously
어떻다	be a certain way	어떻게	in what way; how
이렇다	be this way	이렇게	like this; in this way
그렇다	be that way	그렇게	like that; in that way
저렇다	be that way	저렇게	like that (there); in that way (there)

주말을 즐겁게 보내세요.	Have a nice weekend [lit. Spend your weekend pleasantly]. (즐겁게: pleasantly)
맛있게 드세요.	Enjoy your meal [lit. Eat deliciously].
늦게 왔어요.	I/He/She came late.
이렇게 하세요.	Do it like this.
요즘 어떻게 지내세요?	How are you doing these days?

13.5 Polite suggestion using ...지 그러세요? "Why don't you...?"

The pattern ...지 그러세요? or ...지 그래요? is used when the speaker politely suggests something to the listener. 그러세요 is the honorific polite ending of the verb 그러다 ("to do so"), while 그래요 is the polite ending of the verb 그러다.

같이 가지 그러세요?	Why don't you go together?
좀 쉬지 그러세요?	Why don't you take some rest?

지하철을 타지 그래요?	Why don't you take the subway?
김선생님께 부탁하지 그러세요?	Why don't you ask Mr Kim a favor?
담배를 끊지 그래요?	Why don't you quit smoking?

Exercise 1

The following is the formal polite ending of some ㅎ irregular words. Change the formal polite ending ㅂ니다/습니다 to the polite ending ... 아요/어요.

1 이렇습니다.
2 저렇습니다.
3 어떻습니까?
4 그렇습니까?

Exercise 2

You are working for a wholesale company making electronic products. The following table shows things as compared between last year and this year. Report the changes of state in the following things using ... 아/어지다. You may also use the following adjectives in your answer:

많다 (be a lot)	적다 (be a few)
높다 (be high)	낮다 (be low)
비싸다 (be expensive)	싸다 (be cheap)

	작년 last year	올해 this year
회사 직원수 (number of company employees)	55	50
디지털 카메라 값 (digital camera price)	20–30 만원	10–20 만원
카메라 판매량 (sale quantity of cameras)	21,309	19,456
온라인 주문수 (number of online orders)	950	1034
실직률 (lay-off rate)	1%	3%

1 올해 회사 직원수가 <u>적어졌어요</u>.
2 올해 디지털 카메라 값이 ______________
3 작년보다 올해 카메라 판매량이 ______________
4 올해 온라인 주문수가 ______________
5 작년보다 올해 실직률이 ______________

Exercise 3

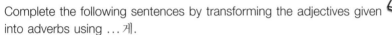

Complete the following sentences by transforming the adjectives given into adverbs using ...게.

Example 주말을 [즐겁다] _____ 보내세요.

1 [맛있다] ______ 드세요.
Enjoy your meal.

2 [편하다] ______ 앉으세요.
Please sit comfortably.

3 주말 [재미있다] ______ 보내셨어요?
Did you have a good weekend?

4 [늦다] ______ 오지 마세요.
Don't come late.

5 영호가 아주 [심하다] ______ 아파요.
Youngho is very severely ill. (심하다: be severe)

Exercise 4 **(CD2; 41)**

Politely urge the listener to do the following using ...지 그러세요? "Why don't you...?"

Example 운전을 배우다 learn to drive
→ 운전을 배우시지 그러세요? Why don't you learn to drive?

1 감기약을 드시다 take cold medicine
2 팩스로 보내다 send (it) by fax
3 제 차로 가다 go by my car
4 유럽으로 여행가다 travel to Europe

Dialogue 2

(CD2; 42)

On a hot summer day, James meets his good friend, Chang-sub at a coffee shop. James has known Chang-sub for a long time. They first met at a college in England when Chang-sub was a study-abroad student. They are talking about the weather. Note the intimate speech style they use in the following dialogue.

창섭	오늘 날씨 되게 덥네. 어제보다 더 더운 거 같아.
제임스	날씨가 너무 더우니까 밖에 나가기가 싫어.
창섭	시원한 냉커피나 한 잔 마실까?
제임스	응, 좋아.
창섭	근데, 오늘 우산 갖고 왔어?
제임스	아니. 안 갖고 왔는데. 왜?
창섭	오늘 오후에 비 오잖아.
제임스	그래? 비 와?
창섭	내일도 비가 오니까 우산 가지고 와.

CHANG-SUB	Onŭl nal-ssi twe-ge tŏm-ne. Ŏ-je-bo-da tŏ tŏ-un-gŏ ka-t'a.
JAMES	Nal-ssi-ga nŏmu tŏ-u-ni-kka pa-kke naga-gi-ga shirŏ.
CHANG-SUB	Shi-wŏ-nan naeng-k'ŏ-p'i-na han-jan mashil-kka?
JAMES	Ŭng, Cho-a.
CHANG-SUB	Kŭn-de o-nŭl u-san ka-ggo wa-ssŏ?
JAMES	Ani. An ka-ggo wan-nŭn-de. Wae?
CHANG-SUB	O-nŭl o-hu-e bi o-ja-na.
JAMES	Kŭrae? Pi wa?
CHANG-SUB	Naeil-do bi-ga onikka u-san kajigo wa.

CHANG-SUB	*The weather is very hot today. It seems it is hotter than yesterday.*
JAMES	*Since the weather is hot, I don't feel like going out.*
CHANG-SUB	*Shall we have a glass of iced coffee or something?*
JAMES	*Yes, that sounds good [lit. that's good].*
CHANG-SUB	*By the way, did you bring an umbrella today?*
JAMES	*No, I didn't bring one. Why?*
CHANG-SUB	*It's going to rain this afternoon, didn't you know?*
JAMES	*Really? It will rain?*
CHANG-SUB	*It's going to rain tomorrow too, so bring your umbrella.*

Vocabulary

날씨	weather
되게	very much (= 아주) 되게 is more colloquial than 아주
더우니까	hot, so; since it is hot 덥다 (be hot) + (으)니까 (because, since)
시원하다	be cool
냉커피	iced coffee
응	yes
우산	umbrella
갖고 오다	to bring (= 가지고 오다) 갖고 가다 (= 가지고 가다): to take (it) somewhere
아니	no
비	rain 비가 오다: to rain
...잖아요	..., you know

Pronunciation tip

In colloquial speech, 같아 is often pronounced 같애 [가태, **ka-t'ae**], and 같아요 is pronounced 같애요 [가태요, **ka-t'ae-yo**].

갖고 오다 and 가지고 오다 can be pronounced 갖구 오다 [가꾸 오다 **ka-kku-o-da**] and 가지구 오다 [**ka-ji-gu o-da**] respectively in daily speech.

More words expressing weather (CD2; 43)

흐리다	be cloudy
맑다	be clear, be sunny
따뜻하다	be warm
덥다	be hot
서늘하다	be cool, be refreshing
쌀쌀하다	be chilly
비가 오다	to rain [lit. rain comes]
바람이 불다	the wind blows

13.6 The intimate speech style, 반말

The intimate speech style or 반말 in Korean is a speech style used when talking to a person whom the speaker feels close to or intimate with. This speech style is often observed from an adult talking to his/her close friend of a similar or younger age, an adult talking to a child, or a child talking to another child.

In this book, three different speech styles have been introduced. Note the different usages of these speech styles:

speech styles	sentence endings	examples
1. Polite style	...아요/어요	가요, 먹어요, 해요
2. Formal polite style	...ㅂ니다/습니다	갑니다, 먹습니다, 합니다
3. Intimate style	...아/어	가, 먹어, 해

The degree of closeness or intimacy can be subjective to speakers and listeners, and thus if the intimate style is inappropriately used, the speaker may sound impolite or rude to the listener.

The following general rules are applied when using the intimate speech style.

1 By deleting the ending 요, one can transform the polite speech style to an intimate one:

만나요.	→	만나.	없어요.	→	없어.
늦었어요.	→	늦었어.	갔어요.	→	갔어.
좋아요?	→	좋아?	어때요?	→	어때?
갈래요?	→	갈래?	마실까요?	→	마실까?
좋네요.	→	좋네.	덥지요?	→	덥지?

2 The intimate style ending for the future tense ...(으)ㄹ 거예요 is ...(으)ㄹ 거야.

할 거예요.	→	할 거야.	갈 거예요.	→	갈 거야.
좋을 거예요.	→	좋을 거야.	먹을 거예요.	→	먹을 거야.

Note:
...(으)ㄹ 거야 is usually pronounced ...(으)ㄹ 꺼야.

3 The intimate style for the "[noun] + 이에요/예요" construction is "[noun] + (이)야."

학생이에요. → 학생이야.
세 시예요. → 세 시야.
제 거예요. → 내 거야.

4 Pay attention to the intimate style words for "yes" and "no."

네 (or 예) → 응 아니오 → 아니

13.7 Expressing reason using ...(으)니까 "since...; because..."

The clause before ...(으)니까 gives the reason for the following clause. This pattern occurs after a verb, adjective, or noun.

consonant-ending verb/adjective + 으니까
vowel-ending verb/adjective + 니까
consonant-ending noun + 이니까
vowel-ending noun + 니까

In casual speech, the colloquial form ...(으)니깐 or ...(으)니까는 is also frequently used.

시간이 없으니까 택시를 탑시다.
As we don't have time, let's take a taxi.
차가 많이 막히니깐 지하철을 타세요.
Since the traffic is very congested, take the subway.

Note that the pattern ...아/어서, which was introduced in Unit 3, also expresses the meaning *because*. While ...아/어서 cannot be followed by a suggestion or command ending, ...(으)니까 is often followed by a suggestion or command ending.

오늘은 바빠서 내일 만나요. (incorrect)
오늘은 바쁘니까 내일 만나요. (correct)
Since I am busy today, let's meet tomorrow.

As ...(으)니까 is often followed by a suggestion or command ending, it will be useful to remember the following construction.

...(으)니까 -(으)세요.	***Since..., please do...***

눈이 많이 오니까 운전 조심하세요. (운전: driving)
Since it snows a lot, be careful driving.
회의중이니까 조용히 하세요. (조용히: quietly)
Since the meeting is in progress, please be quiet.
영화가 아주 재미있으니까 꼭 보세요. (꼭: without fail)
Since the movie is really good, definitely watch it.
음식이 모자라니까 더 주문하세요. (모자라다: be not enough)
As the food is not enough, please order more.

13.8 Expressing indefinite selection ...(이)나 "...or something"

In Unit 11, the function of ...(이)나 indicating "or" was introduced. When ...(이)나 is placed between two nouns, it means Noun 1 "or" Noun 2. When it is placed after a single noun, it has the meaning "Noun or something" or "Noun or that sort." After a noun ending in a consonant, 이 is added.

차나 마실까요?
Shall we drink tea or something?
테니스나 같이 칠까요?
Shall we play tennis or something together?
선물로 꽃이나 살까요?
As a present, shall we buy flowers or something?

13.9 ...기가 싫어요 "I don't like doing..."

The phrase ...기가 싫어요 consists of ...기 (...ing) + 가 (subject marker) + 싫어요 (be dislikable/hateful). The literal meaning of ...기가 싫어요 is "doing something is dislikable/hateful," but it is best translated in English as "I don't like doing something."

Preceded by a verb, ...기 transforms the verb to a noun as shown below:

나가다	to go out	나가기	going out
공부하다	to study	공부하기	studying
일하러 가다	to go to work	일하러 가기	going to work
먹다	to eat	먹기	eating

In this pattern, ...기 serves as the sentence subject, so 가 the subject marker follows. As the subject marker is often deleted in colloquial conversation, ...기 싫어요 is also frequently used.

설거지하기가 싫어요. (설거지하다: to do dishes)
I don't like doing dishes.
운동하기가 싫어요.
I hate working out.
오늘은 일하기 싫어요.
I don't feel like working today.

Similar patterns are made using other adjectives such as:

...기가 좋아요	doing...is good, I like doing...
...기가 편해요	doing...is comfortable/convenient
...기가 불편해요	doing...is uncomfortable/inconvenient
...기가 힘들어요	doing...is difficult/tough
...기가 쉬워요	doing...is easy
...기가 어려워요	doing...is difficult

한국어 배우기가 어려워요.
Learning Korean is difficult.
한자가 많아서 읽기 어려워요.
Since there are many Chinese characters, it is hard to read (it).
지하철역이 가까워서 지하철 타기가 편해요.
As the subway station is close, it's convenient to take the subway.

13.10 ...잖아요 "you know, don't you know?"

The ...잖아요 ending is used when the speaker assumes that the listener also knows or agrees with a particular fact. 잖아요 can be attached to verbs, adjectives, and nouns. When attached to a noun that ends in a consonant, the linking verb 이 is added.

verb/adjective + 잖아요
noun + (이) 잖아요

In English, it can be translated as "you know," "as you know," "don't you know?," or "don't you see?"

A: 왜 우산을 가지고 왔어요?
Why did you bring an umbrella?
B: 오늘 오후에 비 오잖아요.
It will rain this afternoon, you know (don't you know?).

A: 수한씨가 영어를 아주 잘 하네요.
Soohan speaks English very well.
B: 전에 미국에서 오 년 살았잖아요.
He lived in the US for 5 years before, you know (didn't you know?)

Exercise 5

Change the polite speech style in the following conversation to the intimate speech style.

A: 지금 몇 시예요?
B: 한 시 반이에요. 근데, 과장님 이메일 받았어요?
A: 아니오. 아직 이메일 확인 안 했는데요. 왜요?
(확인하다: to check, to confirm)
B: 내일 미팅이 취소됐어요. (취소되다: to be canceled)
A: 아, 그래요? 그럼, 미팅을 언제 하기로 했어요?
B: 다음 주 수요일에요.

Exercise 6

Provide a reason for the following suggestion or command using ...(으)니까.

Example (오늘은 바쁘다) 내일 애기합시다.
(Today is busy) Let's talk tomorrow.
→ <u>오늘은 바쁘니까 내일 애기합시다</u>.
As I am busy today, let's talk tomorrow.

1 (덥다) 에어콘을 켭시다.
(be hot) Let's turn on the air conditioning.

2 (사무실이 지저분하다) 청소합시다.
(The office is messy.) Let's clean.

3 (내일 8시에 회의가 있다) 늦지 마세요.
(to have a meeting at 8 tomorrow) Don't be late.

4 (배가 고프다) 밥 먹고 합시다.
(be hungry) Let's eat and (then) do it.

Exercise 7

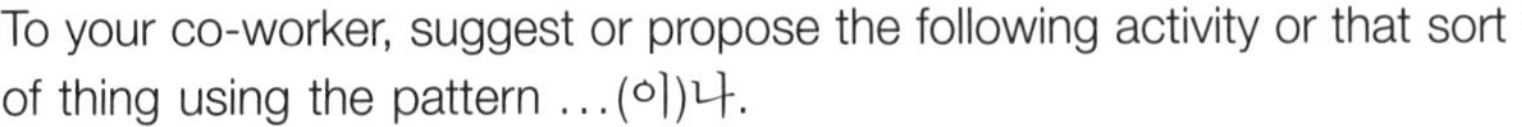

To your co-worker, suggest or propose the following activity or that sort of thing using the pattern ...(이)나.

Example 커피를 마시다 to drink coffee
→ 커피나 마실까요? Shall we drink coffee or something?

1 비디오를 보다 to watch a video
2 쇼핑을 하다 to do shopping
3 시내구경을 하다 to do downtown-sightseeing
4 산책을 하다 to take a walk

Exercise 8

Express your dislikes using...기가 싫어요. Also, explain your dislikes using the expressions given.

Example 피곤하다 (be tired) + 숙제하다 (to do homework)
→ 피곤해서 숙제하기가 싫어요.
I am tired so I don't want to do homework.

1 비가 오다 (to rain) + 모임에 가다 (to go to a gathering)
2 아프다 (be sick) + 출장가다 (to go on a business trip)
3 춥다 (be cold) + 밖에 나가다 (to go outside)
4 차가 많이 막히다 (traffic is busy) + 운전하다 (to drive)

Exercise 9

Complete the dialogues using ...잖아요 "you know, don't you know?"

Example A: 마이클씨가 한국말을 아주 잘 해요.
Michael speaks Korean very well.
B: (부인이 한국사람이다) 부인이 한국 사람이잖아요.
(His wife is Korean) His wife is Korean, you know.

1 A: 김영미씨가 안 보이네요. I don't see Ms Kim Young-mee.
B: (일찍 퇴근했다) ______________________________
She left the office early, didn't you know?

2 A: 은행에 사람이 많네요. There are a lot of people in the bank.
B: (월말이다) ____________________________
You know, it's the end of the month. (월말: the end of a month)

3 A: 비행기값이 정말 비싸요. The airfare is really expensive.
B: (지금 휴가철이다) ____________________________
It's the vacation season now, that's why.

Exercise 10 (Listening) **(CD2; 44)**

Listen to the following conversation between James and his close friend, Chang-sub. Pay attention to the intimate speech style they use and answer the questions in English.

1 Has Chang-sub seen James often lately or not? And why?
2 How does James feel about living in Korea?
3 What does Chang-sub suggest to James in order to improve his Korean?
4 Does Chang-sub watch TV often? Why?

(얼굴: face, 생활: life; living, 두 달: two months, 지나다: to pass, 익숙하다: be familiar, 빨리: fast, 늘다: to improve, 말이 늘다: (one's language) to improve, 드라마: drama)

Cultural point

Korea has four distinct seasons. The spring is warm but short, from early April to May. The summer is very hot and humid, and August is the hottest month (30°–38°C/80°–90°F). The autumn is cool and sunny, beginning around mid-September and lasting until early November. The winter is dry and cold with the temperature ranging from –10°C to 10°C (14°F to 50°F). Over 60 percent of the annual rainfall occurs during the summer. In June and July, there is a particularly rainy period called 장마 *Changma* which is characterized by frequent heavy showers.

Unit Fourteen
가족
Family

In this unit you will learn about:

- Talking about one's family
- Describing people in a photo
- Kinship terms in Korean
- Confirming or stressing a fact using ㄴ 거예요
- Describing one's past discovery or observation using ...더라고요

Dialogue 1

(CD2; 45, 46)

At a dinner gathering, Minsu is showing a few family photos to James.

민수 우리 가족 사진이에요.
제임스 아들하고 딸이 참 귀엽네요. 이 분이 부인이세요?
민수 네. 제 아내예요.
제임스 미인이시네요. 가운데는 부모님이세요?
민수 네. 제 아버지, 어머니세요.
제임스 (Pointing at another photo) 여기 이 분은 누구세요?
민수 제 누나예요.
제임스 이 사진은 어디서 찍은 거예요?
민수 제주도에서 찍은 거예요.
제임스 아, 그래요? 저도 제주도에 가 봤는데, 경치가 아주 좋더라구요.

MINSU Uri kajŏk sajin-i-eyo.
JAMES Adŭ-ra-go tta-ri ch'am kwi-yŏm-ne-yo. I-bu-ni pu-in-i-se-yo?
MINSU Ne. Che a-nae-e-yo.
JAMES Mi-in-i-shi-ne-yo. Ka-un-de-nŭn, bu-mo-ni-mi-se-yo?
MINSU Ne. Che abŏji, ŏmŏni-seyo.
JAMES (Pointing at another photo) Yŏ-gi i-bu-nŭn nu-gu-se-yo?
MINSU Che nu-na-e-yo.
JAMES I saji-nŭn ŏ-di-sŏ tchi-gŭn kŏ-e-yo?
MINSU Che-ju-do-e-sŏ tchi-gŭn kŏ-e-yo.
JAMES A, gŭ-rae-yo? Chŏ-do Chejudo-e ga bwan-nŭn-de, kyŏng-ch'i-ga a-ju cho-t'ŏ-ra-gu-yo.

MINSU *It's my [lit. our] family photo.*
JAMES *Your son and daughter are very cute. Is this person your wife?*
MINSU *Yes. That's my wife.*
JAMES *She is a beauty. Are they your parents in the middle?*
MINSU *Yes. They are my father and my mother.*
JAMES *(Pointing at another photo) Who is this person here?*
MINSU *It's my sister.*
JAMES *Where did you take this photo?*
MINSU *We took it at Cheju Island.*
JAMES *Oh, is that so? I've also been to Cheju Island, and it was very scenic.*

Vocabulary

우리	our, we
가족	family
사진	photo (사진을 찍다: to take a photo)
아들	son
딸	daughter
참	very
귀엽다	be cute 귀엽네요: 귀엽 (be cute) + 네요 (emphatic ending) (pronounced [귀염네요])
분	person (honorific of 사람)
부인	wife (to refer to somebody else's wife)
제	my (humble polite word of 내)
아내	wife (to refer to one's own wife)
미인	a beauty
미인이시네요	She is beautiful. [lit. She is a beauty.] 미인 + (이)시 (honorific marker) + 네요 (emphatic ending)
가운데	the middle, the center
가운데는	가운데(the middle) + 는 (topic marker, "as for")
부모님	parents
여기	here
이 분	this person
누구	who 누구세요?: Who is it? (honorific form of 누구예요?)
누나	(a male person's) older sister
아버지	father
어머니	mother
어디서	at where (= 어디에서)
제주도	Cheju Island
가 봤다	have been (there)
가 봤는데	가 봤다 + 는데 (providing background information, refer to Unit 8)
경치	scenery
...더라구요	sentence ending expressing one's past experience

Grammar points

14.1 Kinship terms

Korean kinship terms are very rich and intricate. Some family terms have two different forms according to the gender of the speaker or the speaker's paternal/maternal sides.

할아버지	grandfather
할머니	grandmother
부모님	parents
아버지	father (아빠: dad, daddy)
어머니	mother (엄마: mom, mommy)
누나	(a male person's) older sister
언니	(a female person's) older sister
형	(a male person's) older brother
오빠	(a female person's) older brother
동생	younger sibling (여동생: younger sister, 남동생: younger brother)
고모	(father's side) aunt
이모	(mother's side) aunt
삼촌	uncle
외삼촌	(mother's side) uncle
사촌	cousin

In Korean, kinship terms rather than names are used to address an older family member or relative. Kinship terms in Korean are also popularly used to refer to non-family members. For example, 할아버지 can be used not only to address one's own grandfather but also to address any old man.

When referring to somebody else's family members, honorific kinship terms can be used as shown in the following examples:

아버님	father
어머님	mother
아드님	son
따님	daughter

When referring to one's own family members, Koreans tend to use 우리 ("our") more frequently than 제 or 내 ("my"). This is because they consider the member as belonging not just to oneself but to the entire family.

우리 어머니	my mother [lit. our mother]
제 어머니	my mother
우리 딸	my daughter [lit. our daughter]
내 아들	my son
우리 언니	my sister [lit. our sister]
우리 남편	my husband [lit. our husband]

14.2 Confirming or stressing the fact using ...ㄴ 거예요 "It is that..."

The pattern "noun-modifying form + 거예요" is very frequently used in colloquial conversation. You may review noun-modifying forms in Unit 10 (i.e., verbs ...는/(으)ㄴ/(으)ㄹ; adjectives ...(으)ㄴ; noun ...(이)ㄴ).

You can use ...ㄴ 거예요 when (1) you want to confirm the fact as shared information or (2) you want to stress or emphasize the fact. Examine the following sentences comparing the ...ㄴ거예요 ending with the ...아요/어요 ending.

지금 떠나요?	Are you leaving now?
지금 떠나는 거예요?	Is it that you are leaving now?
어디서 만났어요?	Where did you meet (him)?
어디서 만난 거예요?	Where is it you met (him)?
영화가 너무 지루했어요.	The movie was very boring. (지루하다: be boring)
영화가 너무 지루한 거예요.	It is that the movie was so boring (so I didn't enjoy it).

More examples follow:

요즘 너무 바쁜 거예요. 그래서 연락 못 드렸어요.
It is that I am so busy these days. So I wasn't able to contact you.

지금 어디 가시는 거예요?
Where is it that you are going now?

지금 뭐 하는 거예요?
What is it that you are doing now?

안 좋은 일이 있는 거예요?
Is it that there is something making you unhappy?

이 그림 직접 그린 거예요? (그림을 그리다: to draw a picture)
Is it that you drew this picture in person?

어제는 너무 피곤한 거예요. 그래서 일찍 퇴근했어요.
It is that I was so tired yesterday. So I left work early.

14.3 Describing one's past discovery or observation using ...더라고요

Preceded by a verb, adjective, or noun, ...더라고요 is used to describe something/someone that the speaker saw, discovered, or experienced in the past. This pattern is mostly used in spoken Korean, and ...더라고요 is often pronounced ...더라구요.

그 식당 음식이 맛있더라구요.
(I found that) the food at that restaurant was delicious.

중국어를 배워 봤는데 좀 어렵더라구요.
I've learned Chinese and (I found that) it was a little difficult.

어제 시장에 사람들이 너무 많더라구요.
There were too many people in the market yesterday.

김선생님이 키가 아주 크시더라구요. (키가 크다: be tall)
(I saw Mr Kim and) he was very tall.

강의가 아주 재미있더라구요. (강의: lecture)
(I found that) the lecture was very interesting.

한과장님이 승진하셨더라구요. (승진하다: to get promoted)
(I found that) Manager Han had been promoted.

영미씨 남자친구가 미남이더라구요. (미남: a handsome man)
Young-mee's boyfriend was handsome [lit. a handsome man].

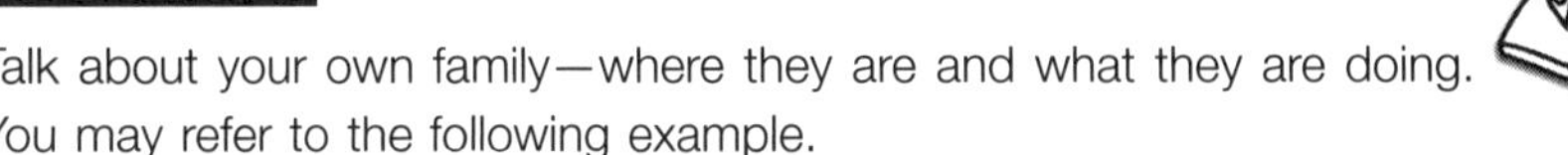

Exercise 1

Talk about your own family—where they are and what they are doing. You may refer to the following example.

Example 우리 가족은 영국에 살아요. 부모님은 런던에 계세요. 저는 형 하나하고 여동생이 하나 있어요. 형은 런던에 있는 은행에서 일해요. 여동생은 지금 맨체스터에 있는 대학교에서 공부해요.

My [lit. our] family lives in the UK. (My) parents are in London. I have one older brother and one younger sister. My older brother is working at a bank in London. My younger sister is studying at a university in Manchester.

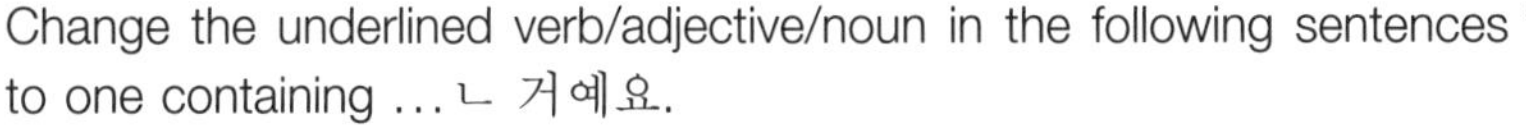

Exercise 2

Change the underlined verb/adjective/noun in the following sentences to one containing ...ㄴ 거예요.

Example 뭐 봐요? What are you watching?
→ 뭐 보는 거예요? What is it you are watching?

1 언제 출장가세요?
When do you go on a business trip?

2 결혼하세요?
Are you getting married?

3 아침에 늦게 일어났어요. 그래서 회사에 늦었어요.
I got up late in the morning. So I was late for work.

4 그 분이 한국말을 너무 잘 하세요. 그래서 아주 놀랐어요.
He speaks Korean so well. So I was very surprised.
(놀라다: to be surprised)

5 과장님이 왜 화가 나셨어요? (화가 나다: to get angry)
Why did the manager get angry?

Exercise 3

Tell your co-worker about your past discoveries and observations using ...더라구요.

Example 영화가 괜찮았어요. The movie was all right.
→ <u>영화가 괜찮더라구요</u>. (I found) the movie was all right.

1 수한씨가 골프를 잘 했어요. (골프: golf)
2 박선생님이 일본어를 잘 하셨어요. (일본어: Japanese language)
3 미라씨 요리 솜씨가 좋았어요. (요리 솜씨: cooking skill)
4 창민씨 여자 친구가 아주 예뻤어요.

Exercise 4 (Listening) (CD2; 47)

The following is a dialogue between James and Mira about their past experiences traveling abroad. Listen and answer the questions in English.

1 Where has Mira traveled abroad?
2 How was the place that Mira traveled to?
3 What country has James been to?
4 How was the place that James traveled to?

(해외여행: travel abroad, ...처럼: like..., 여행하다: to travel, 파리: Paris, 멋있다: stylish, 사람들: people, 친절하다: be kind)

Unit Fifteen

우체국에서

At the post office

In this unit you will learn about:

- Sending mail at the post office
- Expression of intention using ...(으)려고 하다
- How to say "be about to..." in Korean
- Expressions for duration of days
- Expressions for giving and receiving
- Usage of ...아/어 주다 when you do something for someone
- Polite requests using ...아/어 주세요

Dialogue 1

(CD2; 48)

James is trying to send a package to the UK by air mail. The following is a conversation between James and a post office clerk.

직원 어서 오세요. 어떻게 도와 드릴까요?
제임스 저, 이 소포를 영국으로 부치려고 하는데요.
직원 항공우편으로 보내실 거죠?
제임스 네. 얼마나 걸려요?
직원 열흘정도 걸립니다. 안에 뭐가 들어있지요?
제임스 옷하고 기념품이에요.
직원 여기 보내는 사람하고 받는 사람 성함하고 주소를 좀 써 주세요.
제임스 네. 알겠습니다.

CLERK Ŏsŏ o-se-yo. Ŏttŏ-k'e towa tŭril-kkayo?
JAMES Chŏ, i sop'orŭl yŏng-gugŭro puch'i-ryŏgo hanŭndeyo.
CLERK Hang-gong-u-p'yŏ-nŭ-ro bonaesil-kkŏ-jyŏ?
JAMES Ne. Ŏlmana Kŏl-lyŏ-yo?
CLERK Yŏ-rŭl jŏng-do kŏl-lim-ni-da. Ane mwŏ-ga tŭ-rŏ-i-tchi-yo?
JAMES Ot'a-go gi-nyŏm-p'u-mi-e-yo.
CLERK Yŏgi bonaenŭn saram hago bannŭn saram sŏng-ham-hago chuso-rŭl chom ssŏ-ju-se-yo.
JOHN Ne, alge-ssŭm-ni-da.

CLERK *Welcome. How can I help you?*
JAMES *I'd like to send this package to the UK.*
[lit. I intend to send this package to the UK.]
CLERK *You are going to send it via airmail, right?*
JAMES *Yes. How long does it take?*
CLERK *It takes about ten days. What is in there?*
JAMES *Clothes and souvenirs.*
CLERK *Please write down here the sender's and receiver's names and addresses.*
JAMES *Okay. [lit. Yes, understood.]*

Vocabulary

어서 오세요	welcome
어떻게	how
도와 드리다	to help (a polite way of offering help) 도와 주다: to help somebody 도와 드리다: a humble expression of 도와 주다
...(으)ㄹ까요?	shall I/we...? (used when asking listener's opinion, in Unit 6)
소포	parcel, package
영국으로	to the United Kingdom (here, ...(으)로 indicates direction)
부치다	to post, to mail
항공우편으로	by airmail (here, ...(으)로 indicates means)
보내실 거지요?	보내다 (to send) + (으)시 (honorific suffix) + (으)ㄹ 거 (future tense) + 지요? (sentence ending used to confirm or seek agreement, in Unit 13)
얼마나	approximately how long; how much
걸릴까요?	will it take? 걸리다 ([time] to take) + (으)ㄹ까요?
열흘	ten days (= 십일)
...정도	about, approximately (= 쯤)
걸립니다	[time] to take (걸리다 + ㅂ니다)
안에	inside, 안 (inside) + 에 (in)
들어 있다	to be placed in
...지요?	polite sentence ending (see Unit 12)
옷	clothes
기념품	souvenir
보내는 사람	sender, 보내다 + 는 (noun modifier) + 사람
받다	to receive
받는 사람	receiver, 받다 + 는 (noun modifier) + 사람
주소	address
써 주세요	write it for me 쓰다 (to write) + 아/어 주다 (to do for the benefit of someone)

Grammar points

15.1 Expressing intention ...(으)려고 하다 "intend to..."

Verb + (으)려고 하다 is used to express one's intention or plan.

verb base ending in vowel + 려고 하다	가려고 해요.
verb base ending in consonant + 으려고 하다	먹으려고 해요.

이번 여름에 한국에 가려고 해요.
I intend to go to Korea this summer.
오늘부터 술을 끊으려고 해요.
I am going to quit drinking starting today.
다음 주에 설악산으로 등산가려고 해요.
I intend to go hiking to Mt. Sorak next week.

...(으)려고 하다 also has the meaning "be about to..."

비가 오려고 해요.
It's about to rain.
지금 막 떠나려고 하는데요.
I am about to leave now. (막: just about)
기차가 지금 막 출발하려고 해요. (출발하다: to depart)
The train is just about to depart now.

...(으)려고 can be followed by verbs or phrases other than 하다, expressing the meaning "with the intention of doing" or "in an effort to do."

한국에서 일하려고 한국어를 공부해요.
I study Korean to work in Korea.
이거 김선생님께 드리려고 샀어요.
I bought this to give to Mr Kim.

In colloquial speech, ...(으)ㄹ려고 or ...(으)ㄹ려구 such as 갈려고/갈려구 and 먹을려고/먹을려구 are frequently used. However, these colloquial forms are not recommended in writing.

미국에 유학갈려구 요즘 준비하고 있어요.
(Intending) to study abroad in the US, I am preparing for it these days.

15.2 아/어 주다 "to do something for the benefit of someone"

Verb-base + 아/어 주다 expresses the meaning "to do something for the benefit of somebody." When the beneficiary is one of equal status to the giver in terms of social position or age, ...아/어 주다 is used. 드리다 is a humble word for 주다 and ...아/어 드리다 is used when the beneficiary is one of a higher status than the giver. 주시다 is an honorific word for 주다, therefore ...아/어 주시다 is used when a person of higher status does something for the beneficiary. For example:

Giver to Beneficiary

1 **Equal status to equal status** ...아/어 주다
마이클이 존한테 선물을 사 줬어요.
Michael bought a gift for John.

2 **Lower status to higher status** ...아/어 드리다
존이 사장님께 선물을 사 드렸어요.
John bought a gift for his company head.

3 **Higher status to lower status** ...아/어 주시다
사장님께서 존한테 선물을 사 주셨어요.
The company head bought a gift for John.

사주다 사 드리다 사 주시다

Here are some useful expressions with ...아/어 주다/드리다/주시다:

...아/어 주세요.	Please do...for me.
...아/어 주시겠어요?/주실래요?	Would you do...for me?
...아/어 드릴까요?	Shall I do...for you?
...아/어 드리겠습니다/드릴게요.	I will do...for you.

여기 전화번호를 좀 써 주세요.
Please write your phone number here.

한국어를 좀 가르쳐 주실래요?
Would you teach me Korean?

문 좀 닫아 주시겠습니까?
Would you please close the door for me?

한국어를 가르쳐 드릴까요?
Shall I teach you Korean?

제가 점심을 사 드릴게요.
I will buy you lunch.

15.3 Expressions for duration of days

There are two ways of counting days in Korean: (1) using native Korean or (2) using Sino-Korean.

Number of days	Native Korean	Sino-Korean
1 day	하루	일일
2 days	이틀	이일
3 days	사흘	삼일
4 days	나흘	사일
5 days	닷새	오일
6 days	엿새	육일
7 days	이레	칠일
8 days	여드레	팔일
9 days	아흐레	구일
10 days	열흘	십일
15 days	보름	십오일
20 days	스무날	이십일

Of the native Korean words, 하루, 이틀, 사흘, 나흘, 닷새, 열흘, 보름 are most frequently used. As the number of days increases, Sino-Korean is more frequently used to count them.

Exercise 1

The following is a list of what you intend to do next week. Tell your co-worker about it.

Example 설악산에 가다 → <u>설악산에 가려고 해요</u>.
to go to Mt. Sorak I intend to go to Mt. Sorak.

1 박선생님하고 골프를 치다
to play golf with Mr Park
2 부산에 있는 친구를 만나다
to meet a friend in Busan
3 테니스를 배우다
to learn how to play tennis
4 남자친구하고 영화를 보다
to watch movies with my boyfriend
5 롯데 백화점에 가서 쇼핑을 하다
to go to the Lotte department store and shop there
6 민속촌에 놀러 가다
to go to the Folk Village to have fun

Exercise 2

Think about the subject and object in the following sentences and circle the appropriate answer from ...아/어 주다, ...아/어 드리다, and ...아/어 주시다.

1 친구가 저녁을 (만들어 줬어요/만들어 드렸어요/만들어주셨어요.)
My friend cooked/made dinner for me.

2 김과장님께서 제게 책을 (빌려 줬습니다/빌려 드렸습니다/빌려주셨습니다.)
Manager Kim lent me a book.
(제게=저에게=저한테: to me, 빌려 주다: to lend)

3 제가 사장님을 (도와 줬어요/도와 드렸어요/도와 주셨어요.)
I helped the company boss.

Exercise 3

It was your birthday yesterday. Tell your co-worker that (1) your close friend Michael bought you a Korean movie DVD and (2) your mother bought you a sweater. Choose the appropriate verb from 사 주다, 사 드리다, and 사 주시다.

1 마이클이 한국영화 디비디를 ________________
2 어머니께서 스웨터를 ________________

Exercise 4

Offer to do the following for your co-worker. Use ...아/어 드릴게요, "I will do...for you"

Example I will buy you dinner. [저녁을 사 주다]
<u>저녁을 사 드릴게요</u>.

1 I will teach you English. [영어를 가르쳐 주다]
2 I will help you. [도와 주다]
3 I will lend you money. [돈을 빌려 주다]
4 I will take a photo of you. [사진을 찍어 주다]

Exercise 5 **(CD2; 49)**

Express your appreciation to your colleague for things that she did for you. Use "...아/어 주셔서 감사합니다."

Example Thank you for helping me. [도와 주다]
<u>도와 주셔서 감사합니다</u>.

1 Thank you for coming. [와 주다]
2 Thank you for inviting me. [초대해 주다] (초대하다: to invite)
3 Thank you for buying me a gift. [선물을 사 주다]
4 Thank you for teaching me Korean. [한국어를 가르쳐 주다]
5 Thank you for calling me. [전화해 주다]

Exercise 6

Answer the following questions using the correct duration of days.

Example A: 휴가가 며칠이에요? [five days]
How many days is your vacation?
(며칠: how many days)
B: <u>오일이요./닷새요</u>.

1 그 일을 끝내는데 얼마나 걸렸어요? [three days]
How long did it take to finish the work?
2 한국에 얼마동안 계실 거예요? [fifteen days]
How long are you planning to stay in Korea?
3 얼마동안 출장을 가세요? [four days]
How long is your business trip? (출장: business trip)
4 한글을 배우는데 얼마나 걸려요? [one day]
Approximately how long does it take to learn *Hangŭl*?
5 그 학회는 며칠 동안 해요? [two days]
How many days will the conference last?
(학회: academic conference)

Exercise 7 (Listening) **(CD2; 50)**

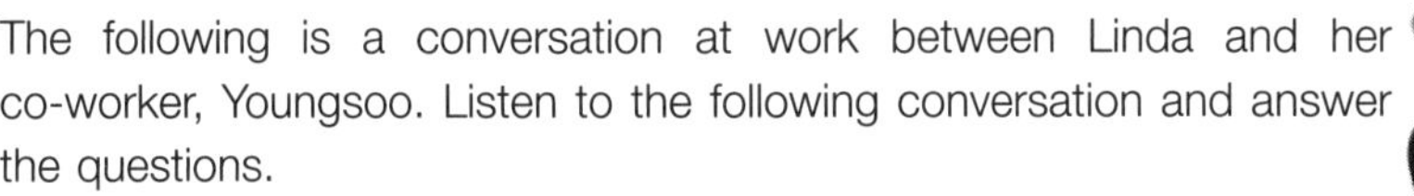

The following is a conversation at work between Linda and her co-worker, Youngsoo. Listen to the following conversation and answer the questions.

1 What is the conversation about?
a. Linda is offering help to Youngsoo.
b. Linda is asking Youngsoo for help.
c. Youngsoo is offering help to Linda.
d. Youngsoo is asking Linda for help.

2 What is Linda planning to do this weekend?
a. see movies with a friend
b. go visit a friend's house
c. go shopping with a friend
d. go on a trip

3 Which place does Youngsoo suggest to Linda? ____________

4 What transportation does Youngsoo recommend to Linda?
a. bus b. taxi c. subway d. walking

5 What number bus goes there?
a. number 17 c. number 28
b. number 19 d. number 48

6 Which subway line goes there?
a. line 1 b. line 3 c. line 5 d. line 7

Cultural point

Post offices in South Korea have a red color sign with a logo of the flying swallow, which symbolizes a messenger delivering news quickly. Postal boxes on the streets are also in the same red color.

There are many types of mail one can use at the post office, including regular mail (보통 우편), priority mail (빠른 우편), express mail (속달), registered mail (등기 우편), and registered express mail (등기 속달). While one can send international mail at any local post office, for a special service like EMS (Express Mail Service), International Post Offices are convenient.

In writing the name and address on mail, Koreans follow a different order. To address mail correctly in the Korean form, first write the address and then the name. The zip code is placed at the bottom of the sender's and receiver's address sections. In writing the address, start with the largest area first and then move down to smaller units such as in an order of City (시), District (구), Town (동), Number (번지).

Here is an example of a Korean mailing address:

서울시 서대문구	Seoul, Sŏdaemoon-Gu
대현동 120 번지	Daehyun-Dong 120
럭키 아파트 101 동 703 호	Lucky APT 101 dong-703 ho
홍길동 앞	Hong, Kil-dong
120-751	120-751

보내는 사람 (sender)

□□□-□□□

우표
stamp

받는 사람 (receiver)

□□□-□□□

Unit Sixteen
은행에서
At the bank

In this unit you will learn about:

- Opening a bank account
- Getting a credit card or debit card
- Asking about the money exchange service
- Useful expressions related to banking
- How to say "말고"
- Expressing availability using ... 돼요

Dialogue 1

(CD2; 51)

James is trying to open a new bank account. He also needs to exchange some money.

제임스	은행 계좌를 만들고 싶은데요.
직원	여기 이것 좀 작성해 주세요. 그리고 도장 가지고 오셨어요?
제임스	네. 여기 있습니다.
직원	얼마 예금하시겠어요?
제임스	오만원이요.
직원	신용카드도 만들어 드릴까요?
제임스	아니오. 신용카드 말고 현금 카드 만들어 주세요.
직원	손님, 여기 통장하고 도장 있습니다.
제임스	아, 그리고 여기 환전 돼요?
직원	네. 됩니다. 환전은 칠번 창구로 가세요.

JAMES	Ŭ-naeng-gejwa-rŭl mandŭl-go shi-p'ŭn-de-yo.
CLERK	Yŏgi i-gŏ-tchom chak-ssŏng-ae chu-se-yo. Kŭrigo do-jang ka-ji-go o-syŏ-ssŏ-yo?
JAMES	Ne. Yŏgi i-ssŭm-ni-da.
CLERK	Ŏlma ye-gŭm-ha-shi-ge-ssŏ-yo?
JAMES	O-ma-nwŏ-ni-yo.
CLERK	Shi-nyong-k'a-dŭ-do man-dŭ-rŏ dŭ-ril-kka-yo?
JAMES	Anio. Shi-nyong-k'a-dŭ mal-go hyŏn-gŭm-k'a-dŭ man-dŭ-rŏ ju-se-yo.
CLERK	Son-nim, yŏgi t'ong-jang-ha-go do-jang i-ssŭm-ni-da.
JAMES	A, kŭrigo yŏgi hwan-jŏn dwae-yo?
CLERK	Ne. Twem-ni-da. Hwan-jŏ-nŭn ch'il bŏn ch'ang-ggu-ro ga-se-yo.

JAMES	*I'd like to open [lit. make] a bank account.*
CLERK	*Please fill out this (form) here (for me).* *And did you bring (your) stamp?*
JAMES	*Yes. Here it is.*
CLERK	*How much do you want to deposit?*
JAMES	*50,000 won.*
CLERK	*Would you like to have a credit card too?* *[lit. Shall I make a credit card for you?]*

JAMES *No. Please get me a debit card, not a credit card.*
CLERK *Mr [lit. Customer], here is your account book and stamp.*
JAMES *Do you also provide a money exchange service here?*
CLERK *Yes, we do. Please go to window number seven.*

Vocabulary

은행	bank
계좌	account (은행 계좌: bank account)
작성하다	to complete writing (a written form or document) 작성해 주세요: 작성하다 + 아/어 주세요
도장	wooden stamp
얼마	how much
예금하다	to deposit (money)
원	won, the unit of Korean currency
만원	10,000 won 오만원: 50,000 won
신용카드	a credit card (= 크레딧 카드)
A 말고 B	not A, but B
현금	cash
현금카드	a debit card [lit. a cash card]
통장	account book
환전	money exchange
되다	to become, to be available
창구	(teller's) window 칠번 창구: window number seven

Other words related to banking (CD2; 52)

돈을 찾다	to withdraw money [lit. to find money]
저금하다	to save money
적금	an installment deposit/saving
대출	money lending/loan
인터넷 뱅킹	internet banking
온라인 뱅킹	online banking
이자	interest
환율	exchange rate
여행자 수표	traveler's check

16.1 Noun A 말고 Noun B "Not A but B"

Used with nouns, A 말고 B ("Not A but B") is typically followed by command, request, or suggestion endings:

커피 말고 녹차 주세요.
Give me green tea, not coffee.
중국 음식 말고 한국 음식 먹읍시다.
Let's eat Korean food, not Chinese food.
보통우편 말고 빠른 우편으로 보내세요.
Send it by express mail, not by regular mail.

In colloquial speech, 말고 is often pronounced [말구 **mal-gu**].

When used with a verb, **Verb A** ... 지 말고 **Verb B** is used, meaning "Don't do A (Verb), but do B (Verb)."

커피 마시지 말고 녹차 드세요.
Don't drink coffee but drink green tea.
영화 보지 말고 뮤지컬 봅시다.
Let's watch a musical rather than watching movies.
안경 쓰지 말고 콘텍트렌즈를 쓰세요.
Don't wear glasses but wear contact lenses.
은행에 가지 말고 인터넷 뱅킹을 이용하세요.
(이용하다: to make use)
Don't go to the bank but use internet banking.

16.2 Expressing availability using ... 돼요? "...available?"

되다 literally means "to become" but it is used in various contexts with the meaning "to be available," "to be operating okay" or "to work fine." For example, in the following dialogue, A is asking B whether the copier is now working fine, after being out of order.

A: 지금 복사기 돼요? Is the copier working now?
B: 아니오. 아직 안 돼요. No. It's still not working.

Here are some more examples with 되다:

[At a café] 여기 인터넷 돼요?
Is internet available here?

[On the phone] 배달 돼요?
Do you deliver? [lit. Is the delivery available?]

[At a restaurant, the waiter says]
죄송합니다. 지금 김치찌개가 안 됩니다.
We are sorry. Right now, Kimchi stew is not available.

민호는 영어랑 일어가 됩니다.
Minho can speak English and Japanese.

일주일 안에 됩니까? (일주일: one week, 안에: inside, within)
Will it be available (or done) within a week?

십만원에 됩니까?
Will that be available at (the price of) 100,000 won?

지금 팩스기가 고장나서 팩스가 안 됩니다.
The fax machine is out of order now, so faxing is not available.

Exercise 1

Answer the following questions using ...말고 or ...지 말고.

Example A: 커피 드실래요? [녹차]
Would you like to have coffee?
B: 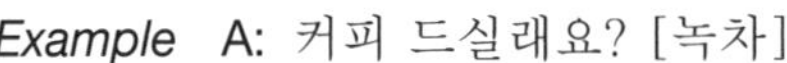커피 말고 녹차 주세요.
Give me green tea, not coffee.

1 맥주 드릴까요? [물] (맥주: beer, 물: water)

2 빨간색 넥타이 드릴까요? [까만색 넥타이]
(빨간색 넥타이 a red necktie)

3 이번 주 토요일에 만날까요? [다음 주 토요일]

4 내일 갈까요? [모레] (모레: the day after tomorrow)

5 오번 버스를 타야 돼요? [십번 버스]

6 경복궁까지 버스를 타고 갈까요? [지하철]

7 비빔밥 먹고 싶어요? [갈비]

Exercise 2

Ask whether the following service is available or functional using ... 돼요 or 됩니까?

Example 환전 money exchange
→ 환전 됩니까? Is money exchange available?

1 에어콘 air conditioning
2 카푸치노 cappuccino coffee
3 과장님하고 통화 telephone communication with the section chief
4 꽃배달 flower delivery

Exercise 3 (Listening) **(CD2; 53)**

James is placing an order with Seoul Restaurant (서울 식당). Listen to the conversation and answer the questions below.

1 What did James order?

2 What is James's address?
   a. Hanyang Apartment 100 dong, number 20
   b. Hanyang Apartment 101 dong, number 210
   c. Hanyang Apartment 102 dong, number 102
   d. Hanyang Apartment 103 dong, number 120

3 How much was the total of his order?
   a. 5,000 won b. 6,500 won
   c. 7,000 won d. 9,500 won

4 What is the expected delivery time for his order?
   a. 10 minutes b. 20 mintues
   c. 30 mintues d. 40 mintues

(주문하다: to order, 주소: address, 전부: all together, ...후에: after..., ...동: building number..., ...호: room number...)

Unit Seventeen

호텔에서

At the hotel

In this unit you will learn about:

- Checking hotel room availability
- Getting familiar with terms used at the hotel
- Asking about a shuttle bus to the airport
- How to say room numbers
- Getting familiar with the honorific formal polite sentence ending
- Talking about one's schedule using ...(으)ㄹ 예정이다

Dialogue 1

(CD2; 54, 55)

James is trying to check in at a hotel. The following is a conversation between James and a front-desk worker at the hotel.

제임스	예약 안 했는데 빈 방 있습니까?
직원	한 분이십니까?
제임스	네.
직원	싱글 룸은 없고 더블 룸 밖에 없는데 괜찮으십니까?
제임스	네. 괜찮습니다.
직원	언제 체크아웃 할 예정이십니까?
제임스	월요일 아침이요. 체크아웃 시간이 언제지요?
직원	열한 시 입니다.
제임스	호텔에서 공항으로 가는 버스 있습니까?
직원	네. 매 시간 있습니다. 여기 카드 키 있습니다. 215 호입니다.

JAMES	Yeyak a-naen-nŭn-de bin-bang issŭm-ni-kka?
CLERK	Han-bun issim-ni-kka?
JAMES	Ne.
CLERK	Singŭl-ru-mŭn ŏp-kko dŏbŭl-rum ba-kke ŏm-nŭn-de kwaen-ch'anŭ-shim-ni-kka?
JAMES	Ne. Kwaen-ch'an-ssŭm-ni-da.
CLERK	Ŏnje ch'ekŭ-aut hal yejŏng i-shim-ni-kka?
JAMES	Wŏryo-il ach'i-miyo. Ch'ekŭ-aut shi-ga-ni ŏnjejiyo?
CLERK	Yŏ-ran-shi im-ni-da.
JAMES	Hote-re-sŏ gong-ang-ŭ-ro ga-nŭn bŏsŭ i-ssŭm-ni-kka?
CLERK	Ne. Mae shigan issŭm-ni-da. Yŏgi k'adŭ-k'i issŭm-ni-da. I-baek-ship-o-ho im-ni-da.

JAMES	*I didn't make a reservation but is there a vacant room?*
CLERK	*Is it for one person?*
JAMES	*Yes.*
CLERK	*There is no single room (available). We only have double room vacancies. Will that be all right?*
JAMES	*Yes, that is fine.*
CLERK	*When are you planning to check out?*
JAMES	*Monday morning. When is the checkout time?*
CLERK	*It's 11 o'clock.*

JAMES	*Do you have a (shuttle) bus that goes to the airport from the hotel?*
CLERK	*Yes. We have (one) every hour.* *Here is (your) key card. It's Room 215.*

Vocabulary

호텔	hotel
예약	reservation
예약하다	to make a reservation
비다	be empty 빈: noun modifying form of 비다
방	room
싱글 룸	a single-bed room
더블 룸	a double-bed room
체크아웃	checkout (= 퇴실)
체크하웃 하다	to check out
...(으)ㄹ 예정이다	be scheduled to...
공항	airport 공항으로 가는 버스: 공항으로 가 + 는 (noun-modifier) + 버스 the bus that goes to the airport
매 시간	every hour (매: every) 매일 every day 매주 every week 매월 every month (= 매달) 매년 every year
카드 키	key card
호	room number 215 호 (이백십오 호) Room 215

Other hotel-related words (CD2; 56)

체크인	check-in (= 입실)
트윈 룸	a twin-bed room (double occupancy)
스위트 룸	a suite room (includes a living room)
온돌방	ondol (heated-floor) room
객실	hotel rooms [lit. guest rooms]
일반실	a standard room

17.1 Honorific formal polite ending …(으)십니다, …(으)십니까?

In Unit 7, you learned the formal polite sentence ending (ㅂ니다/습니다). In the same unit, the honorific formal polite sentence ending was also briefly explained. In this unit, you'll learn more about the honorific formal polite ending.

The honorific formal polite ending is made by attaching the honorific marker …(으)시 or …(이)시 to the formal polite ending … ㅂ니다/습니다. After a verb or adjective base, …(으)시 is attached, while after a noun, …(이)시 is attached. The honorific formal polite ending is used in a formal setting such as at work or at a formal meeting. It is used to refer to somebody who is superior to you (in terms of age or social position) or somebody with whom you have a more formal interaction, even though he/she may be of the same age or the same social position. Note the following honorific formal polite sentence endings for each sentence type.

Present tense

	statement	question	suggestion Let's…	command Please do…
verb base	…(으)십니다	…(으)십니까?	…(으)십시다	…(으)십시오
adjective base	…(으)십니다	…(으)십니까?		
noun	…(이)십니다	…(이)십니까?		

For the past tense:

verb, adjective …(으)셨습니다, …(으)셨습니까?
noun …(이)셨습니다, …(이)셨습니까?

사장님께서 지금 출발하십니다.
The (company) president is departing now.

언제 영국으로 돌아가십니까?
When are you going back to the UK?

같이 가십시다.
Let's go together.

마감 시간을 지켜 주십시오. (마감 시간: deadline; 지키다: to abide by)
Please observe the deadline.

오선생님께서 요즘 건강이 안 좋으십니다.
Mr Oh's health is not good these days.

다음 주에도 많이 바쁘십니까?
Are you very busy next week as well?

몇 분이십니까?
How many people are there?

이 분은 한국 타이어의 김사장님이십니다.
This (person) is President Kim of Korea Tyre.

17.2 ...(으)ㄹ 예정이다 "be scheduled to do..."

This pattern is added to verb bases and translates as "be scheduled to do" or "plan to do."

> 정선생님께서도 오늘 회의에 오실 예정입니다.
> Mr Choung is also scheduled to come and attend today's meeting.
>
> 내년 봄에 미국에 갈 예정입니다.
> I plan to go to the US next spring.
>
> 삼월 십일에 떠날 예정이에요.
> I am scheduled to leave on March 10th.
>
> 울산에 있는 회사를 방문할 예정이에요.
> I am scheduled to visit a company in Ulsan.

Exercise 1

Change the honorific polite sentence ending in the following sentences to the honorific formal polite sentence endings.

Example 뭐 하세요? What are you doing?
→ <u>뭐 하십니까</u>?

1 영어를 아주 유창하게 하세요. (유창하게: fluently)
You speak English very fluently.

2 오늘 신문 보셨어요?
Did you read [lit. see] today's newspaper?

3 오늘 회의에 모두 참석해 주세요.
Everyone, please attend today's meeting.
(모두: all, 참석하다: to present oneself at)

4 박선생님은 제 고등학교 선배세요.
Mr Park is my high school senior.

5 피곤하세요?
Are you tired?

Exercise 2

You are going on a business trip to Ulsan next week. Tell your co-worker the following schedule using ...(으)ㄹ 예정이에요.

월요일오전	울산에 도착하다
Monday a.m.	Arrive in Ulsan
월요일 오후	울산 공장을 둘러보다
Monday p.m.	Look around the Ulsan factory
월요일 밤	울산 호텔에 머무르다
Monday night	Stay at Ulsan Hotel
화요일 오전	조 부장님을 뵈다
Tuesday a.m.	Meet Division Head, Cho
화요일 2 시	서울행 비행기를 타다
Tuesday 2:00 p.m.	Take the airplane to Seoul

월요일 오전에 울산에 도착할 예정이에요. 월요일 오후에 ________
____
____
____
____

(공장: factory, 둘러보다: to look around, 머무르다: to stay, 뵈다: to see, 서울행: bound for Seoul)

Exercise 3 (Listening) **(CD2; 57)**

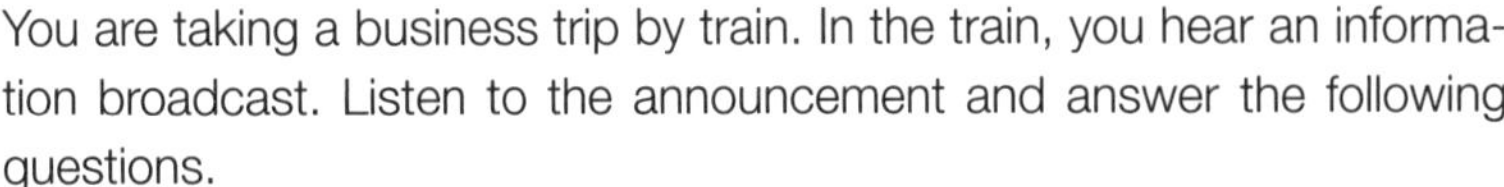

You are taking a business trip by train. In the train, you hear an information broadcast. Listen to the announcement and answer the following questions.

1 What is the train's final destination?

2 When is the train departing from Seoul?

a. 1 minute later b. 3 minutes later
c. 5 minutes later d. 10 minutes later

3 Where will the train first stop and at what time?

4 What is the scheduled arrival time for the final destination?

(저희: our, 열차: train, 이용하다: to use, 대단히: very much, exceedingly, 감사하다/감사드리다: to thank, 출발하다: to depart, 먼저: first, ahead, 도착하다: to arrive, 즐거운: pleasant, enjoyable)

Cultural point

Various types of accommodation are available in Korea, from luxurious hotels to modest guesthouses. In any major city, there are a number of modern hotels providing quality services and amenities including restaurants, bars, beauty shops, conference rooms, wireless internet, business centers, and foreign exchange services. Depending on the class of hotel, rates per night vary: an average of $400 to $500 for deluxe hotels, $80 to $150 for first-class hotels, and $50 to $60 for third-class hotels. For budget travelers, guesthouses or youth hostels may be a good choice, which cost around $15 to $40 and $8 to $40 per night, respectively. Motels and inns (or *Yŏkwan* 여관 in Korean) are also affordably priced, with a rate of about $50 to $80 a night. In big cities, one can also have the option of *Hanok Stay* (staying in a traditional Korean house) which provides foreign tourists with an authentic opportunity to experience the traditional culture and lifestyle of Korea. Most *Hanok* 한옥 houses charge about $100 or less per room with breakfast and laundry services included.

Answer key to exercises

Introduction

Exercise 2

1 ㅔ 2 ㅜ 3 ㅕ 4 ㅐ 5 ㅗ 6 ㅓ

Exercise 4

2
나, 냐, 너, 녀, 노, 뇨, 누, 뉴, 느, 니
다, 댜, 더, 뎌, 도, 됴, 두, 듀, 드, 디
라, 랴, 러, 려, 로, 료, 루, 류, 르, 리
마, 먀, 머, 며, 모, 묘, 무, 뮤, 므, 미
바, 뱌, 버, 벼, 보, 뵤, 부, 뷰, 브, 비
사, 샤, 서, 셔, 소, 쇼, 수, 슈, 스, 시
아, 야, 어, 여, 오, 요, 우, 유, 으, 이
자, 쟈, 저, 져, 조, 죠, 주, 쥬, 즈, 지
차, 챠, 처, 쳐, 초, 쵸, 추, 츄, 츠, 치
카, 캬, 커, 켜, 코, 쿄, 쿠, 큐, 크, 키
타, 탸, 터, 텨, 토, 툐, 투, 튜, 트, 티
파, 퍄, 퍼, 펴, 포, 표, 푸, 퓨, 프, 피
하, 햐, 허, 혀, 호, 효, 후, 휴, 흐, 히

Exercise 6

1 으 2 키 3 우유 4 가루 5 머리
6 바지 7 다리 8 자세히 9 어머니 10 우리나라

Exercise 7

1 가수 2 코 3 주스 4 모래 5 어디에 6 나무

Exercise 13

1 coffee 2 radio 3 banana 4 ice cream
5 America 6 computer 7 fax 8 printer
9 cup 10 coffee shop 11 cake 12 cheese
13 camera 14 chocolate 15 sandwich

Exercise 14

1 집 2 쌀 3 컴 4 물 5 옥
6 원 7 쉽 8 국 9 늑 10 옆

Exercise 16

1 괜찮아요 2 누구예요? 3 겠어요 4 계세요 5 여행
6 빨리 7 외국 8 번호 9 책방 10 좋고

Unit 1 인사 Greetings

Exercise 1

1 안녕하세요? 2 안녕하세요? 3 안녕하세요?

Exercise 2

[Your name] 입니다.

Exercise 3

성함이 어떻게 되세요?

Exercise 4

처음 뵙겠습니다.
반갑습니다.

Exercise 5

1 피터 브라운이에요. 2 한국이에요.
3 존입니다. 4 한국어예요.
5 조문기입니다.

Exercise 6

1 사라예요. 2 존이에요.
3 마이클 밀러예요. 4 이미영이에요.

Exercise 7

1 영국 사람이 아니에요. 2 서울이 아니에요.
3 한국어가 아니에요. 4 스티브가 아니에요.

Exercise 8

1 제임스 스미스입니다.
2 a. (아니오.) 미국 사람이 아니에요. 영국 사람이에요.
   b. (아니오.) 학생이 아니에요.
   c. (아니오.) 존이 아니에요. 제임스예요.
      or (아니오.) 존 밀러가 아니에요. 제임스 스미스예요.

Exercise 9

1 처음 뵙겠습니다.
2 박과장님, 오랜간만이에요.
3 요즘 어떻게 지내세요?

Unit 2 어디 가세요? **Where are you going?**

Exercise 1

1 b 2 b 3 a 4 b 5 a 6 b

Exercise 2

1 가세요? 2 오세요? 3 하세요? 4 있으세요?

Exercise 3

1 하세요. 2 오세요.

Exercise 4

1 은행에 있어요. 2 카페에 있어요.
3 회의실에 있어요. 4 컴퓨터 랩에 있어요.

Exercise 5

1 도서관에 가요. 2 공항에 가요.
3 회사에 가요 4 식당에 가요.

Exercise 6

1 컴퓨터 있어요? 2 컵 있어요? 3 펜 있어요?
4 서울 지도 있어요? 5 핸드폰 있어요?

Exercise 7

1 안 해요. 2 안 바빠요. 3 안 가요. 4 안 가요.

Exercise 8

1 변호사세요? 2 김미라씨세요?
3 과장님이세요? 4 선생님이세요?

Exercise 9

1 성함이 어떻게 되세요? 2 미국 분이세요?
3 무슨 일 하세요? 4 요즘 바쁘세요?

Exercise 10

1 별로 안 많아요. 2 별로 자주 안 가요. 3 별로 자주 안 봐요.

Exercise 11

1 만나요. 만나세요. 2 시작해요. 시작하세요.
3 와요. 오세요. 4 봐요. 보세요.

Unit 3 사무실에서 **At the office**

Exercise 1

1 부장님 2 김선생님 3 과장님 4 박교수님

Exercise 2

1 있으세요? 2 계세요? 3 있으세요? 4 계세요.

Exercise 3

1 많아서 2 있어서 3 좋아서

Exercise 4

1 을 2 가 3 를 4 이 5 을 6 이

Exercise 5

1 은 2 는 3 은

Exercise 6

1 은, 은 2 는, 는 3 는, 는 4 은, 는

Exercise 7

1 언제부터 일을 시작해요?
2 오늘부터 시작해요.
3 내일부터 오세요.
4 두 시부터 일해요.

Exercise 8

저도 영국 사람이에요.

Exercise 9

두 시에 한과장님을 만나요. (or 한과장님을 두 시에 만나요.)

Unit 4 어디 있어요? Where is it?

Exercise 1

1 서울대학교가 어디 있어요?
(or 서울대학교가 어디예요?)
2 영국문화원이 어디 있어요?
(or 영국문화원이 어디예요?)
3 롯데백화점이 어디 있어요?
(or 롯데백화점이 어디예요?)

Exercise 2

1 현대백화점이요?
2 제임스씨요?
3 팩스기요?
4 우체국이요?

Exercise 3

1 이 쪽 2 그 쪽 3 저 쪽 4 왼쪽 5 오른쪽

Exercise 4

1 이 쪽으로 가세요. 그럼, 서울대학교가 보여요.
2 이 쪽으로 가세요. 그럼, 한국은행이 보여요.
3 이 쪽으로 가세요. 그럼, 시청이 보여요.

Exercise 5

sample answers:
1 서울호텔 건너편에 있어요.
2 서울호텔 옆에 있어요.
3 극장 옆에 있어요.
4 서울은행 뒤에 있어요.
5 백화점 옆에 있어요.

Exercise 6

1 극장 2 우체국

Exercise 7

1 지하철 이호선을 타세요. 그리고 신촌에서 내리세요.
2 지하철 삼호선을 타세요. 그리고 경복궁에서 내리세요.
3 지하철 사호선을 타세요. 그리고 사당에서 내리세요.

Exercise 8

1 에서 2 에 3 에서 4 에서 5 에

Exercise 9

1 그리고 2 하고 3 그리고 4 하고

Exercise 10

1 친구 만나러 가요.
2 영화 보러 가요.
3 친구하고 밥 먹으러 가요.
4 옷 사러 가요.

Unit 5 이거 뭐예요? What is this?

Exercise 1

1 샤워하고 있어요.
2 텔레비전을 보고 있어요.
3 김미라씨가 일하고 있어요.
4 저는 점심을 먹고 있어요.
5 저는 한국어를 공부하고 있어요.
6 지호가 커피를 마시고 있어요.

Exercise 2

1 쉬워요, 어려워요
2 가까워요
3 추워요, 추워요
4 더워요, 더워요

Exercise 3

1 들어요 2 들으세요? (or 들어요?) 3 걸어요

Exercise 4

1 커피 안 마시지만 차 마셔요.
2 미국 친구 많지만 한국 친구 안 많아요.
3 일이 재미있지만 조금 어려워요.
4 제임스는 한국말 조금 하지만 수잔은 한국말 아주 잘 해요.

Exercise 5

커피 마시고 있어요.

Exercise 6

바쁘지만 일이 재미있어요.

Exercise 7

1 제 커피예요.
2 수잔 컴퓨터예요.
3 제임스 가방이에요.
4 미라 시계예요.

Exercise 8

1 제임스 친구예요.
2 제 부모님이에요.
3 제 동료예요.
4 제 한국어 선생님이세요.

Exercise 9

1 바빠요 2 예뻐요 3 커요 4 써요

Exercise 10

1 보는데요 2 가는데요 3 하는데요 4 많은데요
5 큰데요 6 예쁜데요 7 재미있는데요 8 바쁜데요

Exercise 11

1 한국어가 쉽고 재미있어요.
2 사무실이 크고 깨끗해요.
3 영화 보고 커피 마셔요.
4 요리를 좋아하고 (요리를) 자주 해요.

Unit 6 몇 시예요? What time is it?

Exercise 1

1 한 시 삼십 분
2 아홉 시 이십오 분
3 네 시 사십오 분

Exercise 2

1 세 사람 2 도우넛 두 개 3 커피 한 잔
4 맥주 다섯 병 5 책 여섯 권 6 종이 네 장

Exercise 3

1 영화를 보기 전에 팝콘을 사요.
2 가기 전에 전화해요.
3 지하철을 타기 전에 표를 사요.
4 일을 시작하기 전에 커피를 마셔요.

Exercise 4

1 몇 시에 갈까요? 2 회사 앞에서 만날까요?
3 언제부터 일을 시작할까요? 4 내일 날씨가 좋을까요?

Exercise 5

1 텔레비전 볼래요? 2 한국 음식 먹을래요?
3 백화점에 쇼핑하러 갈래요? 4 같이 한국어 배울래요?

Exercise 6

1 왔어요 2 시작했어요 3 없었어요 4 만났어요
5 좋았어요 6 봤어요 7 먹었어요 8 바빴어요

Exercise 7

1 들었어요 2 공부했어요 3 재미있었어요
4 만났어요 5 운동했어요 6 먹었어요

Exercise 8

1 일이 많거든요. 2 아팠거든요.
3 요즘 바쁘거든요. 4 한국 회사에서 일하거든요.

Exercise 9

1 팔월 십오일 2 시월 구일 3 삼월 이십일일
4 오월 삼십일 5 십이월 이십사일 6 유월 팔일

Exercise 10

1 커피가 맛있네요. 2 음식이 아주 많네요.
2 방이 아주 깨끗하네요. 4 장미꽃이 아주 예쁘네요.

Unit 7 밖에서 식사하기 Dining out

Exercise 1

1 갈비를 먹어 보세요. 2 노래방에 가 보세요.
3 부산을 여행해 보세요. 4 제 친구를 만나 보세요.

Exercise 2

1 유럽을 여행해 봤어요. 2 소주 마셔 봤어요.
3 민수씨 집에 가 봤어요. 4 맥도날드에서 일해 봤어요.

Exercise 3

1 내일 다시 전화할게요.
2 다음 주에 이메일 할게요.
3 김민수씨를 만나 볼게요.
4 부산으로 출장갈게요.

Exercise 4

1 저는 주말에 영화 보고 싶어요.
제 룸메이트는 주말에 집에서 쉬고 싶어해요.
2 저는 한국에서 일하고 싶어요.
제 룸메이트는 미국에 돌아가고 싶어해요.
3 저는 한국 음식을 주문하고 싶어요.
제 룸메이트는 이태리 음식을 주문하고 싶어해요.
4 저는 아침에 밥을 먹고 싶어요.
제 룸메이트는 아침에 빵을 먹고 싶어해요.

Exercise 5

1 싫어하시 2 약속하시 3 말씀하시
4 드시 5 전공하시

Exercise 6

1 말씀하시겠어요? Would you like to speak?
2 먼저 하시겠어요? Would you like to do it first?
3 한국말로 하시겠어요? Would you like to speak in Korean?
4 이 컴퓨터를 쓰시겠어요? Would you like to use this computer?

Exercise 7

1 어제 김선생님을 만났습니다.
2 회의를 시작하겠습니다.
3 한국말을 몇 년 배웠습니까?
4 학생입니까?
5 어디서 일합니까?

Exercise 8

1 어디 가십니까?	Where are you going?
2 요즘 많이 바쁘십니까?	Are you very busy these days?
3 골프 치십니까?	Do you play golf?
4 김사장님은 지금 안 계십니다.	President Kim is not (here) now.
5 박교수님이십니까?	Are you Professor Park?

Exercise 9

1 밖에 2 만 3 밖에 4 만

Exercise 10

1 소금 좀 주세요./주십시오./주시겠어요?
2 연락처 좀 주세요./주십시오./주시겠어요?
3 한국말 사전 좀 주세요./주십시오./주시겠어요?
4 숟가락하고 젓가락 좀 주세요./주십시오./주시겠어요?

Unit 8 사람 만나기 **Meeting people**

Exercise 1

1 갔습니다 2 일했습니다 3 끝났습니다
4 없었습니다 5 더웠습니다 6 배웠습니다
7 몰랐습니다 8 맛있었습니다 9 먹었습니다
10 끊었습니다

Exercise 2

1 헬스센터에서 운동했습니다.
2 골프를 쳤습니다.
3 부산에 놀러갔습니다.
4 친구하고 같이 영화를 봤습니다.

Exercise 3

1 오 일동안 갑니다.
2 세 달 (or 삼 개월) 있을 거예요.
3 이 년동안 했습니다.
4 사 년동안 유학했습니다.

Exercise 4

1 김선생님도 내일 모임에 올/오실 거예요.
2 스티브는 한국말을 잘 못할 거예요.
3 내일도 날씨가 아주 추울 거예요.
4 지하철이 빠를 거예요.

Exercise 5

기차를 타고 갈 거예요. 부산에 삼 일동안 있을 거예요. 바다를 구경할 거예요. 수영할 거예요. 회를 먹을 거예요. 호텔에서 지낼 거예요.

Exercise 6

1 한국은행에서 근무하시죠?
2 영국에 비가 자주 오죠?
3 서울은 크고 복잡하죠?
4 김민호씨는 학생이죠?

Exercise 7

1 월급을 받으면 뭐 하고 싶어요?
2 대학교를 졸업하면 뭐 하고 싶어요?
3 돈이 많으면 뭐 하고 싶어요?
4 유럽에 여행가면 뭐 하고 싶어요?

Exercise 8

1 이사할 때
2 한국어 공부할 때
3 밤에 운전할 때
4 세일할 때

Exercise 9

1 여동생이 한 명 있는데 대학생이에요.
2 지금 바쁜데 나중에 얘기해요.
3 날씨가 좋은데 어디 놀러 갈까요?
4 마이클은 키가 작은데 농구를 잘 해요.
5 한국어를 공부하는데 조금 어려워요.
6 어제 백화점에 갔는데 사람들이 아주 많았어요.

Exercise 10

1 남대문 시장에 쇼핑하러 갑시다.
2 공원에서 같이 조깅합시다.
3 다음 주 토요일에 모입시다.
4 한선생님도 초대합시다.
5 열한 시에 떠납시다.
6 주말에 등산갑시다.

Exercise 11

[Listening script]

김대리 제임스씨, 점심식사 안 하셨죠?
James, you haven't had lunch, right?

제임스 예, 아직 못했습니다.
No [lit. Yes (that's right)], I haven't yet [lit. I couldn't yet].

김대리 시간 있으시면 같이 식사합시다.
If you have time, let's eat together.

제임스 좋습니다. 어디로 갈까요?
That sounds good. Where shall we go?

김대리 저는 한식이 좋은데 제임스씨는 어떠세요?
I like Korean food, but what about you, James?

제임스 저도 한식이 괜찮습니다.
Korean food is fine with me, too.

김대리 회사 앞에 한식집이 있는데 값이 싸고 맛있어요.
There is a Korean restaurant in front of the office; the food is cheap and delicious.
제임스씨, 요즘도 한국어 수업 들으세요?
James, do you still [lit. these days also] take Korean class?

제임스 아니오, 일 때문에 바빠서 수업을 못 듣습니다.
No, due to my work, I am busy, so I can't take class.
그렇지만, 시간 있을 때 혼자서 공부합니다.
But, when I have time, I study by myself.

Answers:

1 Mr Kim suggests to James that they should go have lunch together if he (James) has time.
2 Food at the Korean restaurant is cheap and delicious.
3 No, because he is busy because of his work.
4 When he has time, he studies by himself.

Unit 9 교통 수단 Transportation

Exercise 1

1 골프를 잘 치려면 연습을 많이 해야 돼요.
2 미국에서 살려면 영어를 알아야 돼요.
3 일찍 일어나려면 일찍 자야 돼요.
4 내일까지 이 일을 끝내려면 오늘 밤을 새야 해요.

Exercise 2

1 건물 안에서 담배를 피우지 마세요.
2 사무실에서 식사하지 마세요.
3 회의중에 핸드폰을 쓰지 마세요.
4 회사에서 술을 마시지 마세요.

Exercise 3

1 제주도로 출장을 가야 돼요.
2 백화점에서 쇼핑해야 돼요.
3 보고서를 써야 해요.
4 친구한테 이메일을 보내야 해요.

Exercise 4

1 햄버거가 샌드위치보다 더 싸요.
(or 샌드위치가 햄버거보다 더 비싸요.)
2 이 아파트가 저 아파트보다 더 작아요.
(or 저 아파트가 이 아파트보다 더 커요.)
3 오늘이 어제보다 더 따뜻해요.
(or 어제가 오늘보다 더 추웠어요.)

Exercise 5

1 문을 좀 닫아 주세요.
Please close the door (for me).
2 문을 좀 열어 주세요.
Please open the door (for me).
3 일곱 시까지 와 주세요.
Please come by 7 o'clock (for me).
4 이메일 주소를 말씀해 주세요.
Please tell me your e-mail address.

Exercise 6

1 모두 앉아 주십시오.
2 조용히 해 주십시오.
3 여기에 주소를 써 주십시오.
4 모두 일어서 주십시오.

Exercise 7

1 회사에서 서울역까지 차로 이십 분 걸려요.
2 대전에서 부산까지 기차로 세 시간 걸려요.
3 집에서 지하철역까지 걸어서 오 분 걸려요.
4 서울대학교에서 시청까지 지하철로 사십 분 걸려요.

Exercise 8

[Listening script]

제임스 미라 씨, 좀 도와 주세요.
Mira, please help me.

미라 무슨 일이에요?
What is it? [lit. What matter is it?]

제임스 다음 주에 대전으로 출장가야 돼요.
Next week, I have to go on a business trip to Daejeon.
대전까지 버스를 탈까요? 기차를 탈까요?
Shall I take a bus to Daejeon [lit. Up to Daejeon]? (Or) Shall I take a train?

미라 버스 타지 마세요. 시간이 많이 걸려요.
Don't take a bus. It takes a long time.
기차가 버스 보다 더 빨라요.
The train is faster than the bus.

제임스 어디서 기차를 타야 돼요?
Where should I take the train?

미라 서울역에서요.
At Seoul Station.

제임스 여기서 대전까지 얼마나 걸려요?
How long does it take from here to Daejeon?

미라 두 시간쯤 걸려요.
It takes about two hours.

Answers:

1 He has to go on a business trip to Daejeon
2 train; because it is faster than the bus
3 about 2 hours

Unit 10 쇼핑 Shopping

Exercise 1

1 화장실을 써도 돼요? 2 구경해도 돼요?
3 물 좀 마셔도 돼요? 4 담배를 피워도 돼요?
5 전화를 써도 돼요? 6 여기 앉아도 돼요?

Exercise 2

1 네. 화장실을 써도 돼요. (or 아니오. 화장실을 쓰면 안 돼요.)
2 네. 구경해도 돼요. (or 아니오. 구경하면 안 돼요.)
3 네. 마셔도 돼요. (or 아니오. 마시면 안 돼요.)
4 아니오. 담배를 피우면 안 돼요. (or 네. 담배를 피워도 돼요.)
5 네. 전화를 써도 돼요. (or 아니오. 전화를 쓰면 안 돼요.)
6 네. 여기 앉아도 돼요. (or 아니오. 여기 앉으면 안 돼요.)

Exercise 3

1 키가 큰 사람
2 예쁜 딸
3 잘 생긴 남자
4 멋있는 옷

Exercise 4

1 추운 2 좋은 3 복잡한 4 부지런한

Exercise 5

1 지금 다니는 학교 the school I'm attending now
2 저기 가는 사람 the person who is going over there
3 좋아하는 꽃 the flower that I like
4 어제 받은 선물 the present that I received yesterday
5 지난 주에 만난 분 the person that I met last week
6 내일 해야 할 일 the work that I have to do tomorrow
7 내일 볼 영화 the movie to watch tomorrow

Exercise 6

1 찾는 2 좋아하는 3 입은 4 먹은 5 가르칠

Exercise 7

1 마이클은 번역을 아주 잘 하는 것 같아요.
2 존은 매운 음식을 잘 먹는 것 같아요.
3 메리는 돈을 잘 버는 것 같아요.
4 미라는 책을 많이 읽는 것 같아요.

Exercise 8

[Listening script]

미라 이거 누구 펜이에요?
Whose pen is this?

제임스 제 거예요.
It's mine.

미라 좀 써도 돼요?
Can I please use it? [lit. Is it okay that I use it a little?]

제임스 네, 쓰세요.
Sure, please use it.
근데, 미라 씨, 저 분 누구세요?
By the way, Mira, who is that person over there?

미라 누구요?
Who do you mean?

제임스 저기 키가 큰 분이요.
The tall person over there.

미라 저 분이요? 한국 전자 김 사장님이세요.
That person over there?
He is President Kim (or CEO) of Korea Electronics.

Answers:

1 James's
2 Mr Kim, the company president of Korea Electronics
3 He is tall.

Exercise 9

[Listening script]

제임스 최민수씨, 바쁜 일이 있어서 내일 약속을 못 지킬 것 같아요.
정말 미안해요.
다음 주에 만나도 괜찮을까요?
Minsu, I have an urgent matter [lit. busy work] so it seems I won't be able to keep our appointment tomorrow. I am really sorry. Will it be okay to meet next week?

최민수 네. 괜찮아요. 제임스 씨 요즘 많이 바쁘신 거 같아요.
Yes, that is okay. It seems you are very busy these days.
제임스 네. 요즘 일이 많아요.
Yes, I have a lot of work these days.
최민수 지금 하는 프로젝트는 언제 끝나요?
When will the project you are currently working on be over?
제임스 이번 주말에 다 끝날 것 같아요.
It seems it will be over this weekend.

Answers:

1 James thinks he won't be able to keep his appointment with Minsu tomorrow.
2 next week
3 by this weekend

Unit 11 여행 Travel

Exercise 1

1 더 큰 집으로 이사갈까 해요.
2 새 차를 살까 해요.
3 내년에 결혼할까 해요.
4 사업을 그만둘까 해요.

Exercise 2

2 살을 빼기로 했어요.
3 담배를 끊기로 했어요.
4 술을 안 마시기로 했어요.
5 아침에 조깅하기로 했어요.
6 돈을 많이 안 쓰기로 했어요.

Exercise 3

1 다섯 시간이나 여섯 시간 걸려요.
2 김밥이나 비빔밥 먹고 싶어요.
3 서울백화점이나 한국백화점에 가요.
4 도서관이나 집에서 공부해요.

Exercise 4

[Listening script]
이번 주 금요일에는 한과장님을 만나기로 했어요.
This Friday, I am scheduled to meet Manager Han.
오전 열한 시에 한과장님 사무실에서 만나기로 했어요.
I am scheduled to meet (him) at his office at 11:00 a.m.
토요일 오전에는 헬스클럽에서 운동을 할까 해요.
On Saturday morning, I am thinking of working out at the fitness center.
토요일 저녁에는 룸메이트랑 같이 요리를 하기로 했어요.
On Saturday evening, I am going to cook together with my roommate.
비빔밥을 만들까 해요.
We are thinking of making *Bibimbap.*
일요일 아침에는 서점에서 책을 읽을까 해요.
On Sunday morning, I am planning to read a book at a bookstore.
일요일 오후에는 영화나 연극을 볼까 해요.
On Sunday afternoon, I am thinking of watching a movie or play.

Answers:
1 This Friday (11:00 a.m.), at Manager Han's office
2 She is planning to work out at the fitness center.
3 She is going to cook with her roommate.
4 She is thinking of watching a movie or play.

Unit 12 전화 On the phone

Exercise 1

1 성함 2 께서 3 께 4 분 5 돌아가셨습니다

Exercise 2

1 스키를 탈 수 있어요/없어요.
2 한국요리를 할 수 있어요/없어요.
3 케이크를 만들 수 있어요/없어요.
4 테니스를 칠 수 있어요/없어요.

Exercise 3

1 미팅을 취소할 수 있을까요?
2 사장님을 뵐 수 있을까요?
3 자료를 좀 볼 수 있을까요?
4 전화를 좀 빌릴 수 있을까요?

Exercise 4

1 뭐든지 2 어디든지 3 누구든지 4 언제든지

Exercise 5

1 번역 좀 부탁합니다. 2 통역 좀 부탁합니다.
3 타이핑 좀 부탁합니다. 4 배달 좀 부탁합니다.

Exercise 6

1 이거 얼마지요? 2 누구시지요?
3 지금 어디지요? 4 오늘이 무슨 요일이지요?

Exercise 7

1 여기서 기다리시지요. 2 안으로 들어가시지요.
3 나오시지요. 4 드시지요.

Exercise 8

[Listening script]

직원 여보세요.
Hello.
제임스 여보세요. 김선영 씨 좀 부탁합니다.
Hello. May I speak to Kim Sun Young?
직원 누구요?
Who?
제임스 김선영 씨요.
Ms Kim Sun Young.
직원 지금 안 계신데요.
She is not (here) now.
점심식사 하시러 나가셨어요.
She went out for lunch.

제임스 아, 그래요? 언제 들어오시지요?
Oh, is that right? When will she return? [lit. When does she come in?]
직원 아마 한 시 반쯤에 들어오실 거예요.
She will come back probably around 1:30.
제임스 그럼, 두 시에 다시 전화 드리겠습니다.
Then, I will call again at 2:00.
직원 네, 알겠습니다.
Okay.
(직원: employee)

Answers:
1 Kim Sun Young
2 She went out for lunch.
3 Around 1:30 p.m.
4 at 2:00 p.m.

Unit 13 날씨 Weather

Exercise 1

1 이래요 2 저래요 3 어때요? 4 그래요?

Exercise 2

2 싸졌어요. 3 적어졌어요.
4 많아졌어요. 5 높아졌어요.

Exercise 3

1 맛있게 2 편하게 3 재미있게 4 늦게 5 심하게

Exercise 4

1 감기약을 드시지 그러세요?
2 팩스로 보내시지 그러세요?
3 제 차로 가시지 그러세요?
4 유럽으로 여행가시지 그러세요?

Exercise 5

A: 지금 몇 시야?
What time is it now?
B: 한 시 반이야. 근데, 과장님 이메일 받았어?
It's 1:30. By the way, did you receive the manager's e-mail?
A: 아니. 아직 이메일 확인 안 했는데. 왜?
No. I haven't checked e-mail yet. Why?
B: 내일 미팅이 취소됐어.
Tomorrow's meeting is canceled.
A: 아, 그래? 그럼, 미팅을 언제 하기로 했어?
Oh, really? Then, when did they/he decide to have the meeting?
B: 다음 주 수요일에.
Next Wednesday.

Exercise 6

1 더우니까 에어컨을 켭시다.
2 사무실이 지저분하니까 청소합시다.
3 내일 8 (여덟) 시에 회의가 있으니까 늦지 마세요.
4 배가 고프니까 밥 먹고 합시다.

Exercise 7

1 비디오를 볼까요? 2 쇼핑을 할까요?
3 시내구경을 할까요? 4 산책을 할까요?

Exercise 8

1 비가 와서 모임에 가기가 싫어요.
2 아파서 출장가기가 싫어요.
3 추워서 밖에 나가기가 싫어요.
4 차가 많이 막혀서 운전하기가 싫어요.

Exercise 9

1 일찍 퇴근했잖아요.
2 월말이잖아요.
3 지금 휴가철이잖아요.

Exercise 10

[Listening script]

창섭 요즘 얼굴 보기가 힘들어. 많이 바빠?
Lately, it's been hard to see you [lit. Lately, seeing your face is hard]. Are you very busy?

제임스 응, 좀.
Yeah, a little.

창섭 한국 생활은 어때?
How's your life in Korea?

제임스 괜찮아. 두 달 지나니까 많이 익숙해졌어.
Okay. After two months, I've adjusted a lot.
근데 한국말이 빨리 안 늘어.
But, my Korean isn't improving fast.

창섭 한국 드라마를 보지 그래?
Why don't you watch Korean dramas?
한국 드라마가 재미있잖아.
You know Korean dramas are fun (to watch).

제임스 바쁘니까 텔레비전 볼 시간이 없어.
Since I am busy, I don't have time to watch TV.

Answers:

1 No. Because James has been very busy lately.
2 He feels he is now very used to it.
3 watch Korean dramas
4 No. Because he is too busy to find time to watch TV.

Unit 14 가족 Family

Exercise 1

Example: 제 가족은 미국에 있어요. 부모님하고 언니는 캘리포니아에 사세요. 오빠는 지금 시카고에서 일해요. 언니는 지금 대학원에 다녀요.
(사세요: honorific form of 살아요 "to live," 대학원: graduate school)

Exercise 2

1 언제 출장가는 거예요?
2 결혼하시는 거예요?

3 아침에 늦게 일어난 거예요. 그래서 회사에 늦었어요.
4 그 분이 한국말을 너무 잘 하시는 거예요.
그래서 아주 놀랐어요.
5 과장님이 왜 화가 나신 거예요?

Exercise 3

1 수한씨가 골프를 잘 하더라구요.
2 박선생님이 일본어를 잘 하시더라구요.
3 미라씨 요리 솜씨가 좋더라구요.
4 창민씨 여자 친구가 아주 예쁘더라구요.

Exercise 4

[Listening script]

제임스 미라씨, 해외 여행 해 봤어요?
Mira, have you traveled abroad?

미라 네. 일본에 가 봤어요.
Yes, I have been to Japan.

제임스 어땠어요?
How was it?

미라 도쿄에 가 봤는데, 서울처럼 아주 복잡하더라구요.
그리고 음식이 아주 맛있었는데 좀 비싸더라구요.
제임스씨는 어디 여행해 봤어요?
I've been to Tokyo, and it was very crowded, just like Seoul. And the food (there) was very delicious, but it was a little expensive. Where have you traveled, James?

제임스 저는 프랑스를 여행해 봤어요.
프랑스 파리가 아주 멋있고 좋더라구요.
그리고 프랑스 사람들도 아주 친절하더라구요.
I've traveled to France. Paris in France was very cool and nice. And French people were also very friendly.

Answers:

1 Tokyo, Japan
2 It was crowded. The food there was delicious but rather expensive.
3 France
4 It was very nice and people there were friendly.

Unit 15 우체국에서 At the post office

Exercise 1

1 박선생님하고 골프를 치려고 해요.
2 부산에 있는 친구를 만나려고 해요.
3 테니스를 배우려고 해요.
4 남자친구하고 영화를 보려고 해요.
5 롯데 백화점에 가서 쇼핑을 하려고 해요.
6 민속촌에 놀러 가려고 해요.

Exercise 2

1 만들어 줬어요. 2 빌려 주셨습니다. 3 도와 드렸어요.

Exercise 3

1 사 줬습니다 or 사 줬어요.
2 사 주셨습니다 or 사 주셨어요.

Exercise 4

1 영어를 가르쳐 드릴게요.
2 도와 드릴게요.
3 돈을 빌려 드릴게요.
4 사진을 찍어 드릴게요.

Exercise 5

1 와 주셔서 감사합니다.
2 초대해 주셔서 감사합니다.
3 선물을 사 주셔서 감사합니다.
4 한국어를 가르쳐 주셔서 감사합니다.
5 전화해 주셔서 감사합니다.

Exercise 6

1 사흘이요/삼일이요.
2 보름이요/십오일이요.
3 나흘이요/사일이요.
4 하루요./일일이요.
5 이틀이요./이일이요.

Exercise 7

[Listening script]

LINDA 영수씨, 저 좀 도와 주시겠어요?
Youngsoo, would you help me?

YOUNGSOO 네, 무슨 일이에요?
Yes, what is it?

LINDA 이번 주말에 친구하고 같이 쇼핑하려고 하는데요.
This weekend, I am planning to go shopping with my friend.
어디에 가면 가방을 싸게 살 수 있어요?
Where can I buy a bag at a cheap price?
[lit. If I go where, can I buy a bag cheap?]

YOUNGSOO 음, 동대문 시장에 가 보세요.
Well, try [lit. try to go] the Dongdaemoon Market.

LINDA 동대문 시장이요?
Dongdaemoon Market?
동대문 시장에 가려면 여기서 몇 번 버스를 타야 돼요?
Which number bus should I take from here to get to the Dongdaemoon Market?

YOUNGSOO 십구번 버스요. 근데, 지하철을 타세요.지하철이 편해요.
The number 19 bus. But take the subway. The subway is convenient.

LINDA 지하철 몇 호선을 타야 돼요?
Which subway line should I take?

YOUNGSOO 여기서 일호선을 타세요.
From here, take line number 1.

LINDA 고마워요.
Thank you.

Answers:

1 b
2 c
3 Dongdaemoon Market
4 c
5 b
6 a

Unit 16 은행에서 At the bank

Exercise 1

1 맥주 말고 물 주세요.
2 빨간색 넥타이 말고 까만색 넥타이 주세요.
3 이번 주 (토요일) 말고 다음 주 토요일에 만나요.
4 내일 말고 모레 가요.
5 오번 버스 말고 십번 버스를 타야 돼요.
6 버스 말고 지하철을 타고 가세요.
7 비빔밥 말고 갈비 먹고 싶어요.

Exercise 2

1 에어콘 돼요?
2 카푸치노 돼요?
3 과장님하고 통화 됩니까?
4 꽃배달 됩니까?

Exercise 3

[Listening script]

종업원 여보세요. 서울 식당입니다.
EMPLOYEE Hello. This is Seoul Restaurant.
제임스 여보세요. 거기 배달 돼요?
JAMES Hello. Do you deliver (food)?
종업원 네. 돼요. 뭐 주문하시겠어요?
EMPLOYEE Yes, we do. What would you like to order?
제임스 비빔밥 하나하고 된장찌개 하나요.
JAMES One Bibimbap and One Twenjangjjigae.
종업원 주소 좀 말씀해 주세요.
EMPLOYEE Please tell me your address.
제임스 한양 아파트 101 동 210 호예요.
JAMES It's Hanyang Apartment building number 101 and room number 210.
종업원 전부 9,500 원입니다. 30 분 후에 배달 됩니다.
EMPLOYEE All together it's 9,500 won. It will be delivered in 30 minutes.
제임스 네, 감사합니다.
JAMES Okay, thank you.

Answers:
1 Bibimbap and Twenjangjjigae
2 b
3 d
4 c

Unit 17 호텔에서 At the hotel

Exercise 1

1 영어를 아주 유창하게 하십니다.
2 오늘 신문 보셨습니까?
3 오늘 회의에 모두 참석해 주십시오.
4 박선생님은 (or 박선생님께서는) 제 고등학교 선배십니다.
(께서는: honorific form of 은/는, see Unit 12)
5 피곤하십니까?

Exercise 2

울산 공장을 둘러 볼 예정입니다. 월요일 밤에는 울산 호텔에 머무를 예정이에요. 그리고, 화요일 오전에는 조 부장님을 뵐 예정입니다. 화요일 두 시에 서울행 비행기를 탈 예정이에요.

Exercise 3

[Listening script]
안녕하십니까?
Hello.
오늘도 저희 열차를 이용해 주셔서 대단히 감사드립니다.
Thank you very much for using our train today.
[lit. Today also, we thank you very much for using our train.]
이 열차는 부산행 열차입니다.
This train is bound for Busan.
5 분후에 서울을 출발할 예정입니다.
It is scheduled to depart from Seoul in five minutes.
먼저 오후 두 시 반에 대전에 도착할 예정입니다.
Our first stop is Daejeon at 2:30 p.m.
그리고, 오후 네 시 반에 부산에 도착할 예정입니다.
We are scheduled to arrive in Busan at 4:30 p.m.

오늘도 즐거운 여행 되십시오.
We hope you enjoy your trip today.
[lit. Today also, become a pleasant trip.]

Answers:

1 Busan
2 c
3 Daejeon at 2:30 p.m.
4 4:30 p.m.

Grammar reference

Sentence endings

The polite sentence ending

	statement	question	suggestion (Let's...)	command (Do...)
verb	...아요/ 어요	...아요/ 어요?	...아요/ 어요	...아요/ 어요
adjective	...아요/ 어요	...아요/ 어요?		
noun	...이에요/ 예요	...이에요/ 예요?		

The honorific polite sentence ending

	statement	question	suggestion (Let's...)	command (Do...)
verb	...(으)세요	...(으) 세요?	...(으)세요	...(으)세요
adjective	...(으)세요	...(으) 세요?		
noun	...(이)세요	...(이) 세요?		

The formal polite sentence ending

	statement	question	suggestion (Let's…)	command (Do…)
verb	…ㅂ니다/ 습니다	…ㅂ니까/ 습니까?	…(으) ㅂ시다	…(으) 십시오
adjective	…ㅂ니다/ 습니다	…ㅂ니까/ 습니까?		
noun	…입니다	…입니까?		

The honorific formal polite sentence ending

	statement	question	suggestion (Let's…)	command (Do…)
verb	…(으) 십니다	…(으) 십니까?	…(으) 십시다	…(으) 십시오
adjective	…(으) 십니다	…(으) 십니까?		
noun	…(이) 십니다	…(이) 십니까?		

Negation ending

affirmative	negative
statement ...아요/어요 ...(으)세요 ...ㅂ니다/습니다 ...(으)십니다 ...이에요/예요 ...(이)세요 ...입니다 ...(이)십니다	 안...아요/어요 = ...지 않아요 안...(으)세요 = ...지 않으세요 안...ㅂ니다/습니다 = ...지 않습니다 안...(으)십니다 = ...지 않으십니다 ...이/가 아니에요 ...이/가 아니세요 ...이/가 아닙니다 ...이/가 아니십니다
question ...아요/어요? ...(으)세요? ...ㅂ니까/습니까? ...(으)십니까? ...이에요/예요? ...(이)세요? ...입니까? ...(이)십니까?	 안...아요/어요? = ...지 않아요? 안...(으)세요? = ...지 않으세요? 안...ㅂ니까/습니까? = ...지 않습니까? 안...(으)십니까? = ...지 않으십니까? ...이/가 아니에요? ...이/가 아니세요? ...이/가 아닙니까? ...이/가 아니십니까?
suggestion/proposition (Let's...) ...아요/어요 ...(으)세요 ...(으)ㅂ시다 ...(으)십시다	 (Let's not...) ...지 말아요 ...지 마세요 ...지 맙시다 ...지 마십시다
command/request (Do...) ...아요/어요 ...(으)세요 ...(으)십시오	 (Don't do...) ...지 말아요 ...지 마세요 ...지 마십시오

Word bases and sentence endings

Present tense

dictionary form	definition	polite ending		formal polite ending	
		regular	honorific	regular	honorific
가다	go	가요	가세요	갑니다	가십니다
오다	come	와요	오세요	옵니다	오십니다
먹다	eat	먹어요	드세요	먹습니다	드십니다
마시다	drink	마셔요	드세요	마십니다	드십니다
만나다	meet	만나요	만나세요	만납니다	만나십니다
자다	sleep	자요	주무세요	잡니다	주무십니다
지내다	spend time	지내요	지내세요	지냅니다	지내십니다
배우다	learn	배워요	배우세요	배웁니다	배우십니다
가르치다	teach	가르쳐요	가르치세요	가르칩니다	가르치십니다
듣다	listen, take	들어요	들으세요	듣습니다	들으십니다
걷다	walk	걸어요	걸으세요	걷습니다	걸으십니다
하다	do	해요	하세요	합니다	하십니다
공부하다	study	공부해요	공부하세요	공부합니다	공부하십니다
사다	buy	사요	사세요	삽니다	사십니다
살다	live	살아요	사세요	삽니다	사십니다
알다	know	알아요	아세요	압니다	아십니다
모르다	not know	몰라요	모르세요	모릅니다	모르십니다
많다	many/much	많아요	많으세요	많습니다	많으십니다
좋다	good	좋아요	좋으세요	좋습니다	좋으십니다
덥다	hot	더워요		덥습니다	
춥다	cold	추워요		춥습니다	
쉽다	easy	쉬워요		쉽습니다	
어렵다	difficult	어려워요		어렵습니다	

dictionary form	definition	polite ending		formal polite ending	
		regular	honorific	regular	honorific
가깝다	close	가까워요		가깝습니다	
바쁘다	busy	바빠요	바쁘세요	바쁩니다	바쁘십니다
예쁘다	pretty	예뻐요	예쁘세요	예쁩니다	예쁘십니다
이다	be	이에요/ 예요	이세요	입니다	이십니다
아니다	not be	아니에요	아니세요	아닙니다	아니십니다
있다	exist; have	있어요	계세요 있으세요	있습니다	계십니다 있으십니다
없다	not exist; not have	없어요	안 계세요 없으세요	없습니다	안 계십니다 없으십니다
그렇다	be so	그래요		그렇습니다	
그러다	do so	그래요	그러세요	그럽니다	그러십니다

Past tense

dictionary form	definition	polite ending		formal polite ending	
		regular	honorific	regular	honorific
가다	go	갔어요	가셨어요	갔습니다	가셨습니다
오다	come	왔어요	오셨어요	왔습니다	오셨습니다
먹다	eat	먹었어요	드셨어요	먹었습니다	드셨습니다
마시다	drink	마셨어요	드셨어요	마셨습니다	드셨습니다
만나다	meet	만났어요	만나셨어요	만났습니다	만나셨습니다
자다	sleep	잤어요	주무셨어요	잤습니다	주무셨습니다
지내다	spend days	지냈어요	지내셨어요	지냈습니다	지내셨습니다
배우다	learn	배웠어요	배우셨어요	배웠습니다	배우셨습니다
가르치다	teach	가르쳤어요	가르치셨어요	가르쳤습니다	가르치셨습니다
듣다	listen, take	들었어요	들으셨어요	들었습니다	들으셨습니다
걷다	walk	걸었어요	걸으셨어요	걸었습니다	걸으셨습니다
하다	do	했어요	하셨어요	했습니다	하셨습니다

dictionary form	definition	polite ending		formal polite ending	
		regular	honorific	regular	honorific
공부하다	study	공부했어요	공부하셨어요	공부했습니다	공부하셨습니다
사다	buy	샀어요	사셨어요	샀습니다	사셨습니다
살다	live	살았어요	사셨어요	살았습니다	사셨습니다
알다	know	알았어요	아셨어요	알았습니다	아셨습니다
모르다	not know	몰랐어요	모르셨어요	몰랐습니다	모르셨습니다
많다	many/much	많았어요	많으셨어요	많았습니다	많으셨습니다
좋다	good	좋았어요	좋으셨어요	좋았습니다	좋으셨습니다
덥다	hot	더웠어요		더웠습니다	
춥다	cold	추웠어요		추웠습니다	
쉽다	easy	쉬웠어요		쉬웠습니다	
어렵다	difficult	어려웠어요		어려웠습니다	
가깝다	close	가까웠어요		가까웠습니다	
바쁘다	busy	바빴어요	바쁘셨어요	바빴습니다	바쁘셨습니다
예쁘다	pretty	예뻤어요	예쁘셨어요	예뻤습니다	예쁘셨습니다
이다	be	이었어요/ 였어요	이셨어요/ 셨어요	이었습니다/ 였습니다	이셨습니다/ 셨습니다
아니다	not be	아니었어요	아니셨어요	아니었습니다	아니셨습니다
있다	exist; have	있었어요	계셨어요 있으셨어요	있었습니다	계셨습니다 있으셨습니다
없다	not exist; not have	없었어요	안 계셨어요 없으셨어요	없었습니다	안 계셨습니다 없으셨습니다
그렇다	be so	그랬어요		그랬습니다	
그러다	do so	그랬어요	그러셨어요	그랬습니다	그러셨습니다

Future tense (probability; conjecture)

dictionary form	polite ending		formal polite ending	
	regular	honorific	regular	honorific
가다	갈 거예요	가실 거예요	갈 겁니다	가실 겁니다
오다	올 거예요	오실 거예요	올 겁니다	오실 겁니다
먹다	먹을 거예요	드실 거예요	먹을 겁니다	드실 겁니다
마시다	마실 거예요	드실 거예요	마실 겁니다	드실 겁니다
만나다	만날 거예요	만나실 거예요	만날 겁니다	만나실 겁니다
자다	잘 거예요	주무실 거예요	잘 겁니다	주무실 겁니다
지내다	지낼 거예요	지내실 거예요	지낼 겁니다	지내실 겁니다
배우다	배울 거예요	배우실 거예요	배울 겁니다	배우실 겁니다
가르치다	가르칠 거예요	가르치실 거예요	가르칠 겁니다	가르치실 겁니다
듣다	들을 거예요	들으실 거예요	들을 겁니다	들으실 겁니다
걷다	걸을 거예요	걸으실 거예요	걸을 겁니다	걸으실 겁니다
하다	할 거예요	하실 거예요	할 겁니다	하실 겁니다
공부하다	공부할 거예요	공부하실 거예요	공부할 겁니다	공부하실 겁니다
사다	살 거예요	사실 거예요	살 겁니다	사실 겁니다
살다	살 거예요	사실 거예요	살 겁니다	사실 겁니다
알다	알 거예요	아실 거예요	알 겁니다	아실 겁니다
모르다	모를 거예요	모르실 거예요	모를 겁니다	모르실 겁니다
많다	많을 거예요	많으실 거예요	많을 겁니다	많으실 겁니다
좋다	좋을 거예요	좋으실 거예요	좋을 겁니다	좋으실 겁니다
덥다	더울 거예요		더울 겁니다	
춥다	추울 거예요		추울 겁니다	
쉽다	쉬울 거예요		쉬울 겁니다	
어렵다	어려울 거예요		어려울 겁니다	
가깝다	가까울 거예요		가까울 겁니다	

dictionary form	polite ending		formal polite ending	
	regular	honorific	regular	honorific
바쁘다	바쁠 거예요	바쁘실 거예요	바쁠 겁니다	바쁘실 겁니다
예쁘다	예쁠 거예요	예쁘실 거예요	예쁠 겁니다	예쁘실 겁니다
이다	일 거예요	이실 거예요	일 겁니다	이실 겁니다
아니다	아닐 거예요	아니실 거예요	아닐 겁니다	아니실 겁니다
있다	있을 거예요	계실 거예요 있으실 거예요	있을 겁니다	계실 겁니다 있으실 겁니다
없다	없을 거예요	안 계실 거예요 없으실 거예요	없을 겁니다	안 계실 겁니다 없으실 겁니다
그렇다	그럴 거예요		그럴 겁니다	
그러다	그럴 거예요	그러실 거예요	그럴 겁니다	그러실 겁니다

Clausal connectives

dic. form	...아/어서 because; since	...ㄴ데 and; but	...고 and	...지만 but	Noun modifying form (present)
가다	가서	가는데	가고	가지만	가는
오다	와서	오는데	오고	오지만	오는
먹다	먹어서	먹는데	먹고	먹지만	먹는
마시다	마셔서	마시는데	마시고	마시지만	마시는
만나다	만나서	만나는데	만나고	만나지만	만나는
자다	자서	자는데	자고	자지만	자는
지내다	지내서	지내는데	지내고	지내지만	지내는
배우다	배워서	배우는데	배우고	배우지만	배우는
가르치다	가르쳐서	가르치는데	가르치고	가르치지만	가르치는
듣다	들어서	듣는데	듣고	듣지만	듣는
걷다	걸어서	걷는데	걷고	걷지만	걷는
하다	해서	하는데	하고	하지만	하는
공부하다	공부해서	공부하는데	공부하고	공부하지만	공부하는

dic. form	…아/어서 because; since	…ㄴ데 and; but	…고 and	…지만 but	Noun modifying form (present)
사다	사서	사는데	사고	사지만	사는
살다	살아서	사는데	살고	살지만	사는
알다	알아서	아는데	알고	알지만	아는
모르다	몰라서	모르는데	모르고	모르지만	모르는
많다	많아서	많은데	많고	많지만	많은
좋다	좋아서	좋은데	좋고	좋지만	좋은
덥다	더워서	더운데	덥고	덥지만	더운
춥다	추워서	추운데	춥고	춥지만	추운
쉽다	쉬워서	쉬운데	쉽고	쉽지만	쉬운
어렵다	어려워서	어려운데	어렵고	어렵지만	어려운
가깝다	가까워서	가까운데	가깝고	가깝지만	가까운
바쁘다	바빠서	바쁜데	바쁘고	바쁘지만	바쁜
예쁘다	예뻐서	예쁜데	예쁘고	예쁘지만	예쁜
이다	이어서/ 여서	인데	이고	이지만	인
아니다	아니어서	아닌데	아니고	아니지만	아닌
있다	있어서	있는데	있고	있지만	있는
없다	없어서	없는데	없고	없지만	없는
그렇다	그래서	그런데	그렇고	그렇지만	그런
그러다	그래서	그러는데	그러고	그러지만	그러는

Conjunctions

그리고: and 그래서: so, therefore
그러면: if so, then (=그럼) 그렇지만: but, however
그러나: however 하지만: but
그런데: but; by the way (=근데)

Korean—English glossary

[ㄱ]	
가격	price
가깝다	be close
가끔	from time to time; occasionally
가다	to go
가르치다	to teach
가방	bag
가수	singer
가위	scissors
가을	autumn
가족	family
...가지	kinds, sorts
가지고 오다	to bring
갈아타다	to change (a vehicle)
갈비	*Kalbi*
감기	cold
감사하다	to thank
감사드리다	to thank (humble polite)
감사합니다	Thank you
갑자기	suddenly
값	price
강의	lecture
갖고 오다	to bring
같이	together
개	dog
...개	piece, object
...개월	months
객실	hotel rooms
거래하다	to do business
거실	living room
거의	almost
걱정	worry, concern
걱정하다	to worry
건강	health
건너편	the opposite side
건물	building
걷다	to walk
걸리다	to take (time)
걸리다	be caught by
걸어서	on foot
겨울	winter
결혼	marriage
결혼하다	to get married
경기	economic conditions
경복궁	Kyŏngbok Palace
경영학	business management studies
경제학	economics
경치	scenery
계속	continuously
계시다	to be, to exist (honorific)
계좌	account
계획	plan
고등학교	high school
고맙다	be thankful
고마워요	Thank you
고모	(father's side) aunt
고장나다	to get out of order
고향	hometown
골프	golf
골프(를) 치다	to play golf
...곳	place

공부하다 study
공사 construction
공원 park
공장 factory, plant
공항 airport
과목 subject; course
과장 section chief; manager
광주 Gwangju
괜찮다 be all right
교수 professor
교육학 education studies
교통 traffic
구 nine
구경하다 to look around, to sightsee
구두 dress shoes
구월 September
국 soup
...권 volume
귀엽다 be cute
그것 that (= 그거)
그냥 just
그래요? Is that so?; Really?
그럼 then; if so
그렇다 be so
그렇지만 but, however
그리고 and
그리다 to draw
그림 picture; drawing
그만두다 to stop; to quit
그저께 the day before yesterday
그제 the day before yesterday
극장 movie theater
근무하다 to work, be on duty
근처 vicinity; in the area
금년 this year
금요일 Friday
기계공학 mechanical engineering
기념품 souvenir
기다리다 to wait
기사 (taxi, bus) driver
기차 train
김밥 *Kimbap*
김치 *Kimchi*
까만색 black
...까지 up to; until
깨끗하다 be clean
...께서 honorific subject marker
...께서는 honorific topic marker
꼭 definitely, without fail
꽃 flower
끊다 to quit; to break off
끝나다 (something) to end, to be over
끝내다 to finish (something)

[ㄴ]

나 I
나가다 to go out
나라 country, nation
나무 tree
나쁘다 be bad
나오다 to come out
나중에 later
나흘 four days
날씨 weather
남다 to remain
남동생 younger brother
남편 husband
낮다 be low
내 my
내년 next year
내리다 to get off (vehicle)
내일 tomorrow
내후년 the year after next year
냉커피 iced coffee
너무 too much; very
네 yes; I see
넥타이 necktie
넷 four

노래방	singing room, karaoke
녹차	green tea
놀다	to play
놀라다	be surprised
놀러 가다	to go to have fun
농구	basketball
농담	joke
농담하다	to joke
높다	be high
누구	who
누나	(a male's) older sister
눈	eye
눈	snow
뉴스	news
뉴욕	New York
늘다	to improve
늦다	be late
늦게	late

[ㄷ]

다	all
다니다	to attend
다르다	be different
다른	other; another; different
다리	leg; bridge
다리미	iron
다섯	five
다시	again
다음	next
닫다	to close
달	month
닭	chicken
담배	cigarette
담배(를) 피우다	to smoke a cigarette
닷새	five days
대구	Daegu
대단히	very much, exceedingly
대리	assistant section chief
대사관	Embassy
대전	Daejeon
대출	money lending
대학교	university
대학생	college student
대학원	graduate school
대학원생	graduate student
댁	house, home (honorific)
더	more
더블룸	double-bed room
덥다	be hot
…도	also
도서관	library
도시	city
도와주다	to help (somebody); to give help
도우넛	doughnut
도장	wooden stamp
도착	arrival
도착하다	to arrive
돈	money
돈을 벌다	to earn money
돈을 찾다	to withdraw money
돌아가다	to return
돌아가시다	to pass away
돕다	to help
동료	colleague
동생	younger sibling
동안	for; during
되게	very much
되다	to become
되다	to be available
둘	two
둘러보다	to look around
뒤	back; behind
드라마	drama
드리다	to give (humble)
드시다	to eat/drink (honorific)
듣다	to listen; to take (class)
들다	to eat; to lift up
들어가다	to go in, enter
들어오다	to come in

들어있다	to be placed in
등기 우편	registered mail
등산	mountain climbing
등산가다	to go mountain climbing
디지털	digital
따뜻하다	be warm
딸	daughter
... 때문에	because of...
떠나다	to leave

[ㄹ]

라디오	radio
라면	ramen, instant noodles
런던	London
룸메이트	roommate
룸키	room key

[ㅁ]

마감	closing
마감 시간	closing time, deadline
... 마리	animal (counter)
마시다	to drink
마음	heart; mind
마음에 들다	be to one's liking
마흔	forty
막	just about
막히다	to be blocked
만	ten thousand
... 만	only
만나다	to meet
만들다	to make
많다	be a lot
많이	a lot
말	words; talk; language
말씀	words; talk (honorific)
말씀하다	to speak (honorific)
맑다	be clear; be sunny
맛있다	be delicious
맞다	be correct
맞다	to fit
맡다	to take charge of
매...	every
매일	everyday
매주	every week
매달	every month
매년	every year
맥도날드	McDonald's
맥주	beer
맨체스터	Manchester
맵다	be spicy
머리	head; hair; brain
머무르다	to stay
먹다	to eat
먼저	first, beforehand
멀다	be far (away)
멋있다	be stylish
며칠	how many days
... 명	person (counter)
명함	business card
몇	how many
몇 번	what number; how many times
모두	all (together)
모래	sand
모레	the day after tomorrow
모르다	to not know
모이다	to get together
모임	gathering, get-together
모자	hat
모자라다	be not enough
목	neck
목요일	Thursday
못	cannot...
못	nail
못하다	cannot do
무슨	what kind of
무엇	what
문	door
문제	problem; question
문화	culture
문화회관	Culture Center
묻다	to ask
물	water

물론	of course
물어보다	to ask
뭐	what
뮤지컬	musical
미국	USA
미남	a handsome man
미안하다	be sorry
미인	a beauty
미팅	meeting
민속촌	Folk Village
[ㅂ]	
바나나	banana
바다	sea, ocean
바로	straight; directly; right away
바이올린	violin
바쁘다	be busy
바지	pants
바꾸다	to change; to transfer
밖	outside
...밖에	only; nothing but
반	half
반갑다	be glad to see
받다	to receive
발	foot
밤	night
밤을 새(우)다	to stay up all night
밥	meal; rice
방	room
방문하다	to visit
배	stomach, belly
배(가)고프다	be hungry
배달	delivery
배우	actor, actress
배우다	to learn
백	one hundred
백만	one million
백화점	department store
뱅킹	banking
버스	bus
...번	time(s)
번역	translation
벌다	to earn
벌써	already
법학	law studies
벗다	to take off (shoes, clothes)
변호사	lawyer
별로	not really
병	bottle
병원	hospital
보고서	report (letter)
보내다	to spend (time)
보내다	to send
보다	to see
...보다	than...
보름	fifteen days
보통	usually; average
보여주다	to show
보이다	be seen
복사	copy; duplicate
복사기	copier
복사하다	to copy; to make a duplicate
복잡하다	be crowded; be complex
봄	spring
뵙다	see (humble polite)
뵈다	see (humble polite)
부모님	parents
부사장	vice-president of a company
부산	Busan
부엌	kitchen
부인	wife
부장	division chief
부전공	minor
부지런하다	be diligent
부치다	to mail
부탁	favor
부탁하다	to ask a favor

...부터	from
북한	North Korea
...분	person (honorific)
...분	minute
...불	dollar
불고기	*Bulgogi*
불편하다	be uncomfortable; be inconvenient
비	rain
비가 오다	to rain
비다	be empty
비디오	video
비빔밥	*Bibimbap*
비싸다	be expensive
비자	visa
비행기	airplane
빌딩	building
빌려주다	to lend
빌리다	to borrow
빠르다	be fast
빨간색	red
빨래	laundry
빨리	fast, quickly
빵	bread
빵집	bakery

[ㅅ]

사	four
사다	to buy
사람	person
사람들	people
사무실	office
사업	business
사원	employee of a company
사월	April
사이즈	size
사장	president of a company
사전	dictionary
사정	situation
사진	photo
사촌	cousin
사호선	line four
사회학	sociology
사흘	three days
산	mountain
산책	walk; stroll
산책하다	to take a walk
살다	to live
살을 빼다	to lose weight
살이 빠지다	to lose weight
삼	three
삼월	March
삼촌	uncle
삼호선	line three
상무	senior executive managing director
새	new
샌드위치	sandwich
생물학	biology
생일	birthday
생활	life, living
샤워하다	to take a shower
서늘하다	be cool
서른	thirty
서울	Seoul
서울역	Seoul Station
서점	bookstore
선물	gift
선배	one's senior, upper class senior
선생	teacher
선생님	teacher (honorific)
설거지	doing dishes
설거지하다	to do dishes
설악산	Mt. Sorak
설탕	sugar
성함	name (honorific)
세일	sale
세일하다	to be on sale
셋	three
셔츠	shirt
소고기	beef

소금	salt
소리	sound
소주	*Soju*, Korean hard liquor
소포	parcel
속달	express mail
속옷	underwear
손	hand
손님	customer; guest
솜씨	skill, deftness
쇼핑하다	to shop
수	number
수업	class
수영	swimming
수영하다	to swim
수요일	Wednesday
숙제	homework
숙제하다	to do homework
숟가락	spoon
술	alcoholic drink
쉬다	to rest
쉰	fifty
쉽다	be easy
스무날	twenty days
스물	twenty
스위트 룸	suite room
스웨터	sweater
스커트	skirt
스키	ski
스키를 타다	to ski
스트레스	stress
승진	promotion
승진하다	to get promoted
...시	...o'clock
시간	hour(s); time
시계	watch
시내	downtown
시원하다	be cool
시월	October
시작하다	to start
시장	market
시청	City Hall
시험	examination
식당	restaurant
식사	eating a meal
식사하다	to eat (a meal)
신다	to put on (shoes)
신발	shoes
신어 보다	to try (shoes) on
신용카드	credit card
신촌	Shinchon
신호등	traffic light
실례지만	Excuse me, but
실직	unemployment, loss of employment
실직률	layoff rate
싫다	be dislikable
싫어하다	to dislike, to hate
심하다	be severe
십	ten
십만	one hundred thousand
십이월	December
십일월	November
싱글룸	single-bed room
싸다	be cheap
쌀쌀하다	be chilly
쓰다	to use
쓰다	to write
...씨	Mr/Ms...

[ㅇ]

아기	baby
아내	wife
아니오	no
아니다	to not be
아니면	or; if not
아들	son
아르바이트	part-time job
아마	probably
아버지	father
아이들	children
아이스 커피	iced coffee
아이스크림	ice cream

아주	very
아직	yet; still
아침	breakfast, morning
아파트	apartment
아프다	be sick
아홉	nine
아흐레	nine days
아흔	ninety
악수	hand-shaking
안	inside
안	not
안경	glasses
안녕하다	be well
안녕하세요?	How are you?
앉다	to sit
알겠습니다	I understand; I see
알다	to know
앞	front
약	medicine
약...	about..., approximately...
약국	pharmacy
약속	appointment; promise
약속하다	to make an appointment; to promise
애기하다	to talk, to speak to
어느	which
어디	where
어떤	what kind of
어떻게	how
어떻다	be a certain way
어렵다	be difficult
어리다	be young
어머니	mother
어때요?	How is it?
어떠세요?	How is it (honorific)
어떻게	how
어서	quickly
어서 오세요	Welcome
억	one hundred million
언니	(a female's) older sister
언제	when; some time
언제든지	whenever
얼굴	face
얼마	how much; how many
얼마나	about how much/ many/long
없다	to not exist, to not have
...에	in/on/at
...에게	to
에어콘	air conditioning
...에 대해서	about; concerning
여기	here
여기(에)서	from here; at here
여덟	eight
여동생	younger sister
여드레	eight days
여든	eighty
여름	summer
여보세요	hello (on the phone)
여섯	six
여쭈다	to ask (humble)
여행	trip, travel
여행가다	to go on a trip
여행자 수표	traveler's check
여행하다	to travel
역	station
역사	history
연극	play
연락	contact
연락처	contact number
연락하다	to contact
연습	practice
연습하다	to practice
열	ten
열다	to open
열심히	diligently, hard
열차	train
열흘	ten days
엿새	six days
영국	UK

영국 사람	a British (person)
영국 문화원	British Culture Center
영문학	English literature studies
영어	English language
영화	movie
옆	beside; (next) side
예	yes; I see
예금하다	to deposit
예쁘다	be pretty
예순	sixty
예약	reservation
예약하다	to reserve
예정이다	be scheduled
오	five
오늘	today
오다	to come
오래	for long
오래간만	after a long while
오른쪽	right side
오빠	(a female's) older brother
오월	May
오이	cucumber
오전	a.m.
오후	p.m.
온돌	heated floor
온돌방	ondol room
온라인	online
올해	this year
옷	clothes
왜	why
외삼촌	(mother's side) uncle
외투	coat
왼쪽	left side
요리	cooking
요리하다	to cook
요일	day of the week
요즘	these days
우리	we; our
우산	umbrella
우체국	post office
운동하다	to exercise, to work out
운전하다	to drive
울다	to cry
울산	Ulsan
웃다	to smile; to laugh
원	won
원피스	(female's) one-piece dress
월급	monthly salary
월말	the end of a month
월요일	Monday
웨이터	waiter
유럽	Europe
유명하다	be famous
유월	June
유창하게	fluently
유창하다	be fluent
유학하다	to study abroad
육	six
...(으)로	to(ward); by; as
은행	bank
은행원	bank employee
음식	food
음악	music
의논하다	to discuss
의사	doctor
의자	chair
이	two
이	this
이것	this (= 이거)
...(이)나	or...
...(이)나	...or something
이다	to be
이따가	later
...(이)랑	with; and
이레	seven days
이렇다	be this way
이름	name
이리	this way
이메일	e-mail
이메일 주소	e-mail address

이모 (mother's side) aunt
이번 this time
이사하다 to move (house)
이용하다 to make use of
이월 February
이자 interest
이 쪽 this way
이태리 Italy (= 이탈리아)
이틀 two days
이호선 line two
익숙하다 be familiar, be used to
...인분 portion per person
인터넷 internet
일 one
일 work
일반 regular, standard
일반실 standard room
일본말 Japanese language
일본어 Japanese language
일어나다 to get up
일어서다 to stand up
일요일 Sunday
일월 January
일찍 early
일하다 to work
일호선 line one
일흔 seventy
읽다 to read
잃다 to lose
잃어버리다 to lose
입 mouth
입다 to wear; to put on
입어 보다 to try (clothes) on
입학 entering a school
있다 to exist, to have

[ㅈ]

자다 to sleep
자료 data
자리 seat
자주 often
자켓 jacket
작년 last year
작다 be small
작성하다 to complete writing
...잔 cup; glass
잘 well
잘못 wrongly
잘생기다 be handsome
잠깐 for a moment
잠깐만 only for a short time
잡수시다 to eat (honorific)
...장 sheet(s) (counter)
장미(꽃) rose
재미없다 be not fun, uninteresting
재미있다 be fun, enjoyable
재작년 the year before last year
재킷 jacket
저금하다 to save money
저 I (humble polite)
저것 that (thing) over there (= 저거)
저기 (over) there
저녁 dinner; evening
저렇다 be that way
저희 we; our (humble)
적금 installment deposit
적다 be a few
전공 major
전공하다 to major
전무 executive managing director
전에 before, previously
전화 telephone
전화를 걸다 to dial the phone
전화번호 telephone number
전화하다 to make a phone call
전자 electronics
전자공학 electronic engineering
점심 lunch
점심식사 lunch meal
점원 clerk

젓가락	chopsticks
...정도	about..., approximately...
정말	really
정장	formal suit
정치학	political science
제	my (humble polite)
제주도	Cheju Island
조깅	jogging
조깅하다	to jog
조금	a little
조심하다	be careful
조용히	quietly
졸업하다	to graduate
좀	a little; please
좁다	be narrow
종이	paper
좋다	be good
좋아하다	to like
죄송하다	be very sorry
주	week
주다	to give
주무시다	to sleep (honorific)
주문	order, odering
주문하다	to order
주말	weekend
주소	address
주스	juice
주시다	to give (honorific)
주차장	parking lot
죽다	to die
준비	preparation
준비하다	to prepare
중간	the middle
중간에	in the middle
중국	China
중국어	Chinese language
중식	Chinese food
즐겁다	be merry, be pleasant
즐겁게	happily, pleasantly
지갑	wallet
지금	now
지나다	to pass
지난	last...
지내다	to spend days
지도	map
지루하다	be boring
지역	area
지역 번호	area number
지저분하다	be dirty, be messy
지키다	to abide by
지하철	subway
직원	employee
직접	directly, in person
집	house, home
...쪽	direction; way
...쯤	about..., approximately...

[ㅊ]

차	car; tea
차가 막히다	traffic is congested
참	very
참석하다	to participate
창구	(teller's) window
찾다	to look for; to find
찾다	to withdraw (money)
책	book
책상	desk
처음	first time; beginning
천	thousand
천만	ten million
체크아웃	checkout
체크아웃 하다	to check out
체크인	check-in
청바지	blue jeans
청소하다	to clean
초	candle
초대	invitation
초대하다	to invite
초콜릿	chocolate
최근	recent (time)
최선	one's best

최선을 다하다	to do one's best
추천하다	to recommend
축하하다	to congratulate
출발	departure
출발하다	to depart
출장	business trip
출장가다	to go on a business trip
춥다	be cold
취소하다	to cancel
층	floor
치다	to hit; to play
치마	skirt
치즈	cheese
친구	friend
친절하다	be kind
친하다	be intimate, be close
칠	seven
칠월	July

[ㅋ]

카드	card
카드 키	key card
카메라	camera
카페	café, coffee shop
카푸치노	cappuccino
칼	knife
캐나다	Canada
커피	coffee
커피숍	coffee shop
컨설턴트	consultant
컴퓨터	computer
컴퓨터 공학	computer science
컴퓨터 랩	computer lab
컵	cup
케이크	cake
켜다	to turn on
코	nose
코미디	comedy
코트	coat
콘텍트렌즈	contact lenses
콜라	cola, coke
크다	be big
크림	cream
클래식	classic
키	height
키가 크다	be tall
키가 작다	be short

[ㅌ]

타다	to ride (vehicle)
타이어	tyre
타이핑	typing
태권도	Taekwondo
택시	taxi
테니스	tennis
텔레비전	television
토요일	Saturday
퇴근하다	to leave one's office
통계	statistics
통역	interpretation
통장	account book
통화	phone communication
투피스	(female's) two-piece suit
트윈룸	twin-bed room
특별하다	be special
티셔츠	T-shirt

[ㅍ]

파리	Paris
파인애플	pineapple
파티	party
판매	selling; marketing
판매량	sale amount
팔	arm
팔	eight
팔다	to sell
팔월	August
팝콘	popcorn
팩스	fax
펜	pen
편하다	be comfortable; be convenient

표	ticket
프랑스	France
프로그램	program
프로젝트	project
프린터	printer
피곤하다	be tired
피아노	piano
피우다	to smoke (cigarette)
필요하다	to need, be necessary

[ㅎ]

...하고	and; with
하나	one
하다	to do
하루	one day
학교	school
학기	school term
학생	student
학회	(academic) conference
한...	about..., approximately...
한국	Korea
한국말	Korean language
한국어	Korean language
한글	the Korean alphabet
한문	Chinese writing
한번	once
한식	Korean food
한식집	Korean restaurant
한자	Chinese characters
...한테	to...
할머니	grandmother
할아버지	grandfather
항공우편	air mail
해결하다	to solve
해외	abroad
핸드폰	cellular phone
햄버거	hamburger
학생	student
합격하다	to pass (an exam)
허락	approval
허락하다	to approve
헬스센터	fitness center
헬스클럽	fitness center
현금	cash
현금카드	debit [cash] card
형	(a male's) older brother
...호	room number...
호텔	hotel
혼자	alone (=혼자서)
화	anger
화(가) 나다	to get angry
화(를) 내다	to show one's anger
화요일	Tuesday
화장실	bathroom
확인하다	to check, to confirm
환율	exchange rate
환전	money exchange
회	raw fish
회계학	studies of accounting
회사	company
회사원	company employee
회의	conference; meeting
회의실	conference room
회의중	meeting in progress
회장	chairman
훨씬	much (more)
휴가	vacation
휴가철	vacation season
흐리다	be cloudy
힘들다	be difficult, be tough

English—Korean glossary

[A]

a few 적다
a lot 많이
abide by 지키다
about how much/long 얼마나
about, approximately... 약...; 한...
about, approximately... ...정도; ...쯤
about; concerning ...에 대해서
abroad 해외
account 계좌
account book 통장
actor, actress 배우
address 주소
after a long while 오래간만
afternoon, p.m. 오후
again 다시
air conditioning 에어콘
airmail 항공우편
airplane 비행기
airport 공항
alcoholic drink 술
all 다
all right 괜찮다
all (together) 모두
almost 거의
alone 혼자, 혼자서
already 벌써
also ...도
a.m. 오전
and ...하고
and 그리고
anger 화
animal counter ...마리
apartment 아파트
appointment; promise 약속
approval 허락
approve 허락하다
April 사월
area 지역
area number 지역 번호
arm 팔
arrival 도착
arrive 도착하다
ask 묻다
ask 물어보다
ask (humble) 여쭈다
ask a favor 부탁하다
assistant section chief 대리
at ...에; ...에서
attend 다니다
August 팔월
aunt (father's side) 고모
aunt (mother's side) 이모
autumn 가을
available 되다

[B]

baby 아기
back; behind 뒤

bad	나쁘다
bag	가방
bakery	빵집
banana	바나나
bank	은행
bank employee	은행원
banking	뱅킹
basketball	농구
bathroom	화장실
be	이다
be a lot	많다
be a certain way	서늘하다
be cool	어떻다
be not	아니다
be scheduled	예정이다
be seen	보이다
be that way; be like that	저렇다
be this way; be so	이렇다
be to one's liking	마음에 들다
be well	안녕하다
beautiful person	미인
because of...	...때문에
become	되다
beef	소고기
beer	맥주
before, previously	전에
beside; (next) side	옆
Bibimbap	비빔밥
big	크다
biology	생물학
birthday	생일
black	까만색
blocked	막히다
blue jeans	청바지
book	책
bookstore	서점
boring	지루하다
borrow	빌리다
bottle	병
bread	빵
break off; quit	끊다
breakfast	아침
bridge	다리
bring	가지고 오다
bring	갖고 오다
British Culture Center	영국 문화원
British person	영국 사람
building	건물
building	빌딩
Bulgogi	불고기
bus	버스
Busan	부산
business	사업
business card	명함
business trip	출장
busy	바쁘다
but, however	그렇지만
buy	사다

[C]

café	카페
cake	케이크
call by telephone	전화하다
camera	카메라
Canada	캐나다
cancel	취소하다
candle	초
cannot...	못
cannot do	못하다
cappuccino	카푸치노
car	차
card	카드
careful	조심하다
cash	현금
catch; caught by	걸리다
cellular phone	핸드폰
chair	의자
chairman	회장
change (a vehicle)	갈아타다
change, transfer	바꾸다
cheap	싸다
check-in	체크인
check out (verb)	체크아웃하다

checkout	체크아웃
cheese	치즈
Cheju Island	제주도
chicken	닭
children	아이들
chilly	쌀쌀하다
China	중국
Chinese characters	한자
Chinese food	중식
Chinese language	중국어
Chinese writing	한문
chocolate	초콜릿
chopsticks	젓가락
cigarette	담배
city	도시
City Hall	시청
class	수업
classic	클래식
clean	깨끗하다
clean	청소하다
clear; be sunny	맑다
clerk	점원
close	가깝다
close	닫다
closing	마감
closing time, deadline	마감 시간
clothes	옷
cloudy	흐리다
coat	외투
coat	코트
coffee	커피
coffee shop	커피숍
cola, coke	콜라
cold	감기
cold	춥다
colleague	동료
college student	대학생
come	오다
come in	들어오다
come out	나오다
comedy	코미디
comfortable	편하다
company	회사
company employee	회사원
complete writing	작성하다
computer	컴퓨터
computer lab	컴퓨터 랩
computer science	컴퓨터 공학
conference (academic)	학회
conference room	회의실
confirm, check	확인하다
congested (traffic)	차가 막히다
congratulate	축하하다
construction	공사
consultant	컨설턴트
contact	연락
contact	연락하다
contact lenses	콘텍트렌즈
contact number	연락처
continuously	계속
convenient	편하다
cook	요리하다
cooking	요리
cool	시원하다
copier	복사기
copy, duplicate	복사
correct	맞다
country, nation	나라
cousin	사촌
cream	크림
credit card	신용카드
crowded; complex	복잡하다
cry	울다
cucumber	오이
culture	문화
Culture Center	문화 회관
cup	컵
cup; glass	…잔
customer; guest	손님
cute	귀엽다

[D]

Daegu 대구
Daejeon 대전
data 자료
daughter 딸
day after tomorrow 모레
day of the week 요일
deadline, closing time 마감시간
debit [cash] card 현금카드
December 십이월
definitely, without fail 꼭
delicious 맛있다
delivery 배달
depart 출발하다
department store 백화점
departure 출발
deposit 예금하다
desk 책상
dial the phone 전화를 걸다
dictionary 사전
die 죽다
different 다르다
different 다른
difficult 어렵다
difficult, tough 힘들다
digital 디지털
diligent 부지런하다
diligently, hard 열심히
dinner 저녁
direction; way …쪽
directly, in person 직접
dirty, messy 지저분하다
discuss 의논하다
dislikable 싫다
dislike, hate 싫어하다
division chief 부장
do 하다
do business 거래하다
do dishes 설거지하다
do homework 숙제하다
do one's best 최선을 다하다
doctor 의사
dog 개
doing dishes 설거지
dollar …불
door 문
double-bed room 더블룸
doughnut 도우넛
downtown 시내
drama 드라마
draw 그리다
dress shoes 구두
drink 마시다
drive 운전하다
driver (taxi, bus) 기사

[E]

early 일찍
earn 벌다
earn money 돈을 벌다
easy 쉽다
eat 먹다
eat 들다
eat (a meal) 식사하다
eat (honorific) 잡수시다
eat/drink (honorific) 드시다
eating a meal 식사
economic conditions 경기
economics 경제학
eight 여덟
eight 팔
eight days 여드레
eighty 여든
electronic engineering 전자공학
electronics 전자
e-mail 이메일
e-mail address 이메일 주소
Embassy 대사관
employee 직원
employee of a company 사원

empty	비다
end of a month	월말
end, be over	끝나다
English language	영어
enter	들어가다
entering a school	입학
Europe	유럽
every	매...
everyday	매일
every week	매주
every month	매달
every year	매년
examination	시험
exceedingly, very much	대단히
exchange rate	환율
Excuse me, but	실례지만
executive managing director	전무
exercise, work out	운동하다
exist	있다
exist (honorific)	계시다
expensive	비싸다
express mail	속달
eye	눈

[F]

face	얼굴
factory, plant	회사
familiar, be used to	익숙하다
family	가족
famous	유명하다
far (away)	멀다
fast	빠르다 (adjective)
fast	빨리 (adverb)
father	아버지
favor	부탁
fax	팩스
February	이월
fifteen days	보름
fifty	쉰
finish (something)	끝내다
first, beforehand	먼저
first time; beginning	처음
fit	맞다
fitness center	헬스센터, 헬스클럽
five	다섯
five	오
five days	닷새
floor	층
flower	꽃
fluent	유창하다
fluently	유창하게
Folk Village	민속촌
food	음식
foot	발
for a long time	오래
for a moment	잠깐
for, during	동안
formal suit	정장
forty	마흔
four	넷
four	사
four days	나흘
France	프랑스
Friday	금요일
friend	친구
from	...부터
from here; at here	여기(에)서
from time to time	가끔
front	앞
fun, enjoyable	재미있다

[G]

gathering, get-together	모임
get angry	화(가) 나다
get married	결혼하다
get off (vehicle)	내리다
get together	모이다
get up	일어나다

gift 선물
give 주다
give (honorific) 주시다
give (humble) 드리다
glad to see 반갑다
glasses 안경
go 가다
go mountain climbing 등산가다
go on a business trip 출장가다
go on a trip 여행가다
go out 나가다
go to have fun 놀러 가다
golf 골프
good 좋다
graduate 졸업하다
graduate school 대학원
graduate student 대학원생
grandfather 할아버지
grandmother 할머니
green tea 녹차
Gwangju 광주

[H]
half 반
hand 손
handsome 잘생기다
handsome man 미남
hair; head; brain 머리
hamburger 햄버거
happily, pleasantly 즐겁게
hat 모자
have, possess 있다
head; hair; brain 머리
health 건강
heart; mind 마음
heated floor 온돌
height 키
hello (on the phone) 여보세요
help 돕다
help, give help 도와주다
here 여기
high 높다
high school 고등학교
history 역사
hit; play 치다
hometown 고향
homework 숙제
honorific subject marker . . . 께서
honorific topic marker . . . 께서는
hospital 병원
hot 덥다
hotel 호텔
hotel rooms 객실
hour(s); time 시간
house, home 집
house, home (honorific) 댁
how 어떻게
How are you? 안녕하세요?
however, but 그렇지만
How is it? (honorific) 어떠세요?
How is it? 어때요?
how many 몇
how many days 며칠
how many times 몇 번
how much; how many 얼마
hungry 배(가)고프다
husband 남편

[I]
I 나
I (humble polite) 저
ice cream 아이스크림
iced coffee 냉커피
iced coffee 아이스 커피
improve 늘다
inconvenient 불편하다
in the middle 중간에
inside 안
installment deposit 적금

interest	이자	**[L]**	
internet	인터넷	language	말
interpretation	통역	last...	지난
intimate, close	친하다	last year	작년
invitation	초대	late	늦다 (adjective)
invite	초대하다	late	늦게 (adverb)
iron	다리미	later	나중에
Italy	이태리 (=이탈리아)	later	이따가
[J]		laundry	빨래
jacket	자켓, 재킷	lawyer	변호사
January	일월	layoff rate	실직률
Japanese language	일본말	learn	배우다
Japanese language	일본어	leave	떠나다
jog	조깅하다	leave one's office	퇴근하다
jogging	조깅	lecture	강의
joke	농담	left side	왼쪽
joke	농담하다	leg	다리
juice	주스	lend	빌려주다
July	칠월	library	도서관
June	유월	life, living	생활
just	그냥	like	좋아하다
just about	막	line four	사호선
[K]		line one (subway)	일호선
Kalbi	갈비	line three	삼호선
karaoke	노래방	line two (subway)	이호선
key card	카드 키	listen; to take (class)	듣다
Kimbap	김밥	little; a little	조금 (=좀)
Kimchi	김치	live	살다
kind	친절하다	living, life	생활
kinds, sorts	...가지	living room	거실
kitchen	부엌	London	런던
knife	칼	look around	둘러보다
know	알다	look for; find	찾다
Korea	한국	lose	잃다; 잃어버리다
Korean alphabet	한글	lose weight	살을 빼다
Korean food	한식	lose weight	살이 빠지다
Korean language	한국말	low	낮다
Korean language	한국어	lunch	점심
Korean restaurant	한식집		
Kyŏngbok Palace	경복궁		

[M]

mail; post	부치다
major (noun)	전공
major (verb)	전공하다
make	만들다
make a copy	복사하다
make an appointment	약속하다
make a phone call	전화하다
make use of	이용하다
Manchester	맨체스터
map	지도
March	삼월
market	시장
marriage	결혼
May	오월
McDonald's	맥도날드
meal; rice	밥
mechanical engineering	기계공학
medicine	약
meet	만나다
meeting	미팅
meeting, conference	회의
meeting in progress	회의중
middle	중간
minor	부전공
minute	...분
Monday	월요일
money	돈
money exchange	환전
money lending	대출
month	달
monthly salary	월급
months	...개월
more	더
morning	아침
mother	어머니
mountain	산
mountain climbing	등산
mouth	입
move (house)	이사하다
movie	영화
movie theater	극장
Mr/Ms...	...씨
Mt. Sorak	설악산
much (more)	훨씬
music	음악
musical	뮤지컬
my	제
my	내

[N]

nail	못
name	이름
name (honorific)	성함
narrow	좁다
neck	목
necktie	넥타이
need, necessary	필요하다
new	새
news	뉴스
New York	뉴욕
next	다음
next year	내년
night	밤
nine	구
nine	아홉
nine days	아흐레
ninety	아흔
no	아니오
North Korea	북한
nose	코
not	안
not enough	모자라다
not exist	없다
not fun, uninteresting	재미없다
not have	없다
not know	모르다
not really	별로
November	십일월
now	지금
number	수

[O]

o'clock ...시
October 시월
of course 물론
office 사무실
often 자주
older brother (a female's) 오빠
older brother (a male's) 형
older sister (a female's) 언니
older sister (a male's) 누나
on foot 걸어서
on sale 세일하다
once 한번
ondol room 온돌방
one 일
one 하나
one day 하루
one hundred 백
one hundred million 억
one hundred thousand 십만
one million 백만
one-piece dress 원피스
one's best 최선
one's senior 선배
online 온라인
only ...만
only; nothing but ...밖에
open 열다
opposite side 건너편
or ...(이)나
or; if not 아니면
order (verb) 주문하다
order, ordering 주문
our 우리
our 저희 (humble polite)
out of order 고장나다
outside 밖

[P]

pants 바지
paper 종이
parcel 소포
parents 부모님
Paris 파리
park 공원
parking lot 주차장
participate 참석하다
part-time job 아르바이트
party 파티
pass away 돌아가시다
pass (an exam) 합격하다
pass (by) 지나다
pen 펜
people 사람들
person 사람
person (counter) ...명
person (honorific) ...분
pharmacy 약국
phone communication 통화
photo 사진
piano 피아노
picture, drawing 그림
piece, object ...개
pineapple 파인애플
place ...곳
placed in 들어있다
plan 계획
play 연극
play 놀다
pleasant; marry 즐겁다
pleasantly; happily 즐겁게
please 좀
p.m. 오후
political science 정치학
popcorn 팝콘
portion per person ...인분
post office 우체국
practice 연습
practice 연습하다

preparation 준비
prepare 준비하다
president of a company 사장
pretty 예쁘다
price 가격
price 값
printer 프린터
probably 아마
problem 문제
professor 교수
program 프로그램
project 프로젝트
promise 약속하다
promoted 승진하다
promotion 승진
put on (shoes) 신다

[Q]

quickly 어서
quietly 조용히
quit 그만두다

[R]

radio 라디오
rain 비 (noun)
rain 비가 오다 (verb)
ramen, instant noodles 라면
raw fish 회
read 읽다
really 정말
Really?; Is that so? 그래요?
receive 받다
recent (time) 최근
recommend 추천하다
red 빨간색
registered mail 등기 우편
regular, standard 일반
remain 남다
report (letter) 보고서
reservation 예약
reserve 예약하다
rest 쉬다
restaurant 식당
return 돌아가다
rice; meal 밥
ride (vehicle) 타다
right side 오른쪽
room 방
roommate 룸메이트
room number... ...호
rose 장미(꽃)

[S]

sale 세일
sale amount 판매량
salt 소금
sand 모래
sandwich 샌드위치
Saturday 토요일
save money 저금하다
scenery 경치
school 학교
school term 학기
scissors 가위
sea; ocean 바다
seat 자리
section chief 과장
see 보다
see (humble polite) 뵈다, 뵙다
sell 팔다
selling; marketing 판매
send 보내다
senior executive managing director, division chief 부장
Seoul 서울
Seoul Station 서울역
September 구월
seven 일곱
seven 칠
seven days 이레

seventy	일흔
severe	심하다
sheet(s) (counter)	...장
Shinchon	신촌
shirt	셔츠
shoes	신발
shop	쇼핑하다
short	키가 작다
show	보여주다
show one's anger	화(를) 내다
sick	아프다
sightsee; look around	구경하다
singer	가수
single-bed room	싱글룸
sit	앉다
situation	사정
six	여섯
six	육
six days	엿새
sixty	예순
size	사이즈
ski	스키
ski	스키를 타다
skill; deftness	솜씨
skirt	스커트, 치마
sleep	자다
sleep (honorific)	주무시다
small	작다
smile; laugh	웃다
smoke (cigarette)	피우다
snow	눈
so	그렇다
sociology	사회학
Soju, Korean hard liquor	소주
solve	해결하다
son	아들
sorry	미안하다
(very) sorry	죄송하다
sound	소리
souvenir	기념품
speak (honorific)	말씀하다
special	특별하다
spend (time)	보내다
spend (days)	지내다
spicy	맵다
spoon	숟가락
spring	봄
stand up	일어서다
standard room	일반실
start	시작하다
station	역
statistics	통계
stay	머무르다
stay up all night	밤을 새(우)다
stomach	배
straight; directly; right away	바로
stress	스트레스
student	학생
studies of accounting	회계학
studies of business management	경영학
studies of education	교육학
studies of English literature	영문학
studies of law	법학
study	공부하다
study abroad	유학하다
stylish	멋있다
subject; course	과목
subway	지하철
suddenly	갑자기
sugar	설탕
suite room	스위트 룸
summer	여름
Sunday	일요일
surprised	놀라다
sweater	스웨터
swim	수영하다
swimming	수영

[T]

Taekwondo	태권도
take a shower	샤워하다
take a walk	산책하다
take in charge	맡다
take off (shoes, clothes)	벗다
take (time)	걸리다
talk; speak to	얘기하다
tall	키가 크다
taxi	택시
tea	차
teach	가르치다
teacher	선생
teacher	선생님 (honorific)
telephone	전화
telephone number	전화번호
television	텔레비전
ten	십
ten days	열흘
ten million	천만
ten thousand	만
tennis	테니스
ten	열
than	...보다
Thank you	감사합니다 (formal)
Thank you	고마워요 (casual)
thankful	고맙다
that	그것 (=그거)
that (thing) over there	저것(=저거)
the day before yesterday	그저께
the day before yesterday	그제
then; if so	그럼
there; over there	저기
these days	요즘
thirty	서른
this	이
this	이것 (=이거)
this direction	이 쪽
this time	이번
this way	이리
this year	금년, 올해
thousand	천
three	삼
three	셋
three days	사흘
Thursday	목요일
ticket	표
time(s)	...번
tired	피곤하다
to (somebody)	...에게
to (somebody)	...한테
to(ward); by; as	...(으)로
today	오늘
together	같이
tomorrow	내일
too much; very	너무
traffic	교통
traffic light	신호등
train	기차, 열차
translation	번역
travel	여행하다
traveler's check	여행자 수표
tree	나무
trip, travel	여행
try (clothes) on	입어 보다
try (shoes) on	신어 보다
T-shirt	티셔츠
Tuesday	화요일
turn on	켜다
twenty	스물
twenty days	스무날
twin-bed room	트윈룸
two	둘
two	이
two days	이틀
two-piece suit	투피스

typing 타이핑
tyre 타이어

[U]
UK 영국
Ulsan 울산
umbrella 우산
unemployment, loss of employment 실직
uncle 삼촌
uncle (mother's side) 외삼촌
uncomfortable 불편하다
understood 알겠습니다
underwear 속옷
university 대학교
until...; up to... ...까지
USA 미국
use 쓰다
use; make use of 이용하다
usually; average 보통

[V]
vacation 휴가
vacation season 휴가철
very 아주
very 참
very much 되게
vice-president of a company 부사장
vicinity, near place 근처
video 비디오
violin 바이올린
visa 비자
visit 방문하다
volume ...권

[W]
wait 기다리다
waiter 웨이터
walk 걷다
walk; stroll 산책
wallet 지갑
warm 따뜻하다
watch 시계
water 물
we; our (humble) 저희
we; our 우리
wear, put on 입다
weather 날씨
Wednesday 수요일
week 주
weekend 주말
Welcome 어서 오세요
well 잘
what 무엇 (=뭐)
what kind of 무슨
what kind of 어떤
what number 몇 번
when; some time 언제
whenever 언제든지
where 어디
which 어느
who 누구
why 왜
wife 부인 (someone else's)
wife 아내 (one's own)
window (teller's) 창구
winter 겨울
with ...하고
with; and ...(이)랑
withdraw money 돈을 찾다
won (Korean currency) 원
wooden stamp 도장
words; talk (honorific) 말씀
work 일
work 일하다
work; be on duty 근무하다
worry 걱정하다

worry; concern 걱정
write 쓰다
wrongly 잘못

[Y]
year after next 내후년
year before last 재작년
yes; I see 네, 예
yet; still 아직
young 어리다
younger brother 남동생
younger sibling 동생
younger sister 여동생

Grammar index

U: Unit
D: Dialogue
G: Grammar point